METS
BY THE
NUMBERS

METS
BY THE
NUMBERS

A Complete Team History
of the Amazin' Mets by Uniform Number

JON SPRINGER & MATTHEW SILVERMAN

Skyhorse Publishing

Skyhorse Publishing books may be purchased in bulk at special discounts for sales promotion, corporate gifts, fund raising, or educational purposes. Special editions can also be created to specifications. For details, contact Special Sales Department, Skyhorse Publishing, 555 Eighth Avenue, Suite 903, New York, NY 10018 or info@skyhorsepublishing.com.

www.skyhorsepublishing.com

10 9 8 7 6 5 4 3 2 1

Library of Congress Cataloging-in-Publication Data
    Springer, Jon.
    Mets by the numbers : a complete team history of the amazin' Mets
by uniform number / Jon Springer & Matthew Silverman.
        p.   cm.
    Includes index.
    ISBN 978-1-60239-227-4 (alk. paper)
    1. New York Mets (Baseball team)—History.   2. Baseball players—
New York (State)—New York.   I. Silverman, Matthew, 1965–   II. Title.

GV875.N45S67   2007
796.357'64097471—dc22

                                                    2007044257

Printed in the United States of America

To Dad

CONTENTS

FOREWORD

Willie Mays was one of the greatest baseball players of all time; perhaps the best of all those living today.

Kelvin Torve, as I recall, is a very nice person.

These two gentlemen should never be confused as baseball players, but in the early 1990s they were, and it makes for the delicious type of anecdote that fills this entertaining book.

Mays, of course, played most of two seasons with the Mets in 1972 and 1973. Following his retirement, the Mets did not issue his famous No. 24 to any other player, although the number was never officially retired. Then, in 1990, Torve, a career minor leaguer, spent some time with the Mets. For no apparent reason, when he took the field for his first game as a Met, he did so wearing No. 24.

This, of course, was surprising, and all these years later, Charlie Samuels, the Mets affable equipment manager, and Jay Horwitz, the team's vice president of media relations, recall the incident and shake their heads while chuckling, wondering why they allowed Torve to have Willie's number. What they really get a kick out of is why people care, but they do; and that's the reason you're reading this book.

Torve's heist of the famous number was a short-lived issue. He wore No. 39 from his second week on, through parts of the 1990 and 1991 seasons, but it's a fun piece of Mets trivia. The far more deserving Rickey Henderson wore the number during his time with the Mets and donned it again as a coach. Torve is now free to wear it in whatever line of work he pursues today.

I've always enjoyed keeping track of uniform numbers. They define players in a variety of ways, so much so that players' nicknames are occasionally a reflection of the numbers they wear. Some members of the 1986 Mets referred to manager Davey Johnson not as "Skip," or "Davey," but as simply "Number 5."

On a couple of occasions when I worked on the air with Tom Seaver, I called him "41." I did so to pay tribute to a man who actually took part in a no-hitter for the New York Mets, but little did Tom know I wasn't referring to him. I know, I know, the Mets have never pitched a regular season or postseason no hitter, but for the sake of this discussion, spring training counts. That's how we come to Gordon Richardson.

Richardson had been a part of the St. Louis Cardinals' world championship team in 1964, but by the next spring he was a Met. In March 1965, at Al Lang Field in St. Petersburg, Richardson, wearing No. 41, combined with Gary Kroll to no-hit the Pittsburgh Pirates. I don't remember what number Kroll wore, and if I did, I wouldn't tell you. You'll just have to read the whole book. But I can tell you that Richardson was the last Met to wear No. 41 before Seaver began his Hall of Fame career in 1967.

You're not the only one who cares about uniform numbers. They mean a lot to the guys who wear them, too. That's why, when the great Warren Spahn joined the Mets in 1965, Ed Kranepool gave up the No. 21, presenting it to Spahn, and took No. 7, the number he would wear throughout the rest of his Mets career. To this day, no matter who wears 7 for the Mets, I always think of Kranepool.

Ron Swoboda will always be remembered as No. 4, but he wore 14 as a rookie in 1965. The next year, longtime Cardinals third baseman Ken Boyer joined the Mets, and Swoboda surrendered 14. Following the trade of Boyer to the Chicago White Sox during the 1967 season, number 14 became available for its original owner, Gil Hodges.

Hodges wore the number the night the Mets played their first game in the National League, on April 11, 1962, and reclaimed it when he was named manager for the 1968 season. Less than three years after leading the Mets to the 1969 world championship, Hodges passed away, and his number was retired.

Only three Mets, plus Jackie Robinson, have had their numbers retired by the Mets, but in my opinion there should be more. I've long felt that Keith Hernandez's No. 17 should be on the outfield wall because he was clearly the soul of the team that provided the best series of seasons the franchise has enjoyed. One could also make the case for Dwight Gooden's 16, and Darryl Strawberry's 18, although their personal problems have precluded that honor to this point. I would argue that Jerry Koosman, the winningest left-handed pitcher in Mets history, is worthy of his No. 36 being considered for retirement as well.

That's one of the fun things about tracking uniform numbers. They provide great fodder for debate, as well as trivia. Which brings us back to Willie Mays. I have never felt that the Mets should retire his number. He was a great player—as a Giant—but some Met, at least in my opinion, probably should have worn 24 long before Kelvin Torve. That number is still essentially preserved in Mets mothballs, but if someday the Mets decide to honor Willie for his contributions to baseball in New York as a Giant as well as a Met by permanently retiring it, I say go for it.

If that day ever comes, Jim Beauchamp should be part of the ceremonies. Someone had to give 24 to Willie when he became a Met. You probably remember that Beauchamp took No. 5 after Mays came aboard. If you didn't, that's all right. That's what this book is all about. Have fun.

—**Howie Rose**
June 2007

INTRODUCTION

When he last managed to articulate his message, I embraced him.
He had come out of the steamy depths to tell me ever-so-bravely that
he, too, was a Daffodil-11.
   "My brother," I said.

                                        —Kurt Vonnegut, *Slapstick*

Where do you start? You start with 1. That was Richie Ashburn making his way to the plate at old Busch Stadium (née Sportsman's Park) to face Larry Jackson of the Cardinals on April 11, 1962. No. 1 stood in the batter's box and lifted a fly to Curt Flood in center. One down. And the Mets were on their way.

The Mets wore their road grays that first night and blue pinstripes two afternoons later at the Polo Grounds, on Friday the 13th. With only a handful of changes, those would be the uniforms the club would wear for the next fifteen years. But, oh, the number of people that would wear them, some for only a few days.

Figuring that broadcasting Phillies games would involve slightly less misery than another season with the Mets, Ashburn retired following the Mets' inaugural season in 1962, but his uniform didn't. No. 1 went first to Cliff Cook, whose bad back forced him out, then to Duke Carmel, who insulted Casey Stengel, assuring another No. 1 would soon arrive. Then another. And another. And so on. Yesterday's Mookie Wilson is yesteryear's Richie Ashburn is today's Luis Castillo. And tomorrow never knows.

Since a uniform number can be worn by only one player at any one point of time, it can and does define that player's unique moment in team history. Isolate the number, and you have a broader history—what Vonnegut called an "artificial extended family"—linking one player's moment to the next's. Reverse-engineer a progression of uniform numbers and a history of transactions and the front-office philosophies behind them are laid bare. Find the point where a player changes uniforms and you'll find a story there to tell. The players in the uniform and the gaps in between them: that's what this book is about.

Uniform numbers lend the only uniqueness to players who otherwise are all dressed alike. According to Jack Looney's *Now Batting, Number . . .*, instances of teams wearing numbers date to the nineteenth century. The

Cleveland Indians formally introduced the practice in 1916, and the St. Louis Cardinals followed a few years later. But it didn't really take off until the Yankees in 1929 assigned their players numbers that corresponded to their position in the batting order, which is how Babe Ruth became 3 and Lou Gehrig 4, and so on. By 1932, all major league teams were doing it.

That makes baseball uniform numbers at least seventy-five years old. But in a sport obsessed with statistics, they may just be the final frontier. The data contained in this book is completely unofficial, gathered the only way it could have been—over a lifetime of fandom and refined with the help of scorecards, old newspapers, photos, and video—and presented in a way that's never been done before. Yet uniform numbers are perhaps the official stat of the true fan, whether they use them as mnemonics (the locker combination goes Strawberry-Koosman-Carter, 18-36-8) or plunk down $200 for a jersey with authentic digitry.

We hope this book sheds new light on some forgotten numerical history (the five Mets who wore No. 41 *before* Tom Seaver) while digging deeper into the familiar lore (revealing something about Kelvin Torve *other than* the fact he once wore No. 24). And while we expect this will be a useful reference book, we're hoping a little harder that it's also fun to read. There is no quiz at the end. As Casey said, you could look it up.

How to Read This Book

This book was assembled during the 2007 season, so statistics are as current as publishing allows. To cut down on confusion, the data set includes only those numbers assigned to players on the active roster in-season, whether they played or not, as well as primary coaches and managers as listed on an official scorecard. That means: Rube Walker, yes; Batboy Jim, no. Garth Brooks, no; Mac Suzuki, yes.

The lists of statistical leaders and a progression of numbers that accompany each chapter are based on the performances of players only on the dates that they wore or have worn that number (in Chapter 7, for example, Ed Kranepool's numbers don't jibe with his career Met stats because the three seasons he spent wearing No. 21 are counted separately and listed in that chapter). In a few cases where precise dates are unknowable (George Theodore's switch from 18 to 9, for example), we made our best estimate based on the data we gathered and don't figure to be off by much. Players are in **bold** in a chapter if they actually wore the number, and years given refer only to the seasons he wore those digits.

"Number of times issued" means the number of times a number was issued to a new or returning player nonconsecutively. For example, Greg McMichael in Chapter 36 counts for one player but two issues since No. 36 was reissued between the time he left the team and when he returned.

Career statistical leaders are based on a minimum of 100 plate appearances or 100 innings pitched. Statistics formatted (.273/.358/.505, 34 HR, 98 RBI) refer to batting average/on-base percentage/slugging percentage, home runs, and RBI. There aren't batting and pitching leaders for every number, but it will become clear to the reader soon enough that some numbers are pitchers' numbers and some are dominated by hitters. And some numbers are still waiting for their first good player.

Dates that accompany each player in the progression refer to the years (partial or full) that the player performed for the Mets. Dates in parenthesis indicate the starting or ending date for players *only in those cases where there were multiple issues of the same jersey in the same year.* For an even more detailed look at precise dates (as well as a continually updated progression), consult mbtn.net or metsbythenumbers.com. Corrections and comments, plus any book-related inquiries, may also be directed to the site.

Finally, we have included an all-time alphabetical roster for quick reference.

The words *exhaustive*, *obsessive* and, hopefully, *lively* may be used to describe this effort, but after forty-five years it's about time Mets history was spun in a new way. The team—and the fans—deserve it.

#1: LEADING OFF: MOOKIE WILSON

"**N**umber 1 is my number because . . . that's the number they gave me in spring training."

Turned out to be a pretty apt decision, at least when it came to **Mookie Wilson** (1980–89), who would become the epitome of No. 1, arguably the most beloved Met of all time, and, appropriately, the leadoff hitter in a discussion of numerical Mets history.

Selected by the Mets in the second round of the 1977 amateur draft, Wilson arrived in September of 1980 displaying all the characteristics fans expect in a No. 1: aggression at the plate, speed and daring on the base paths, range in center field, and an enthusiasm worthy of his number.

Years of cheerful service through the lean early '80s were rewarded when Wilson found himself at the plate for the most important turn at bat in Met history. His 10th inning, Game 6 confrontation with Bob Stanley of the Red Sox in the 1986 World Series would produce the most important wild pitch in team history (Brad Clontz's in 1999 rates second) and, of course, a slow ground ball destined to roll past Bill Buckner and into baseball's collective consciousness forever.

After the arrival of Lenny Dykstra, and a concurrent shoulder injury in 1985, Wilson would increasingly be platooned in left field and center field, and with judicious use his on-base percentage improved during the second five years of his ten-year stay at Shea. He was traded in the disastrous bloody summer of 1989, but not before becoming the Mets' all-time leader in stolen bases (281) and triples (62), records that still stand as of the writing of this book.

Since Earle Combs of the Yankees donned No. 1 in 1929, helping usher in the practice of uniform numbers throughout baseball, No. 1 has traditionally been associated with scrappy, speedy, leadoff hitters.

Richie Ashburn led off the very first Mets game in 1962 wearing No. 1. He flew out to center, though later in the game he singled and scored the first run in Mets history. A future Hall of Famer, Ashburn certainly possessed No. 1–like qualities, although many, particularly his speed and once-pristine fielding, had eroded by the time he'd reached the Mets. Nevertheless, the 35-year-old Ashburn was probably the Mets' best overall player in their inaugural season, with a .424 on-base percentage—he was 27 plate appearances shy of qualifying but would have been the NL's leader that year—and a .306 batting average. His retirement following the '62 season left the Mets in want of a dependable leadoff hitter—and center fielder—for years to come.

Lance Johnson joined the Mets in 1996 as a free agent signee from the Chicago White Sox. He subsequently and unexpectedly set team records that year for hits (222), runs (117), and triples (21) in a season. He had trouble repeating that performance in 1997 and feuded with manager Bobby Valentine before being sent back to Chicago (this time, to the Cubs) in the first trade of Steve Phillips's reign as general manager.

Johnson, who was known as "One-Dog" to teammates in reference to his uniform number, suited up in No. 51 for the Mets just once—on September 1, 1996—while the Mets inducted Mookie Wilson into the club's Hall of Fame. "We had to do what we could to make his day perfect," Johnson told the *New York Times* afterward.

Over the eighteen years between Ashburn and Wilson, No. 1 went to twelve men. **Cliff Cook** and his replacement, **Duke Carmel**, in 1963 combined to hit .229 in reserve outfield duty. Low-average slugging third baseman **Charley Smith** (1964–65) followed and led the '64 Mets in home runs with 20. **Eddie Bressoud** (1966) was a stopgap shortstop peddled to St. Louis following the 1966 season for middle infield reserve **Jerry Buchek** (1967–68). Minor league vets **Kevin Collins** and **Bobby Pfeil** split reserve duties with the 1969 Mets.

The 1970s brought more brief visitors: part-timers **Lute Barnes** (1972–73), **Gene Clines** (disappointing compensation in exchange for Duffy Dyer in 1975), **Leo Foster** (1976), **Sergio Ferrer** (1978–79), and, making a pre-managerial appearance, **Bobby Valentine** (1977–78).

The post-Mookie era would bring the Mets two of their great disappointments and shame to the No. 1 jersey. **Tony Fernandez** (1993) should have worked out but didn't: the four-time All-Star shortstop was acquired in an off-season trade with the Padres, and he got off to a brutal start with the '93 Mets, hitting .225 and looking like he'd rather be waiting for a bus than playing baseball. Exasperated, the Mets un-loaded him in mid-June to Toronto, where he'd starred his first eight seasons in the majors. He promptly hit .306 for the Blue Jays, including 18 triples in 94 games, and won a World Series ring. Booooo.

BOBBY VALENTINE

Fernandez's arrival prompted **Vince Coleman** (1991–92) to change his number from 1 to 11, but he was a loser in any disguise. Signed to a rich free-agent deal just as Darryl Strawberry departed to the Dodgers, "Vincent Van Go" showed only traces of the speed that made him a three-time 100-base stealer with St. Louis. He brought precious little else to the Mets' lineup while battling hamstring injuries, beat reporters, and team authorities. He is remembered best for throwing an M-100 firecracker from a car outside Dodger Stadium in 1993, injuring three bystanders, including a two-year-old girl.

When Wilson joined Bobby Valentine's coaching staff in 1997, he wore No. 51 until Lance Johnson was traded in August, and he suited up again in 1 through the 2002 season. While Wilson remained in the organization as a minor league coach, the Mets appeared to take No. 1 out of circula-tion. But **Esix Snead** wore it during his brief stay in 2004; and in 2005, they turned it over to rookie **Anderson Hernandez**. An injury to incum-bent second baseman Kaz Matsui made Hernandez the opening-day second baseman in 2006. But despite making a catch that will play on

Mets highlight reels for years, Hernandez failed to hit well enough to hold onto the job.

Slap-hitting aging speedster **Luis Castillo** (2007) joined the Mets in time to participate in their late-season collapse, although that was hardly his fault. Castillo provided excellent defense at second base and some key offensive contributions despite wobbly knees. Knees that fans will be seeing for a long time.

Other Mets who wore No. 1 include reserve outfielders **Chuck Carr** (1990), **Lou Thornton** (1990), and **Ricky Otero** (1994), plus infield prospects **Kevin Baez** (1993), and **Fernando Viña** (1994).

Number of times issued: 26 (25 players, 1 coach)

Longest tenured: Mookie Wilson (10 seasons, 1,116 games)

Best single seasons: Lance Johnson, 1996 (.333/.362/.479, 21 triples, 50 stolen bases); Wilson, 1982 (.279/.314/.369, 55 RBI, 58 stolen bases); Richie Ashburn, 1962 (.306/.424/.393)

Career statistical leaders: Home runs (Wilson 60), RBI (Wilson 342), batting average (Johnson .326)

Mets by the Lineup

Mookie Wilson matched his uniform number to his slot in the starting lineup in 681 regular-season games during his career with the Mets, the most times a uni number has aligned with a batting order slot in Met history.

Following is a list of Met players whose jersey number aligned with their slot in the batting order most often (through 2007). Note that in more than 1,300 games, Bud Harrelson never once batted third, and that no Met No. 9 has ever batted ninth in a starting lineup (although Todd Hundley, Ty Wigginton, and Todd Zeile have been candidates as designated hitter).

1. Mookie Wilson   681 games
2. Phil Linz   34 games
3. Richie Hebner   11 games
4. Rusty Staub   250 games
5. David Wright   245 games
6. Mike Marshall   37 games
7. Hubie Brooks   115 games
8. Chris Cannizzaro   58 games

#2: MARVELOUS MARV AND THE TERRIBLE TWOS

A catcher who couldn't throw, a manager in disguise, a reviled acquisition, and a man whose initials were M.E.T., but whose play was B.A.D. Mets who have worn No. 2 are remembered for reasons they might not have wanted.

Take **Marvin Eugene Throneberry** (please!), the very first Met player to suit up in No. 2, acquired with the best of intentions but destined to become a lasting symbol of the futility and lovability of the dreadful-but-endearing '62 Mets.

Throneberry, who arrived in a trade with Baltimore in May 1962, was the kind of player the young Mets were willing to take a chance on: he'd shown good power in the minor leagues, hitting 40 home runs in consecutive seasons with the Yankees' Denver farm team. Although he'd since bounced to the Kansas City A's and Baltimore Orioles organizations, the Mets' brass felt Throneberry could thrive if given the everyday opportunity he'd never really had. The Mets then willingly parted with the first player they'd selected in the expansion daft, Hobie Landrith, to acquire him.

"Marvelous Marv" would hit .238 with 16 home runs for the '62 Mets, but where he really excelled was in the area of pitiable comic relief. He committed a league-leading 17 errors at first base. He famously interfered with a base runner in the field, and missed first base on a triple in halves of the same inning. His earnest struggles struck a chord with Mets fans anxious to cheer for anything.

Throneberry was considerably less popular with the front office following a contract squabble prior to the 1963 season. He was farmed out by May, never to return to the big leagues. His legend lived long after his career, thanks in part to a magnificent portrayal of himself in Miller Lite beer ads.

Dark glasses, a black hat, and a fake mustache weren't part of the official uniform, but when manager **Bobby Valentine** (1996–2002) donned them during a 1999 game, he wasn't supposed to be there anyway. His reappearance in the Shea dugout in disguise following an ejection came during a remarkable week in which the manager must have felt he had nothing to lose: three members of his hand-picked coaching staff had just been fired, eliciting Valentine's offer to put his own head on the chopping block if the Mets didn't improve over their next 55 games. They would go 40-15 over that stretch.

No man since Casey Stengel embodied the role of Mets manager quite like Valentine, who in six-plus years as the team's manager proved one of the most charismatic and divisive personalities in Mets history. While his tenure was marked with feuds with players (Todd Hundley, Pete Harnisch, Bobby Bonilla), the media (Murray Chass, Marty Noble), and general manager Steve Phillips, Valentine was rarely outmanaged by the other guy and was always fascinating to think along with. Astutely dubbed "The New Perfesser" by the *Village Voice*, Valentine won 536 games as a Mets manger, second only to Davey Johnson's 595.

Mackey Sasser hit well enough to be a capable backup for catcher Gary Carter, but a mystifying throwing ailment prevented him from being Carter's successor. An adequate receiver with an otherwise strong throwing arm, Sasser suffered from an inability to return the ball to his pitcher in one try: delays while he repeatedly pumped his arm before throwing frustrated Sasser and his teammates alike, but opponents took little pity, swiping bases on him with impunity.

The condition seemed to worsen after the Mets let Carter go, leading to the Mets use seven different catchers in 1990—six of whom couldn't hit—and Sasser's eventual conversion to a utility player. The free-swinging lefty compiled a .283 career average as a Met with good doubles power. He hit .307 over 100 games in 1990.

That the Nolan Ryan-for-**Jim Fregosi** swap was the worst deal in Mets history is barely debatable—the question remains where it ranks among bad trades in baseball history.

When the swindle was orchestrated in December of 1971, the Mets were confident they got the better of it. After all, Fregosi (1972–73) was a six-time All-Star shortstop with the Angels and viewed as the long-awaited answer to the Mets' third-base whirligig, which was already becoming famous. They had Wayne Garrett around but didn't trust him, Tim Foli wasn't yet ready, and **Bob Aspromonte** (1971), the starter for most of the 1971 season and Fregosi's predecessor in the No. 2 jersey, had been released. Above all, the Mets believed they were contenders and could afford to go for it with a veteran, even if it meant the sacrifice of a few young prospects.

But they hadn't done their homework. An injured foot requiring surgery in 1971 had convinced the Angels that their 29-year-old star player was rapidly approaching the breakdown stage. The recently acquired Leo Cardenas would be their 1972 shortstop whether they traded Fregosi or not. If Ryan's frequent injuries and famous wildness—a fact driven home by dreadful performances near the end the 1971 season—warranted a trade, Fregosi was probably the wrong target and came very expensively, given the Angels' lack of leverage. And then there was the fact that Fregosi had never played an inning of third base in his 1,392-game major league career.

Fregosi never regained his form. Injuries limited him to 101 games in 1972, when he batted just .232 with five home runs, the worst numbers of his career. By 1973 he'd fallen out of favor with fans and management and was dealt to the Rangers in mid-season. The bounty? Undisclosed cash payment.

The Terrible Twos also included outfielder **George Altman** (1964), the prize in the Roger Craig trade who saw his career take a sudden turn for the worse with the Mets. Shortstop **Jose Oquendo** (1983–84) provided dazzling fielding but a weak bat as a teenager for Bambi's Bandits in 1983; he'd develop into an excellent utility player and later a regular second baseman with the Cardinals. **Chuck Hiller** (1965–67) served as the poor-fielding, left-handed-hitting piece of a second-base platoon in the mid-1960s and hung around the organization for decades afterward as a coach and organizational instructor.

Fiery ex-Phillie **Larry Bowa** (1985) played the last games of his career during the Mets' 1985 stretch drive and continues to hold down the short-stop position on the "They were Mets?" all-time squad. **Roy Staiger** (1976–77) was a well-regarded prospect but showed little beyond a strong glove at third base. **Kevin Elster** (1986) made his debut on the last day of August in 1986—just in time to become an instant World Champion. He wore numbers other than 2 for the balance of his Mets career. **Jimmy**

Piersall was assigned No. 2 when he joined the Mets in 1963, but he switched to 34 after two days. Ex-Yankee socialite infielder **Phil Linz** spent the final two years of his career as a Mets backup.

Other 2s: Reserve infielders **Brock Pemberton** (1974–75), **Phil Mankowski** (1980, 1982), and **Bill Almon,** a former #1 overall pick by the San Diego Padres (1987); and short-lived outfielders **Doug Saunders** (1993); **Tom Grieve** (1978), future Texas GM who traded away Sammy Sosa; **Wayne Housie** (1993); and **Damon Buford** (1995).

Number of times issued: 22 (19 players, 1 manager, 2 coaches)

Longest tenured: Bobby Valentine (manager; 7 seasons, 1,003 games), Mackey Sasser (5 seasons, 420 games)

Best single season: Mackey Sasser, 1990 (.307/.344/.426)

Career statistical leaders: Home runs (Marv Throneberry 16), RBI (Sasser 133), batting average (Sasser .283)

How Low Can You Go?

On July 3, 1962, at Candlestick Park in San Francisco, Marv Throneberry allowed a pop fly to drop untouched on the infield grass for an RBI single, one of 15 Giants hits supporting Jack Sanford's complete-game effort in a 10-1 rout of the Mets. Nothing terribly unusual about that—Throneberry frequently made mind-bogglingly bad plays, the '62 Mets were routinely battered, and the Giants were on their way to the NL pennant. A mismatch on paper was borne out on the field. But it was on paper—specifically, the Met lineup card—where it got interesting.

1 Ashburn RF
10 Kanehl CF
11 Woodling LF
16 Taylor C
4 Neal 2B
2 Throneberry 1B
18 Mantilla 3B
7 Chacon SS
15 Jackson P

Add the uniform numbers together and you have 84—then and still, the lowest combined uniform starting lineup in Mets history.

This lineup's historical importance was of course not recognized at the time, and it was definitely lost on the man who wrote it. Manager Casey Stengel exited the ballpark during the fourth inning, leaving direction of the team to coach Cookie Lavagetto. Later it was revealed that Stengel had traveled eighty miles to Stockton, California, to recruit amateur free-agent pitcher Bob Garibaldi of Santa Clara University. Garibaldi was among the most sought-after collegians in the country that summer, but the meeting, like the game that day, was a low point: Garibaldi the next day announced he'd signed with the Giants. The '62 Mets had lost again.

#3: WHEN YOU SAY BUD

Over a thirteen-year playing career with the Mets, **Bud Harrelson** never wore a uniform number other than 3 and never played an inning at any position but shortstop.

A Mets constant who distinguished himself with feistiness and hustle, Harrelson (1965–77) is easily the team's all-time No. 3, a jersey otherwise populated by journeymen. As a Met, Harrelson earned two world championship rings (one as a coach), two All-Star Game appearances, a Gold Glove, and had a second, shorter, and considerably more difficult, career as a Mets manager.

Harrelson was a star in the field but not in the highlight reels. Steady but rarely breathtakingly so, he positioned himself superbly, caught whatever was hit near him, and threw accurately and on time. At the plate he consistently provided meager but reliable production, supplementing a near complete lack of power (7 career home runs) with good on-base skills, general heads-up play, and the ability to reach base via the bunt.

Part of Casey Stengel's "Youth of America," Harrelson signed with the Mets out of San Francisco State University shortly after he turned nineteen years old in 1963. So impressed was Stengel with the young infielder at spring camp in 1964 that the manager lobbied, albeit unsuccessfully, to take him north. It wouldn't be until 1967 that Harrelson established himself as the Mets' everyday shortstop.

In the championship season of 1969, Harrelson was one of only four regular starters under manager Gil Hodges' platoon system—Cleon Jones in left, Tommie Agee in center field, and Jerry Grote behind the plate were the others—embodying the baseball truism about strong defense up the middle winning championships. Fans recall Harrelson best for his dusty brawl with Pete Rose during the 1973 National League Championship Series: Harrelson, although giving away size to Rose, acquitted himself well as the Mets—similar longshots themselves—defeated the mighty Reds.

Ironically, Harrelson's career as a manager was a case of decent statistics hiding a shaky day-to-day performance. Given the unenviable task of succeeding Davey Johnson, Harrelson struggled to hold together fragments of a crumbling dynasty and lasted less than two seasons despite his teams achieving an overall winning mark. Although strongly influenced by Gil Hodges, Harrelson appeared to lack his managerial idol's presence and confidence, and his tenure is not remembered fondly.

Harrelson was on the coaching lines (wearing No. 23) while a successor in the No. 3 jersey, **Rafael Santana,** replicated Harrelson's role as the no-hit, good-glove shortstop on a Mets championship team. Santana (1984–87) lasted four years as a Met, three as a starter, although it's difficult to imagine how. Reliable defensively, Santana was a poor hitter, providing little of the extras in terms of speed or on-base skills that Harrelson could.

By the time **Carl Everett** (1995–97) had begun to realize his tremendous potential, he was already on his way out. A first-round draft pick of the Yankees out of Hillsborough High in Tampa, Dwight Gooden's alma mater, Everett had all the tools but had already worn through two organizations when he arrived in an astutely orchestrated trade with Florida following the 1994 season. Everett really began to blossom in 1997, providing explosive power, clutch hits, and ability in any outfield position, becoming one of the most promising young players on the suddenly contending Mets. Then Shea Stadium day-care staff alerted authorities of their concerns the Everett family may have been abusing their children.

The incident—which for a time cost the Everett's custody of their two kids—didn't sit well with the family-friendly image the Mets were promoting. Everett was unloaded cheaply, to Houston for doomed reliever John Hudek, following the 1997 season. Everett would go on to greater accomplishments on the field with the Astros and Red Sox and even grander displays of temper and curious behavior.

Vance Wilson (1998–2004) one day will tell his grandkids that he backed up the two greatest catchers of his era—Mike Piazza with the Mets and Ivan Rodriguez with the Tigers. Through 2006 they totaled twenty-four All-Star appearances and seventeen Silver Sluggers between them. Not bad for a 44th-round draft pick who didn't arrive in the majors to stay until age twenty-nine.

Wilson provided hard-nosed play, good defense, and respectable power in a fine job succeeding Piazza's similarly well-liked and valuable caddy, Todd Pratt. Wilson was exposed some when pressed into an everyday role following Piazza's injury in 2003 and was sent to the Tigers in exchange for Anderson Hernandez following the 2004 season.

Richie Hebner arrived reluctantly on the eve of the 1979 season and overnight became the third baseman he no longer was and the cleanup hitter he was never suited to be. His offseason job as a gravedigger, however, was a perfect match for the dreary '79 Mets.

A hardscrabble New Englander who might have also made a career as a hockey player, Hebner was a mainstay of the terrific Pirates teams of the early 1970s but had already been transitioned to a first baseman by Philadelphia when the Mets acquired him (for pitcher Nino Espinosa in a deal that certainly didn't go New York's way). Hebner knocked in four runs in his Met debut but things went downhill from there. A target of fan abuse and a symbol of a futile franchise, he was unloaded shortly after his only season in New York for outfielder Jerry Morales and third baseman Phil Mankowski.

Left-handed-hitting French Canadian slugger **Tim Harkness** replaced Marv Throneberry at first base for the Mets in 1963. While his overall numbers were unimpressive (10-41-.221), Harkness is remembered for hitting two extra-inning walk-off home runs that season, including a 14th-inning grand slam to stun the Cubs. His trade to Cincinnati in 1964 for Bobby Klaus stunned teammates and Harkness alike, resulting in Harkness refusing to report to the Reds' farm team in San Diego until the Mets reluctantly provided him a $2,000 bonus.

Gus Bell was the 1962 Mets' opening-day right fielder but lasted just five weeks in a Met uniform before being sent to Milwaukee as the player to be named in the previous winter's trade for Frank Thomas. Bell (1962) was one of the better power hitters in the National League in the 1950s, but he was all but washed up when the Mets selected him in the expansion draft. He hit .149 in 100 at-bats for the Mets. Another expansion draftee, **Ed Bouchee,** suited up in No. 3 after Bell disappeared in '62. Bouchee (1962) was a burly power-hitting first baseman with bad hands, suiting him perfectly to be a backup to Throneberry.

Billy Cowan (1965) was acquired from the Cubs to be the Mets' everyday center fielder in 1965. Despite a good glove, Cowan proved to be an abysmal free-swinger (.179 batting average, .205 on-base percentage, 5 walks, and 45 strikeouts in 162 plate appearances) and was traded in August. Reserve infielder **Mike Cubbage** wore No. 3 in 1981 but No. 4 when he took over briefly as Mets manager a decade later. **Miguel Cairo** had a good reputation as a reserve when he arrived in 2005 but spent entirely too much time making starts for injured teammates.

Veteran reservist **Damion Easley** was a terrific pinch hitter whose stint with the 2007 Mets ended in dual tragedy: A gruesome ankle injury ended his season in August and its repercussions by year-end rendered him the dubious distinction as having played the most games in the majors without appearing in a postseason series—1,593 and counting.

Also, short-lasting reserves were **Sergio Ferrer** (1978), **Mario Ramirez** (1980), **Junior Noboa** (1992), **Darrin Jackson** (1993), and **Luis Rivera** (1994).

Number of times issued: 21 (17 players, 2 coaches, 1 manager, 1 DNP)

Longest tenured: Bud Harrelson (13 seasons, 1,322 games)

Best single season: Harrelson, 1970 (.243/.351/.309, 95 walks, 23 stolen bases, 8 triples)

Career statistical leaders: Home runs (Carl Everett 27), RBI (Harrelson 242), batting average (Richie Hebner .268)

Step Right Up and Teach the Mets

Promoting from within was a few years in coming for the Mets. The early coaching staff mostly played when John McGraw ruled the Polo Grounds. Casey Stengel, who'd been 33 when he'd starred for McGraw's Giants in the 1923 World Series, kept the Mets beat writers in stitches at his old stomping grounds. Crabby coach Rogers Hornsby scared the pants off the greenhorns, while pitching coach Red Ruffing could regale the beleaguered staff with tales of playing with Babe Ruth. It was all good stuff, but it didn't translate into wins.

The first Mets to join the coaching ranks were players at the end of the line. Yogi Berra and Warren Spahn served as part-time players and full-time coaches in 1965. Berra, just fired by the Yankees despite winning a pennant as a rookie manager, caught just five games; Spahn flew the coop after three months, 12 losses and untold headaches working with the hopeless pitching staff. He opted to pitch a few final games in San Francisco and did not coach in the majors again until 1972. Rusty Staub was a player-coach in 1982, but his role soon changed to unofficial advisor and official pinch hitter.

Gil Hodges was the first former Met to manage in the majors. He first managed expansion Washington in 1963 and then, fittingly, took over the Mets in 1968. (Both the Senators and Mets traded players to acquire him as manager.) Hodges was also the first former Met to manage a world champion. Eight former Mets have followed him as manager at Shea, with varying degrees of success. Six of them, like Hodges, were infielders. Unlike Hodges, though, five apprenticed as coaches for the club.

Player	Position	Number	Coach	Number	Manager	Number
Yogi Berra	C	8	1965–71	8	1972–75	8
Warren Spahn	P	21	1965	21		
Gil Hodges	1B	14			1968–71	14
Joe Pignatano	C	5	1968–81	52		
Roy McMillan	SS	11	1973–75	51	1975	51
Willie Mays	OF	24	1974–79	24		
Joe Torre	1B	9			1977–81	9
Bud Harrelson	SS	3	1982, 1985–90	53, 23, 3	1990–91	3
Rusty Staub	OF	4, 10	1982	10		
Bobby Valentine	2B	1	1983–85	53, 22, 26	1996–2002	2
Mike Cubbage	3B	3	1990–96	4	1991	4
Chuck Hiller	2B	2	1990	22		
John Stephenson	C	49, 19, 12	1992–93	51, 32		
Dallas Green	P	27			1993–96	46
Bob Apodaca	P	34	1996–99	34		
Mookie Wilson	OF	1	1997–2002	51, 1		
Randy Niemann	P	46, 40	1997–99, 2001–02	45, 48, 52		
Al Jackson	P	15, 38	1999–2000	54		
John Stearns	C	16, 12	2000–01	12		
Sandy Alomar Sr.	SS	5	2005–07	2		
Willie Randolph	2B	12			2005–07	12
Rickey Henderson	OF	24	2007	24		
Howard Johnson	3B	20, 44	2007	52		

Note: Position refers to primary position as a Met. **Bold** indicates manager (including interim managers). Coach and manager only include years in those capacities as Mets.

#4: RUSTY, NAILS, AND MOJO

It's the destiny of the Met No. 4 jersey to be on the back of a fan favorite who stars in a post-season, only to be sent away in a baffling trade shortly afterward.

Naturally, it's happened four times.

Rusty Staub (1972–74) was one of the most complete ballplayers of his time; packaging power, on-base ability, clutch hitting, and fear-some defense in right field (he led the National League in assists in 1974 and '75).

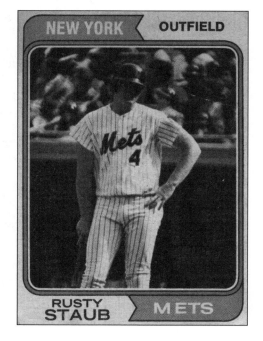

Acquired from Montreal just prior to the 1972 season for Ken Singleton, Tim Foli, and Mike Jorgensen, the left-handed-hitting Staub was leading the Mets in home runs and RBI before a fractured hand requiring surgery inter-rupted his season and derailed any hopes for the once-prom-ising Mets. Staub returned in 1973 to set a then-team record with 36 dou-bles and provide 3 home runs as the Mets upset the favored Cincinnati Reds in the playoffs. In the 1973 World Series, Rusty led all hitters with a .423 batting average despite playing with a shoulder damaged so badly in a collision with the right-field wall at Shea that he was forced to throw underhand.

As he had been in prior stops in Houston and Montreal, Staub was a great fan favorite, which made his trade to Detroit for Mickey Lolich following the 1975 season all the more infuriating. Approaching 10-and-5 rights (ten years of major league service, five with one club) giving him the power to veto a trade, a front office skittish about the newly won gains of the players association figured to act while they still controlled their hitting star's destiny. The Mets would right that mistake six years later, however, and Rusty would write an exciting final chapter to his career . . . as we'll see in Chapter 10.

He wasn't much of an outfielder any other day, but his diving catch of Brooks Robinson's liner in Game 4 of the 1969 World Series helped make **Ron Swoboda** an all-time Mets hero.

"Rocky" socked 19 homers as a 21-year-old rookie in 1965 (wearing No. 14, which he set aside for Ken Boyer in 1966). Though he never followed through on his early promise, Swoboda (1966–70) had a flair for the unexpected: it was his pair of two-run homers that defeated the Cardinals despite Steve Carlton striking out 19 Mets in September 1969. His 8th-inning double brought in the go-ahead run in Game 5 of the World Series to set the stage for Kooz, Cleon, and the rampage at Shea that followed. And along with teammate Tom Seaver, Swoboda became something of a spokesman for the champion Mets and what they represented in those turbulent times. Swoboda left unhappy after a 1971 trade to Montreal (Don Hahn came in exchange). He eventually returned to New York, first as a Yankee, then as a sportscaster of some renown.

Robin Ventura is always going to evoke mixed feelings. Signed as a free agent in 1999, Ventura (1999–2001) was a legitimate MVP candidate (he finished sixth in the voting, just ahead of teammates Mike Piazza and Edgardo Alfonzo) and a team leader who introduced "Mojo Risin'" to the Met vocabulary. He capped his first year as a Met with the unforgettable "grand slam single" that dramatically ended Game 5 of the '99 NLCS. But the goodwill generated by that first season would be severely tested by the two injury-plagued and disappointing campaigns to follow. His stock had dropped so low by the end of 2001 (21-61-.237) that the Mets felt comfortable trading him to the Yankees for three-time All-Star David Justice, leaving conflicted Mets fans the choice of either cheering for his continued mediocrity or rooting against the comeback they all believed he had in him. Predictably, his results as a Yankee were a mix of good and terrible. Justice, on the other hand, never played a single game for the Mets. One week after the Ventura trade, the Mets dealt him to Oakland for pitchers Mark Guthrie and Tyler Yates.

In Michael Lewis's bestseller *Moneyball*, Billy Beane, the Oakland general manager, described former farmhand roommate **Lenny Dykstra** as "perfectly designed emotionally to play the game of baseball." Who could disagree?

Hyperactive and pint-sized, Dykstra (1985–89) wore No. 4 but played like a No. 1. He hit .278 with 104 doubles and 116 stolen bases as a Met and shined in the 1986 postseason: his home run off Dave Smith in the bottom of the ninth inning won Game 3 of the NLCS against Houston, and his leadoff triple off Bob Knepper sparked the 9th-inning rally that tied that series' epic and decisive Game 6. His leadoff home run in Game 3 of the World Series at Fenway Park was the first step in the Mets' climb out of a deep hole against Boston.

In June of 1989, Dykstra, his giant wad of chewing tobacco, and Roger McDowell were dispatched to Philadelphia for Juan Samuel in a deal that to this day draws wails of regret from Mets fans. He'd go on to lead the Phillies into the 1993 World Series, finishing second in the National League MVP voting to Barry Bonds that year.

The 1989 Dykstra trade was highlighted that September as Samuel struggled to get out of the .230s and career minor-leaguer **Lou Thornton** was patrolling the Shea outfield in Dykstra's old No. 4. Inexplicably, Thornton would return briefly in 1990 in the No. 1 jersey of another displaced favorite, Mookie Wilson.

Former Brooklyn hero **Duke Snider** hit 14 homers in a nostalgia tour as a Met in 1963. As strange as it must have been for old Dodgers fans to see the Duke calling the Polo Grounds home, it was even stranger watching him don a Giants uniform in 1964.

Snider was batting in the 1979 Old-Timers' Day game at Shea Stadium when the tape covering the nameplate on his No. 4 jersey peeled away revealing . . . BOISCLAIR. One of those bit players whom Met fans tend to remember vividly, **Bruce Boisclair** (1976–79) was a gangly outfielder with a wide left-handed stance who enjoyed some success as a part-timer and pinch hitter (.293, 21 doubles, 4 HR, 44 RBI in 307 ABs in 1977) and considerably less success as an outfielder.

Original Mets second baseman **Charlie Neal** might be considered the franchise's first-ever big-money goof. The inviting left-field deck of the Polo Grounds—not to mention his Dodger bloodlines—persuaded the Mets to trade Lee Walls and $75,000 of George Weiss's "mad money" to Los Angeles for the pull-hitting infielder following the expansion draft. But Neal aged quickly (the early Mets had a way of doing that to people) and was shuffled off quietly in 1963.

Utility man **Bob Bailor** (1981–83) was the key player sent to the Dodgers in 1983 (along with reliever Carlos Diaz) in exchange for a portly minor-league southpaw named Sid Fernandez. That remains one of the shrewdest deals the Mets have ever made.

The rest of the Gang of Four were utility infielders and reserves: **Wayne Graham** (1964), best known for managing Rice University's baseball team wearing the uniform number of his manager, Casey Stengel; **Jose Moreno** (1980); **John Valentin** (2002); **Chris Woodward** (2005–06); and **Ben Johnson** (2007). Johnson, who batted all of .185 in 27 at bats in '07, was all the Mets had to show for trading two young relievers—Heath Bell and Royce Ring—who they desperately could have used.

Number of times issued: 17 (14 players, 3 coaches)

Longest tenured: Ron Swoboda (5 seasons, 602 games), Lenny Dykstra (5 seasons, 544 games)

Best single season: Robin Ventura, 1999 (.301/.379/.529, 32 HR, 120 RBI)

Career statistical leaders: Home runs (Ventura 77, Swoboda 50), RBI (Ventura 265, Swoboda 254), batting average (Dykstra .278, Staub .273)

Now Playing at the Drive-In

Former No. 4 Rusty Staub enjoyed a fifteen-year reign as the Mets' all-time single-season RBI leader. Over the next sixteen years, his one-time record of 105 RBI, set in 1975 (while wearing No. 10) and tied by Gary Carter in 1985, would be bested eleven times.

Despite the help of 265 RBI from Robin Ventura and 254 from Ron Swoboda, No. 4 collectively ranks no better than seventh on the Met all-time list of runs batted in by uniform number. (Rusty's No. 10 was weighed down by too many Reys—Ordoñez and Sanchez—to make anyone's list.) David Wright's third straight 100-RBI season enabled No. 5 to push past long-time leader No 18, where Darryl Strawberry's 733 RBI still rank as the highest individual total in Mets history. (Moises Alou spent too much time on the DL to hold off the inevitable.) And 15 caught 18 as well. Following are the top 10 uniform numbers by RBI through 2007:

No.	RBI	Notes
5	1,345	David Wright's 24/7 presence translates into 365 RBI; John Olerud (291) and Steve Henderson (227) stand at second and third
18	1,318	Strawberry with 733; Joel Youngblood with 216
15	1,318	George Foster edges Jerry Grote (361 to 357), but Carlos Beltran (306) will soon change that
20	1,300	Howard Johnson 626; Tommie Agee 265
7	1,285	Kranepool leads with 555; Hubie Brooks (259) and Jose Reyes (242) together don't reach the total of the seventeen-year Met
9	1,228	Todd Hundley 388; Gregg Jefferies 205
4	1,192	Ventura 265, Swoboda 265; Staub 188
25	1,052	Bobby Bonilla 275; Frank Thomas 173
12	1,051	John Stearns 302
22	1,018	Kevin McReynolds 456

#5: MR. WRIGHT

There are moments when you can't help but think **David Wright** will be the last Met to wear the No. 5 jersey. Like his eye black and his attitude, Wright wears it well.

A between-round "sandwich pick"—compensation for having lost Mike Hampton to free agency the previous winter—Wright was the 38th overall selection in the 2001 amateur draft and forced his way to the majors a little more than three years later. Had Wright been given a choice of uniform number, he may have taken No. 8 in honor of his boyhood idol, Cal Ripken of the Orioles. But Mets equipment managers had another recent vintage Hall of Fame infielder in mind when they issued Wright No. 5: George Brett of the Kansas City Royals.

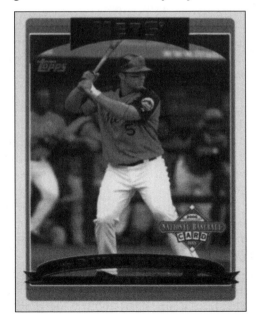

Where talented young players tend to have positive character attributes assigned to them regardless of their actual character, Wright appears to be very much the genuine article; the organization man who's too good to be fake. When fans wailed in 2005 that Willie Randolph had the temerity to bat him seventh in the lineup, Wright diffused any controversy by humbly explaining it offered him opportunities to learn. He paid respect to veterans, granted interviews, made promotional appearances, signed autographs for kids, remained a bachelor, started a charity foundation, and signed a long-term contract that could keep him in a Mets uniform through 2013.

There's no telling by then where he'll rank among the club's all-time offensive leaders, but he's off to an historically good start. In his first three-and-a-half years he posted top-ten Mets seasons in hits (twice), doubles (three times), and RBI. And through 2007 Wright was the second in Mets history (for players with 1,000 at-bats) in batting average (.311), slugging percentage (.533), and on-base percentage (.388). That certainly makes up for the odd errant throw from third base (and he still won the '07 Gold Glove).

One of the men Wright one day may chase down is a predecessor in the No. 5 jersey, **John Olerud** (1997–99). A brilliant bit of thievery brought Olerud to New York. Misinterpreting the first baseman's legendary patience at the plate as a lack of aggression, the Blue Jays took pedestrian starter Robert Person off the Mets' hands and paid $5 million (not Canadian dollars, either) of Olerud's $6.5 million 1997 salary. Olerud hammered home the folly of this deal by having the best three-year stretch of his career with the Mets, amassing 63 home runs, 291 RBI, and a .315/.425/.501 line: His batting and on-base percentages through 2006 were the highest in Mets history and his slugging ranked fourth all-time.

In 1998, Olerud shattered Cleon Jones's twenty-nine-year-old club record for batting average in a season, hitting .354. Olerud also came through when it counted. He hit .438 in the Mets' 1999 Division Series win over Arizona, including a home run in the crucial Game 1 victory over Randy Johnson, and .296 in the following NLCS against Atlanta with two home runs. Sadly, it would be his Mets swan song, as he departed for Seattle as a free agent following the season.

Olerud complemented his uniform by wearing a flapless batting helmet in the field. This was not a fashion statement but rather a precaution—and a message to his mother he'd be careful out there—after having suffered a brain aneurysm while in college.

Style, however, was the specialty of Olerud's successor in the No. 5 jersey, the flamboyant free-swinging Japanese outfielder **Tsuyoshi Shinjo**. Shinjo (2001, 2003) wore gigantic orange sweatbands and seemingly couldn't help but add flair to his motions: he hopped before catching every fly ball, and his home runs were frequently accented with a casually arrogant flip of the bat (especially arrogant given that he homered once every 50 or so at-bats as a Met).

Although imported primarily to be a reserve, injuries and ineffectiveness among regular starters provided Shinjo more playing time than the brass might have imagined in 2001. He responded by being perhaps the team's most exciting player that year, getting 10 home runs, 23 doubles, and 56 RBI in 400 at-bats. The Mets traded him and utility infielder Desi Relaford to San Francisco following the '01 season for left-handed starting pitcher Shawn Estes, but they missed Shinjo's contributions in 2002 enough to re-sign him in 2003, dressing him again in the No. 5 jersey. However, the 2003 go-round was considerably less effective (1 HR, .193 batting average in 114 at-bats) and injury-riddled. Shinjo returned to Japan, where he revived his career as the Jim Palmer of the East: he models the men's underwear brand Gunze and, going far beyond the Orioles' Hall of Famer, Shinjo made plans to model nude. When last seen clothed as a Nippon Ham Fighter, his triple-wide sweatbands came in patterns like argyle.

Casey Stengel famously explained that without a catcher, a team would have a lot of passed balls. And with that, the Mets chose lefty-swinging catcher **Hobie Landrith** with their very first pick in the 1961 expansion draft. A 31-year-old veteran of four organizations, Landrith (1962) in fact allowed three passed balls in a Mets career that lasted less than a month before he was shipped to Baltimore for Marv Throneberry.

There was no shortage of passed balls. The No. 5 jersey subsequently went to other reserve catchers: **Joe Pignatano,** an ex-Dodger who famously hit into a triple play in the last game of the 1962 season and then retired to a long career as a bullpen coach, cultivating the first tomato crop in Shea's right-field pen; **Norm Sherry,** yet another Dodger backup, acquired following the 1962 season and destined for pinch-hitting duties in 1963, his final season; and **Chris Cannizzaro,** who switched from No. 8 in 1965 for the Mets to make room for another veteran New York catcher playing out the last days of his career, Yogi Berra.

Ed Charles, who arrived early in 1967 and lasted through 1969, became the first wearer of the No. 5 jersey to make it more than one season for the Mets. The veteran third baseman, known as the "Glider" for his running style, served as a platoon third baseman—and unofficial poet laureate. He led the 1968 Mets with 15 home runs.

Charles's retirement after the 1969 season triggered one of the most foolish trades in team history when the Mets packaged young outfielder Amos Otis and pitcher Bob D. Johnson to Kansas City for **Joe Foy**.

The trade was a masterpiece of poor timing and wasted resources. Before the 1969 season the Mets had been so high on Otis they wouldn't part with him even though there were indications they might have pried Joe Torre loose from Atlanta if they had. Instead they tried making a third baseman out of Otis, but that experiment failed, leaving Otis unhappy, unproductive (.158 in 93 at-bats as an outfield reserve and pinch hitter), and in Gil Hodges's doghouse.

Only when Otis's value to the Mets was clearly down did they shop him. They chose a questionable target in Foy, who, while talented, came with questions about his attitude and associates, and whose value was mainly as a base stealer (and not a particularly efficient one with 37 steals in 54 attempts in 1969). Foy subsequently flopped as a Met (.236, 6 HR, 22 SB in 35 attempts, rumors of involvement with drugs, benching by Hodges) and was let go in the Rule 5 draft the following winter. Otis, naturally, went on to five All-Star appearances and a solid seventeen-year major league career.

Steve Henderson did the best he could to relieve the emptiness Mets fans felt from the Tom Seaver trade in which he was acquired, but Hendu could only do so much. Called to the majors for the first time following the trade, Henderson (1977–80) immediately took over left field, hit .295 with 12 home runs and a team-leading 65 RBI in just 99 games. He narrowly lost the Rookie of the Year vote to Andre Dawson of Montreal. But "Stevie Wonder" never much improved on his rookie season over the ensuing three years. His career highlight as a Met was a game-winning, three-run homer to cap a 7-6 comeback win over San Francisco, briefly convincing fans that the "magic" was indeed back in 1980. He was traded following that season for a second helping of Dave Kingman.

Davey Johnson managed in the Mets' greatest era (1984–90) and is still the team's winningest manager (595-417), as well as the all-time leader in games managed. He also holds the best winning percentage (.588) and had five consecutive 90-win seasons.

Sandy Alomar Sr. spent only two months of his fifteen-year career with the Mets in 1967 but during that period conceived his son Roberto, who'd play for the Mets 35 years later. Both Alomars, by the way, would be traded to the White Sox in August (thirty-six years apart), and the Mets would be better off without both: the father batted .000, and the son seemed to exude about that much enthusiasm. Senior came back to the Mets as part of Willie Randolph's coaching staff in 2006 and would be joined by another son, Sandy Jr., in 2007. **Mike Howard** (1981–83) was the opening-day right fielder for the 1983 Mets, but his future evaporated with the call-up of 21-year-old man child Darryl Strawberry later that spring.

Francisco Estrada appeared in only two games for the 1971 Mets but holds the record for games caught in the Mexican League during his 26-year career there. Free-swinging lefty power hitter **Jeromy Burnitz** (1993–94) wore No. 5 in his first go-round with Mets. Utility infielder **Mike Phillips** (1975–77) was acquired as insurance for the injured Bud Harrelson and had his moments for the Mets, including hitting for cycle at Wrigley Field in June of 1976.

Others: pinch-hitting specialist **Jim Beauchamp** (1972–73); fleet outfielder **Shaun Fitzmaurice** (1966); reserve outfielder **Jim Gosger** (1973); backup catcher **Charlie O'Brien** (1991); utility man **Jeff McKnight** (1992); catching prospect **Brook Fordyce** (1995); and reserve outfielders **Chris Jones** (1995–96) and one-time Dartmouth quarterback **Mark Johnson** (2000, 2002), who traded years with Shinjo. Catcher **Jerry Moses** was included on the 1975 active roster but never appeared in a game for the Mets.

Number of times issued: 27 (23 players, 1 manager, 1 DNP)

Longest tenured: Manager Davey Johnson (7 seasons, 1,102 games), David Wright (4 seasons, 543 games), Steve Henderson (4 seasons, 497 games)

Best single seasons: John Olerud, 1998 (.354/.447/.551, 22 HR, 93 RBI); David Wright, 2007 (.325/.416/.546, 30 HR, 107 RBI, 34 SB)

Career statistical leaders: Home runs (Wright 97, Olerud 63), RBI (Wright 365, Olerud 291), batting average (Olerud .315, Wright .311)

Just Your Average Mets

In their 45-year history, the Mets have never had a league batting champion. Part of that is a result of having spent so many years in Shea Stadium, a place that park-effect experts say depresses hitting for average more than it depresses hitting for power. But a lot of it has to do with a general lack of quality hitters for most of those years. Consider that from 1972 through 1983, no Met placed even among the top ten in batting average in the National League.

John Olerud, whose .354 batting average in 1998 is the Met standard, finished second that year to Larry Walker of Colorado, who hit .360. The Mets have had two third-place finishes (Cleon Jones in 1969 and Dave Magadan in 1990), one fourth (Lance Johnson in 1996), and a fifth, (Keith Hernandez in 1986), but overall, the Mets are not average when it comes to average: their batting champions come around just as often as their no-hitters.

Among Mets uniform numbers, Olerud and David Wright help No. 5 make a respectable showing when it comes to batting average. The twenty-three men to wear No. 5 have combined for a .275 batting average (that's 2,662 for 9,690), best among Met uni numbers not dominated by one player. Here are the top five through 2007:

No.	AB	Hits	Avg.	Note
31	3,809	1,112	.292	Mike Piazza (.292 career) accounts for 91.3 percent of all No. 31 at-bats.
13	4,604	1,303	.283	Edgardo Alfonzo (.292 career) accounts for 84.6 percent of all No. 13 at-bats.
5	9,690	2,662	.275	Olerud (.315 career) and Wright (. 311 career) set the pace.
29	2,692	728	.270	Dave Magadan hit .290 wearing 29; .291 wearing 10.
17	8,582	2,297	.268	Keith Hernandez (.297 career) and Felix Millan (.274 wearing 17) lead the way.

#6: THE SIX-PACK

How do you become the most-often-issued uniform number in Mets history? Put a lot of short-lived rubbish in the uniform, of course. Six is the most popular number in Mets history, issued thirty-three different times—often, it seems, for no apparent reason.

Virtually the only exception is filthy little second baseman **Wally Backman,** who, were it not for exceptional grit and a champion in manager Davey Johnson, might well have suffered the same fleeting fate of the thirty-one other men who have worn the No. 6 jersey.

After hitting .548 as a seventeen-year-old high school shortstop in Beaverton, Oregon, the Mets selected Backman in the first round of the 1977 amateur draft (Mookie Wilson went in the second round). Listed at 5-foot-9 and 160 pounds, Backman (1981–88) relied on hustle, a good batting eye, and nominal switch-hitting skills (he consistently struggled from the right side) to reach the majors by 1980, but physical calamities and his own fiery temper kept him from staying there.

Backman debuted in September of 1980 (wearing No. 28), hitting .323 as a replacement for the injured Doug Flynn at second base, but he railed at being stuck behind veteran Frank Taveras at shortstop in 1981. Backman briefly staged a retirement when sent to the minors that season and was not invited back when play resumed following the strike. In 1982, Backman split time with Bob Bailor at second base but was lost for the season after breaking his collarbone in a bicycle accident. In 1983, frustrated at backing up the smoother-fielding yet weaker-hitting Brian Giles, Backman was yo-yo'ed between New York and the Tidewater farm club three times in the season's first two months and publicly campaigned for a trade.

Yet Backman's May 1983 demotion turned out to be the break his career needed, pairing him up at Tidewater with Davey Johnson, a believer in offense who would become the Mets' manager in 1984. "The Mets sent down Backman and Ron Gardenhire and kept Brian Giles and Jose Oquendo," Johnson recalled in the *New York Times*, "and I thought they improved my ball club and hurt theirs."

With Johnson installed at Shea Stadium in '84, Backman finally got a chance to play every day and rewarded his manager's faith with the best stretch of his career during the Mets' best era. Paired with Lenny Dykstra atop the Mets' lineup, the two diminutive speedsters terrorized opposing pitchers while setting up the big guns that followed. Although often platooned—Backman was a .164 hitter as a Met from the right side as opposed to .306 from the left—he always seemed to find his way into a key spot in a tight game. Backman was traded to Minnesota following the 1989 season and left behind a .283 career batting average and a .353 on-base percentage over nine years with the Mets.

The rest of the Met six-pack is virtually empty as evidenced by multiple issues in 1962 (**Jim Marshall, Cliff Cook, Rick Herrscher**), 1964 (**Larry Burright, Bobby Klaus**), 1966 (**Lou Klimchock, Jim Hickman**),1967 (**Bart Shirley, Bob W. Johnson**), 1990 (**Mike A. Marshall, Alex Treviño, Darren Reed**), 1997 (**Manny Alexander, Carlos Mendoza**), 1998 (**Rich Becker, Tony Phillips**), and 2004 (**Ricky Gutierrez, Gerald Williams, Tom Wilson, Jeff Keppinger**).

The less said of the above group the better, including as it does extremely brief visitors (Jim Marshall, Herrscher, Shirley, Mendoza, and Wilson), guys better known by other uni numbers (Cook, Hickman, Treviño, Reed, Williams), and regrettable and/or disappointing pickups (Klaus, Mike Marshall, Becker, Phillips). Johnson was a notable exception: picked up on the cheap early in the 1967 season, Johnson surprisingly hit .348/.377/.474 as a pinch hitter and utility man in 230 at-bats and was deftly parlayed to Cincinnati shortly after the season ended for Art Shamsky.

Even those who didn't split a 6 with others during a season had short stays at Shea. **Al Weis** was a rare survivor in the shackles of No. 6. A skinny reserve middle infielder who rarely showed any power, he nevertheless hit the game-tying home run in the 7th inning of the Mets' decisive Game

5 victory in the 1969 World Series. He earned the Babe Ruth Award, a World Series MVP given each winter by the New York baseball writers chapter that is separate from the traditional Series MVP presented after the final game; Donn Clendenon took the better-known Series MVP prize in '69. In four years as a Met, Weis achieved a .191 batting average, a .252 on-base percentage, and hit 4 home runs. But he'll always have Game 5.

Melvin Mora, a Venezuelan soccer player who arrived with the Mets by way of Houston and Taiwan, was a revelation in 1999 spring training and arrived later that year to spark the Mets. He scored the run that forced a one-game playoff with Cincinnati. His throw from left field to nail Jay Bell at home plate in the 8th inning of the decisive Game 4 of the Division Series against Arizona proved one of the most pivotal defensive plays in Mets history. The Mets never seemed to know what to do with Mora (1999–2000), whose ability at so many positions undermined his efforts to establish himself at one. Shortstop, however, was not one of them, and when Rey Ordoñez was injured in 2000, the Mets sacrificed Mora to Baltimore for the surer hands of Mike Bordick in a trade they'd live to regret. Bordick did not re-sign with the Mets after their World Series loss to the Yankees, while Mora would eventually blossom into an All-Star third baseman with the Orioles.

Spunky outfielder **Timo Perez** (2000–03) appeared nearly as suddenly as Mora, and like Mora, he'd play an important role in a Met playoff drive, providing a spark as an injury replacement for fast-fading outfielder Derek Bell. However, Perez's inexcusable base-running mistake in the pivotal Game 1 of the World Series—he failed to run hard from second base on a two-out double off the top of the wall by Todd Zeile and was thrown out at home in a play that excruciatingly shifted the momentum of the entire World Series—may prove to be the biggest gaffe in Mets history. It arguably out-boners baseball's more celebrated postseason goofs from Merkle to Snodgrass to Pesky to Buckner. Perez had some success as an outfield reserve over the next few seasons, but he was often injured and was finally swapped to the White Sox just prior to the 2004 season.

Left-handed-hitting **Joe Orsulak** (1993–95) always gave an honest day's work. He rarely homered, walked, or struck out while hitting .276 over three years at Shea. He had the look of a gritty nineteenth-century outfielder stuck in a bad 1990s Mets outfield. Orsulak inherited No. 6 from **Darryl Boston** (1991–92), similarly effective and similarly pedestrian, although more the type your mom would call a bad influence.

Others: **Greg Harts** (1973), **Rich Puig** (1974), **Mike Vail** (1976–77), **Jose Cardenal** (1979–80), and **Carlos Baerga** (1995). See No. 8 for more on the Baerga bust.

Ruben Gotay tried on No. 6 in '07 and looked good in regular playing time at second base. Like Backman, though, he's a switch-hitter who can't hit right-handed, and like Keppinger, the man he was traded for, the Mets seem somewhat inclined to look for others to play the position despite his ability to sting the ball.

Number of times issued: 33 (all to players)

Longest tenured: Wally Backman (9 seasons, 765 games)

Best single season: Backman, 1986 (.320/.376/.385, 18 doubles, 13 stolen bases)

Career statistical leaders: Home runs (Timo Perez 18, Joe Orsulak 17), RBI (Backman 156; Perez 114, Orsulak 114), batting average (Bob W. Johnson .348, Ruben Gotay .295, Jeff Keppinger .284).

The Joy of Six

Just ask Darren Reed or Lou Klimchock—unpopular players are often the cause of popular numbers. Following is a list of the jersey numbers most frequently issued to players in Mets history through 2007. For a list of the least issued numbers, see Chapter 30.

No.	No. of Players to Wear It	Notes
6	33	Issued a team-record four times in 2004
34	30	Longest tenure: Danny Frisella (1970–72)
17	30	20 position players, 10 pitchers
35	29	Longest tenure: Rick Reed (5 years)
19	28	Bobby Ojeda (5 years) served longest of Sons of Ken MacKenzie
38	28	12 players in 9 years between Roger Craig (1963) and Buzz Capra (1971)
43	28	Issued twice in '66, '97, '98, and '02
11	27	26 position players, 1 pitcher
33	27	14 pitchers, 13 position players
26	26	One All-Star starter: Dave Kingman (1976)
29	26	Best player to wear it gave it up too soon: Ken Singleton
1	25	Everyone wants to be No. 1; most should think twice

#7: STEADY EDDIE

When **Ed Kranepool** hung up his No. 7 jersey for the last time, the event drew little notice (to be fair, a lot of things that happened in Flushing in 1979 were like that). There was no tearful retirement press conference, just a quiet refusal by the Mets to offer a 1980 con-tract—a sentiment subsequently echoed by the twenty-five other clubs declining to select Kranepool in the free-agent draft that fall. "There was talk of giving him a day at Shea Stadium last season," a Met publicist told the *New York Times* the following spring, "but nothing ever came of it."

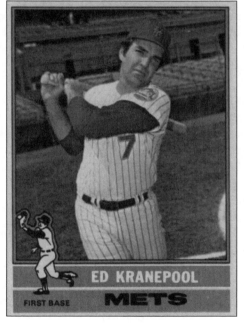

It was hardly the usual farewell to a player who, at the time, held virtually every meaningful offensive record in the history in the franchise, including games, hits, doubles, RBI, and home runs. He was also a local boy, the team's first high-profile amateur signee, the only player to spend every year of the franchise as an active player, and the senior player on the team for thirteen years running. But Kranepool's career was anything but usual.

Kranepool signed with the Mets for a reported $85,000 bonus shortly after graduating from James Monroe High in the Bronx in June of 1962. The talent-starved team gave the seventeen-year-old opportunities almost immediately, as Kranepool split brief visits to the minors between stretches on the Mets' bench, before assuming a starting role at first base in 1965.

Smart-aleck Mets fans of the era once flashed a placard asking whether Ed Kranepool was over-the-hill. Who knew? Kranepool's career as an everyday player might have peaked as a twenty-year-old in 1965, when he played a career-high 153 games and was named to the All-Star team for the first and only time. Kranepool had fair power, but he was slow afoot, nobody's idea of a defensive wizard, and occasionally appeared disinterested and surly.

The Mets for their part seemed to be forever looking to replace him. He'd be displaced as the Mets' first baseman in 1969, waived and sent to the minor leagues in 1970, only to rebound with his best overall season in 1971 (14-58-.280/.340/.447 in 421 at-bats). From there he became a part-time outfielder/first baseman and effective pinch hitter for the balance of his career, a role for which he finally won the admiration of fans. Kranepool hit .396 as a pinch hitter between 1974 and 1978, including .486 in 1974.

Of all the team-leading career statistics Kranepool's longevity built for him, his safest record is the longevity itself. No Met spent more time occupying the same jersey number than Kranepool, and it's not even close. Even discounting the 208 games Kranepool played at the beginning of his Mets' career wearing No. 21—no, he wasn't born wearing 7—his 1,645 games in No. 7 provides a cushion of 323 games over Bud Harrelson's lengthy tenure in No. 3. That's nearly two full seasons.

While Darryl Strawberry toppled his power and production records, that some of his other club records (hits, doubles, and total bases) still stand today is a testament to Kranepool, certainly, but also a comment on the team that employed him all those years.

The Mets finally came around to inducting Kranepool into their Hall of Fame in 1990. By then, his uniform number had been redistributed freely. Doomed third baseman/shortstop **Hubie Brooks** (1981–84, 1991) was the first to don it again. Brooks, a line-drive hitter with a reputation for clutch hitting, arrived along with the wave of promising early '80s Mets and looked, like Kranepool, like he'd be a longtime occupant of the jersey. But Brooks was sacrificed in the Gary Carter trade so that his comrades would taste a world championship. The championship contender Brooks helped build was already in decline (as was Brooks) by the time the Mets reacquired him as an outfielder in 1991.

Future National League MVP **Kevin Mitchell** was only a rookie in 1986 when he played five positions during the year and then capped the season by coolly lining a two-out single to keep the Mets' slim hopes alive in the epic World Series Game 6. It was Mitchell who crossed the plate with the tying run on Bob Stanley's wild pitch that Mookie Wilson so deftly jackknifed away from. Amid rumblings that he was a bad influence, Mitchell was dispatched after the season in the Kevin McReynolds trade.

The Mets may never have had a player as exciting as **Jose Reyes**, although it wasn't all that long ago that some questioned whether he was worth all the hype. Arriving with great promise as a nineteen-year-old in 2003, Reyes fought injuries and a botched conversion to second base in 2004 and struggled to reach base often enough to be effective in 2005 before a breakout 2006 (30 doubles, 17 triples, 19 home runs, a .300 batting average, and, importantly, a .354 on-base percentage). Reyes set a previously unimaginable mark of 77 walks in 2007 and along the way mercifully wiped Roger Cedeño's name from the Mets record books: His 78 stolen bases established a new team record and marked the first time a

Met had led the National League (and the majors) in stolen bases. At his current pace, Reyes ought to own franchise-leading marks in stolen bases and triples, and be approaching marks for runs scored, by the time his contract expires in 2010. Look out, Ed Kranepool.

Few jobs in baseball are lonelier than Mike Piazza's understudy, but catcher **Todd Pratt** (1998–2001) sure made the most of limited stage appearances. His heart-stopping home run off the edge of Steve Finley's glove in deepest center field in the 10th inning in Game 4 of the Mets' upset of Arizona in the 1999 Division Series ranks among the most dramatic and unexpected thrills in team history. In July 2001, the Mets shipped Pratt off to the Phillies for **Gary Bennett** (2001) in a straight-up uni/catcher's gear swap. Bennett had just one plate appearance as a Met, and he doubled.

Juan Samuel (1989) arrived for Lenny Dykstra and Roger McDowell in a trade signaling the impending crumble of the Mets' would-be 1980s dynasty. It was a bad fit all around. Comfortable playing second base and wearing No. 8, the Mets played Samuel in center field and dressed him in No. 7 (Gary Carter still had 8 then). An all-or-nothing kind of hitter, Samuel gave the Mets almost nothing (.228/.299/.300 in 86 games), and he was shuffled off to Los Angeles following the season for Mike Marshall in a spiral of decreasing returns.

Daryl Boston (1990) was claimed by the Mets when the White Sox waived him early in the 1990 season, and he provided competent production at a position ravaged by the trades of Lenny Dykstra and Mookie Wilson the year before. Boston would switch to No. 6 when Hubie Brooks returned in 1991.

Other Magnificent Sevens included fringe players **John Christensen** (1985), **Clint Hurdle** (1987), **Chuck Carr** (1990), **D. J. Dozier** (1992), **Jeff McKnight** (1993), **Charlie Greene** (1996), and **Jason Phillips** (2002). All but Dozier, a two-sport player who also lined up in the Minnesota Vikings backfield, and Greene spent at least some of their Mets careers in a number other than 7.

Number of times issued: 20 (18 players, 1 coach)

Longest tenured: Ed Kranepool (15 seasons, 1,645 games)

Best single season: Jose Reyes, 2006 (.300/.354/.487, 19 HR, 17 triples, 64 stolen bases)

Career statistical leaders: Home runs (Kranepool 106), RBI (Kranepool 555), batting average (Reyes .284, Kevin Mitchell .277, Darryl Boston .273)

Seven-Eleven

If you went to any Mets game, ever, there's a better than 50-50 chance you'd see a No. 7, a No. 11, or a No. 15 on the field. Ed Kranepool appeared in more games wearing No. 7 than every No. 8 in team history. Jose Reyes has logged at least 150 games a year for three years running. It's no wonder then, that through 2007, No. 7 is the most frequently appearing number in team history. Close behind is No. 11, which has appeared in 3,740 Mets games through 2007.

Following is a list of the most frequent appearances in a game by uniform number through 2007, and the percentage of all Mets games in which that number appeared.

No.	Games/Percentage of Games Appearing	Notes
7	3,845/52.6%	With 160 games in 2007, Jose Reyes pushed 7 past 11 (and Ramon Castro's 52-game season) for the all-time team lead.
11	3,740/51.1%	The Mets have had at least one player wearing No. 11 in all but three seasons (1967, 1968, and 2002).
15	3,663/50.1%	Jerry Grote squatted for 1,235 of these.
17	3,433/46.9%	Keith Hernandez, with 880 games, leads the pack.
4	3,272/44.7%	Ron Swoboda, with 602 games, leads.
25	3,238/44.3%	Pedro Feliciano (98 games in two years wearing No. 25) has become a workhorse.
6	3,226/44.1%	Wally Backman had nearly twice the games of the next highest finisher, Timo Perez.
3	3,167/43.3%	Bud Harrelson's 1,322 games leads the way.
5	3,151/43.1%	David Wright has appeared in more games wearing No. 5 (543) than any other Met.
9	3,127/42.8%	Todd Hundley, with 719 games, including 150 catching in 1996 alone.
20	3,118/42.6%	Howard Johnson: 1,149 games in No. 20.
18	3,117/42.6%	All 1,109 of Darryl Strawberry's Mets games came while wearing No. 18.
12	3,103/42.4%	John Stearns played a team-high 718 games in No. 12.
23	3.028/41.4%	Doug Flynn leads with 636 games.
1	2,974/40.7%	Mookie Wilson: 1,116 games, all in No. 1.

#8: THE KID

Like many big deals, getting **Gary Carter** into a Mets uniform was a strenuous exercise in give-and-take.

To receive the catcher who would change a promising 1984 Mets team into a true contender in 1985 and beyond, the Mets had to surrender four players to the Expos: infielder Hubie Brooks, just then coming into his own; catcher Mike Fitzgerald; and prospects Herm Winningham, an outfielder, and Floyd Youmans, a pitcher. Parting with Brooks would leave the Mets an infielder short, so in the days prior to making the Carter deal, general manager Frank Cashen made a separate trade, sending pitcher Walt Terrell to Detroit for young third baseman Howard Johnson.

Once the Mets and Expos agreed to the terms of the trade, they had to seek Carter's approval. As a player dealt in the midst of a multiyear contract, Carter had the right to demand a trade: he'd waive that right in exchange for the Mets extending his no-trade clause through the expiration of the contract in 1989. But where Carter was concerned, one thing was nonnegotiable.

"One thing I have to have," he told Cashen, "is No. 8."

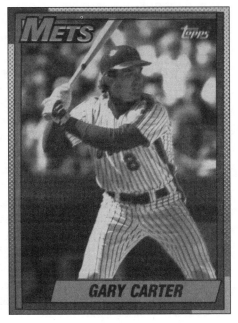

Sorry, John Gibbons. Wear something else, Ronn Reynolds.

No. 8 was Carter's lucky number. It represented both his birthday (April 8) and wedding day (February 8). "I'll never wear anything else," he said. For the Mets, he represented No. 8 with class, charisma, and passion through the life of his contract, and he was vital in achieving the objective the Mets had in mind when they acquired him.

Carter's line single started the two-out, 10th-inning Game 6 World Series rally in 1986, and earlier in that contest, he provided the 8th-inning sacrifice fly that allowed the game to go into extra innings. In all he drove in 9 runs in the '86 World Series, including the tying run in the 6th inning of Game 7, and hit 3 home runs.

Carter was celebrated, and sometimes criticized, for his enthusiasm and attraction to the limelight, earning him the nicknames the "Kid" for the joy he took on the field and "Camera Carter" among detractors for his seeming love of attention. The Kid announced his arrival in New York by hitting a 10th-inning, walk-off home run off Neil Allen of the Cardinals on opening day in 1985, en route to a 32-100-.281 season, probably his best as a Met. He was also the only Met ever to pitch Ivory soap.

More than half of the Mets players to wear No. 8 have been catchers. **John Gibbons**, whose shot at succeeding Mike Fitzgerald as a starter ended when Carter was acquired, was one such 8. The future Blue Jays manager and Ted Lilly sparring partner reappeared briefly in Nos. 43 and 35 later in his Mets career.

It all got started with **Chris Cannizzaro**, who was 23 years old and stuck behind Tim McCarver in the Cardinals organization when the Mets selected him in the 1961 expansion draft. Cannizzaro was a fine defender, but the Mets never liked his bat enough to make him anything more than a backup. He hit .311 in limited duty with the Mets in 1964; when used in 54 more games the next year he batted .183. Cannizzaro did not play much in the majors until the 1969 expansion draft opened up yet more new markets for mediocre backstops, when he signed with the San Diego Padres.

In 1965, Cannizzaro saw his uniform number pushed aside for **Yogi Berra**, acquired by the Mets as a player-coach. Berra kept the former designation for all nine of his plate appearances as a Mets player, but he would also occupy No. 8 as a coach until 1971 and as a manager from '72 to 1975.

Named to the manager's position while the Mets were still reeling from the death of Gil Hodges, Berra would never be confused with his predecessor as a manager (his teams went 292-296 over three-plus seasons) or strategist (starting Tom Seaver on short rest in Game 6 of 1973 World

Series), but he nonetheless took a flawed squad to Game 7 of the World Series in 1973, proving "It ain't over till it's over."

Berra's lengthy tenure as a Mets staffer had kept No. 8 out of circulation for fifteen years before **Dan Norman** (1979–80), an outfielder acquired in the Tom Seaver trade, received the assignment in 1979. Though considered a valuable prospect at the time, Norman (who spent the first part of his Mets career in No. 33) would see the least action of the four men received in that regretful deal.

The infrequently issued No. 8 was in heavy rotation in 1982. Switch-hitting backup catcher **Rick Sweet,** whose surname described his afro and accompanying mustache, spent the early part of the 1982 season in No. 8 before being sold to Seattle. In late June that year the Mets turned the jersey over to journeyman infielder **Phil Mankowski** (who'd appeared in 1980 wearing No. 2), while Hubie Brooks overcame a hamstring injury. Finally in September, the Mets recalled Class AA catcher **Ronn Reynolds** (1982–83), who remained a Mets backup in No. 8 until the early part of the 1983 season (and he returned in 1985 wearing No. 9, thanks to Carter).

Reserve outfielder **Dave Gallagher** (1992–93) was the first Met to be issued No. 8 following Carter's 1989 departure, and he had some success as a pinch hitter for the dreadful Jeff Torborg teams of 1992 and 1993. In 2001, **Desi Relaford** won a job as an infield backup, was terrific in a utility role (8-36-.302), and was sent to San Francisco with outfielder Tsuyoshi Shinjo in the aforementioned deal for pitcher Shawn Estes. Relaford's perfect inning of mop-up pitching on May 17, 2001, leaves him the lowest-numbered Met to ever toe the rubber.

Like a lot of veteran American League infielders en route to the Mets (Fernandez, Alomar, Sanchez, et al.), **Carlos Baerga** (1997–98) suffered an accelerated career decline at Shea. His acquisition for Jeff Kent was a pretty bad deal for the Mets. (Baerga spent most of his first two months as a Met in 1996 playing first base, wearing No. 6, and being hurt.) And to think it seemed like the Mets were getting the better second baseman . . . if only for a moment.

Number of times issued: 14 (11 players, 4 coaches, 1 manager)

Longest tenured: Gary Carter (5 seasons, 600 games)

Best single season: Carter, 1985 (.281/.365/.488, 32 HR, 100 RBI)

Career statistical leaders: Home runs (Carter 89, Carlos Baerga 16), RBI (Carter 349, Baerga 89), batting average (Desi Relaford .302, Baerga .273)

Out of Circulation: A Modest Proposal

Between the firing of Davey Johnson, the sudden resignation of general manager Joe McIlvaine, the ongoing Darryl Strawberry contract squabble, and the general sense of despair as the 1980s, success began transitioning into 1990s struggles, perhaps it was easy to overlook a certain breach of Mets uniform etiquette in 1990.

That's when the Mets promoted journeyman infielder Kelvin Torve and outfitted him in No. 24—apparently unaware that by doing so they'd broken a promise made by deceased owner Joan Payson that the team would leave No. 24 unoccupied as a tribute to Payson's favorite player, Willie Mays.

When fans and writers revolted, Torve was soon dressed in the less controversial No. 39. (Although it appeared an honest mistake had been made, one lesson was that fans are often better stewards of team history than the team itself.)

The Torve incident highlighted the oddity of numbers that have not been officially retired by the club but have been taken out of circulation, on a temporary or semipermanent basis. Mays's 24, Gary Carter's No. 8, and, currently, Mike Piazza's No. 31 are a few such examples of uniform limbo affecting the Mets.

While several players wore No. 8 in the years following Carter's departure, the uniform appeared to get scarce around the time the "Kid" was receiving consideration for the Hall of Fame and has been conspicuously unissued since his induction at Cooperstown in 2003. Some observers pegged this as a signal that the Mets would "officially" retire No. 8 in honor of Carter (as the Expos did), but as of this writing, no such plans have been announced. As for 24, it remains in limbo, save for the Met tenure of Rickey Henderson, who insisted on wearing 24 when he joined the Mets but first sought and received an OK from Mays. (Henderson reappeared in 24 as a Met coach in 2007.)

The Mets have retired only three numbers (Casey Stengel's 37, Gil Hodges' 14, and Tom Seaver's 41) and took Jackie Robinson's 42 out of circulation when it was retired throughout organized baseball in 1998, but the club has seemingly been judicious about the reissue of many others over the years.

Whether the retirements are too few is a matter of fierce debate in some circles, with one fringe believing that reissuing numbers like 1, 17, and 36 amounts to an affront to the dignity of Mookie, Keith, or Jerry, while the other side feels that uniform number retirement is the ultimate honor and only deserving for those rarest of athletes who spend the majority of their careers with the Mets and receive Hall of Fame enshrinement, or contribute to team history in profound or unique ways. As the Mets go, the Retired Numbers Club is about as exclusive as it gets. Others, say in the Monument section north of Queens, have slashed numbers out of existence like a Presidents' Day mattress sale.

A look to pro soccer might provide the most satisfying resolution to this dilemma. In that game, tradition holds that recycling the number of a former great to a current or newly arriving player glorifies the former while sending wishes of success and confidence to the latter. Thus, Pelé is reborn through Romário. Maradona through Riquelme. This keeps the standards for number retirement reassuringly high—what does it say about Babe Ruth that Reggie Jackson receives the same ultimate honor from the Yankees?—while also honoring the heritage of the team.

Nothing raises fan clamor to retire a number like seeing the Graeme Lloyds of the world running around in Keith Hernandez's former uniform (Hernandez himself appears taken aback occasionally). Fans—Keith, too—might be satisfied instead to see the Mets show the courage to issue No. 17 to the next slick-fielding, line-drive-hitting first baseman that arrives in the organization. Until such time, we're stuck with the likes of David Newhan.

#9: TODD, TODD, TORRE & TY

A prodigy whose clubhouse chemistry went nuclear. The veteran signee who couldn't quite replace his popular predecessor. A young power hitter lost amid inept veterans. The ornery catcher who went from the record books to the "Where are they now?" files in a flash. The inauspicious debut of a future Hall of Fame manager.

Your No. 9 Mets: slightly imperfect.

"I don't believe anyone can deny the fact that I have consistently taken it on the chin for the last three years," wrote **Gregg Jefferies**, in an infamous 1991 fax read aloud to listeners of WFAN, New York's influential sports radio station and broadcast home of the Mets. The open letter, an act of desperation from a player suffering effects of a chilly reception from teammates and fans, was recited amid laughter and ultimately served only as another shot on the chin and further isolation to a would-be phenom.

Given a little more maturity and humility, and a more supportive work environment, Jefferies (1987–91) might have been the great player he was pegged to be after tearing through the Mets' minor league system. The team had rarely produced a better hitter. He arrived, however, to a clubhouse with a low tolerance for golden boys and quick to resort to derisive anonymous quotes and humiliating pranks. And in stark contrast to his hitting, Jefferies had shoddy defensive skills, assuring that wherever he was positioned, he replaced a more capable fielder. That eroded the confidence of his teammates. Only when he was installed at first base did his hitting come around; unfortunately, that was in St. Louis several years after leaving New York an unhappy casualty of his own hype.

Jim Hickman was the last survivor of the expansion draft and the team's all-time leader in home runs when he was traded by the Mets following the 1966 season, with Ron Hunt, to the Dodgers for Tommy Davis. Hickman's career until then included infrequent moments of greatness (he was the first Met to hit three home runs in one game and the first Met to hit for the cycle) amid frequent struggles with the strikeout. The Mets also wavered on finding him a permanent home in the field, using him in all three outfield positions and at third base. Hickman (1962–66) was also notable for having worn three different uniform numbers in his Mets career: Although he spent the majority of his time in No. 9, manager Wes Westrum took No. 9 in 1966, forcing Hickman to change to No. 27. And after returning from a midseason injury and seeing 27 redistributed, he became No. 6.

In 1992, tough guy **Todd Hundley** switched from No. 49 to No. 9 to honor his father, former Mets nemesis Randy Hundley. In time, Todd Hundley developed into the best power-hitting catcher the club ever produced. A two-time All-Star, Hundley (1992–98) set the team standard for home runs in a season with 41 in 1996, which also set the all-time record for catchers. He then toughed out a painful elbow injury to lead the Mets' improbable but doomed run at the 1997 playoffs. That injury, though, essentially finished his career with the Mets, who acquired Mike Piazza while Hundley was recovering on the disabled list.

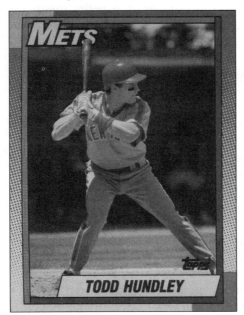

TODD HUNDLEY

Gamely but lamely, Hundley attempted to reestablish his career as an outfielder. He played sparingly and was shipped to Los Angeles following the 1998 season.

Todd Zeile's signature moment for the Mets came up one enormous inch too short. His drive in Game 1 of the 2000 World Series at Yankee Stadium hit the top of the wall and bounced back onto the field, where it transformed into an inning-ending, spirit-crushing, momentum-demolishing event that perfectly suited Zeile's tenure with the Mets. Given the unenviable challenge of replacing the popular John Olerud at first base, Zeile (2000–01) actually performed adequately in 2000 and especially well in the postseason. But Mets fans didn't want comparable, they wanted better. And that was something Zeile could not provide.

Zeile's poor showing in 2001 attracted boo-birds and prompted the team to conduct another experiment with far worse results: the Mo Vaughn acquisition.

Zeile returned in 2004 for his final professional season, this time as a reserve wearing his more familiar No. 27. No. 9 by then belonged to **Ty Wigginton,** a tough product of the Mets' farm system who filled in admirably in the absence of an actual third baseman in 2003. Wiggy, however, was playing on borrowed time, pending the arrival of David Wright. Sure enough, Wigginton (2002–04) was traded only weeks after Wright's 2004 arrival.

Although his Mets and major league careers were brief, gangly, free-spirited outfielder **George Theodore** is one of the most memorable Mets characters of all time. An accomplished minor league slugger who had only scant success in the big leagues, Theodore distinguished himself by expressing his thoughts on philosophy, poetry, and metaphysics, and his geeky appearance (tall, slim, eyeglasses, curly hair) endeared him to fans who recognized him as one of their own. Theodore, who debuted in No. 18 before switching to 9 early in the 1973 season as a tribute to boyhood idol Ted Williams ("I thought it might help my batting," he said), further proved his worth by overcoming a broken hip sustained in a frightening collision with Don Hahn.

Theodore's popularity extended to the minor leagues, where the Visalia Mets in 1974 dressed their mascot, a dog named Emerson Boozer, in Theodore's old No. 19 as a tribute to him.

Joe Torre, the one-time National League Most Valuable Player long coveted by the Mets, was finally acquired near the end of his playing career in 1975. Torre in 1977 transitioned to player-manager just as the front office was packaging Tom Seaver in a trade that would cripple the organization for as long as Torre would manage. As a result, Torre (who officially retired as a player weeks into his managerial tenure) oversaw one of the bleakest stretches in Met history and was fired after compiling a five-year record of 286-420. He'd go on to considerable success as a manager in Atlanta, St. Louis, and finally the Bronx.

Torre was the second Met manager to wear No. 9; **Wes Westrum** was the other. Although Westrum was Casey Stengel's choice to succeed him as manager, he lacked Stengel's charisma with the press, failed to get along with some of his players, and resigned late in 1967 when it was clear a contract renewal was not in the cards. Westrum holds the distinction of managing the Mets out of the cellar for the first time as well as its first sub-100 loss season, in 1966.

Other Met 9s, slightly more imperfect: Reserve catcher **J. C. Martin** (1968–69), best remembered for his creative base running in the triumphant 1969 World Series, as well as reserve catchers **Bill Sudakis** (1972), **Bruce Bochy** (1992), **Ronn Reynolds** (1985), and **Mike DiFelice** (2007); reserve infielders **Phil Mankowski** (1982) and **Craig Brazell** (2004); and outfielders **Mark Bradley** (1983), **Jerry Martin** (1984), and **Ricky Ledee** (2006–07). **Randy Bobb**, a reserve catcher, appeared on the active roster in September of 1970, but he never appeared in a Mets game.

Number of times issued: 18 (17 players, 1 DNP, 2 managers)

Longest tenured: Todd Hundley (8 seasons, 793 games), Joe Torre (as manager, 5 seasons, 706 games)

Best single seasons: Hundley, 1996 (.259/.356/.550, 41 HR, 112 RBI, 32 doubles); Hundley, 1997 (.273/.394/.549, 30 HR, 86 RBI)

Career statistical leaders: Home runs (Hundley 124, Jim Hickman 56, Gregg Jefferies 42), RBI (Hundley 395, Jefferies 205, Hickman 195), batting average (Ty Wigginton .270, Joe Torre .267)

The Constant 9

Lest any Mets fan forget, No. 9 stood for the television home for the Mets from the team's inception in 1962 through 1998. In the days before cable, WOR-TV was the only place to see the Mets unless you were at Shea Stadium or caught them on the road. The club's high and low comedy was expertly described on Channel 9 by the trio of Ralph Kiner, Lindsey Nelson, and Bob Murphy through 1978, the longest-running broadcasting trio the game has seen.

Channel 9 taught Mets history. Whether it was through the mouths of Kiner, Nelson, and Murphy—they alternated between TV and radio (what a concept!)—or via the highlight films that Channel 9 popped on the air the moment the tarp hit the field, a fan learned something new about the club with every broadcast, even when old stories were all there was to offer when the present club offered little worthy of note.

Channel 9 was busy. The station had broadcast the Dodgers and Giants—and even the Phillies during the baseball void—and filled the Mets-free hours with the Knicks, Nets, Rangers, Islanders, Cosmos, and pro wrestling when it was the WWF (and WWWF). There was no local news we needed to stay turned for or hustle off the air to catch. Non-sports fixtures included *Romper Room*, the "Million Dollar Movie," and racy Thames Television imports. About the only thing that could make a young fan smile after another Mets loss were the words "And coming up after Mets baseball, it's *The Benny Hill Show*."

Kiner's Korner was named for the short porch in Forbes Field that Kiner the Pirate made famous with his numerous blasts, but in New York the name lived on long after the Pittsburgh park came down. The Mets postgame interview show featured a familiar set with the names of major league teams in a woodcut-like font behind the heads of the guests. You could tell that being on *Kiner's Korner* was often as big a thrill for the players as it was for those watching at home, loving every extra second of baseball exposure on TV. The show enabled fans to find out what the ballplayer was like beyond what could be conveyed in a newspaper story.

Casey Stengel set the standard when he literally brought the house down—à la Mr. Magoo—on the very first show when the Mets manager forgot to take off his microphone upon walking off the set. The anything-can-happen nature of live TV pervaded the show, even as technology became more sophisticated. After reading a few out-of-town scores, Kiner ended the show with, "And if you can't make it out to the ballpark, we hope to see you right back out there." As if any of us would dare disappoint him.

#10: THEY BROUGHT THE FUNK

He played every position except pitcher and catcher in 1962—and as things turned out, he could probably have done those at least as well as his teammates. **"Hot Rod" Kanehl** was the first Mets utility player, one of the first heroes of Mets fans, and the first to wear the No. 10 jersey.

Admired by manager Casey Stengel ever since he'd had him at a Yankee training camp in the late 1950s, Kanehl (1962–64) nearly didn't make it to the Mets. A dispute over the rights to his contract erupted as the minor league Syracuse franchise transitioned from control of the Twins to the Mets over the 1961–62 off-season, with each organization claiming the rights to Kanehl. Commissioner Ford Frick ruled in the Mets' favor in February of 1962.

Kanehl's grit, hustle, and versatility helped obscure meager statistical output: a .241 batting average and just 32 extra-base hits in nearly 800 at-bats over three seasons.

Poor stats, hidden or otherwise, happen to be a common characteristic of the No. 10 brotherhood. There has been flash and occasional sizzle from the 10-spot, but few have ever put together the whole package wearing that number. Out-making has generally been more prolific than output.

Rey Ordoñez (1998–2002) drove a hard bargain to be the franchise's most spectacular defensive player. Acquired by the Mets in a special lottery following a defection from the Cuban national team, Ordoñez came around at precisely the wrong moment for an all-glove, no-hit shortstop. Stars like Nomar Garciaparra and Alex Rodriguez were redefining expectations at the position, and statistical measures revealing just how poorly Ordoñez compared to them were becoming the language of the common fan. Ordoñez was another Mark Belanger in a game where Mark Belanger, the eight-time Gold Glove Orioles shortstop, no longer had a place.

Tantalized by a 60-RBI season in 1999, the Mets signed Ordoñez to a four-year contract that would turn out to be one of the bigger mistakes in the Steve Phillips era. Injured in 2000, Ordoñez never developed any further as a hitter. In fact, he regressed. Later it was revealed that he was older by more than two years than the Mets had initially believed. Suddenly on the wrong side of thirty, it was less of a surprise when his once-legendary fielding skills fell into decline. When he uttered a few unkind words about the fans, any lingering debate over the value of offense vs. defense turned to a near unanimous call for his removal, which the Mets were only too eager to answer, trading him to the Tampa Bay Devil Rays for two players to be named later.

Rey Sanchez (2003) succeeded Ordoñez and was expected to provide good defense and a steady bat and to mentor shortstop-to-be Jose Reyes. The new Rey failed miserably on all three counts and is best remembered today for receiving a haircut during a blowout loss early on the Art Howe watch. This Rey's unreliability assured that Reyes would arrive ahead of schedule.

Rusty Staub wore No. 10 in Houston and in Montreal but patiently waited three seasons while backup catcher **Duffy Dyer** occupied the jersey for the Mets. Dyer (1968–74) might have been a better hitter than the man he understudied for a half-dozen years, Jerry Grote. With Grote missing a good part of the 1972 season with an injury, Dyer reached career highs with 17 doubles and 8 home runs in 363 plate appearances; that's more homers than Grote ever hit in a single year and stood as the club record for catchers until Gary Carter came around. In '73, Dyer's pinch-hit, run-scoring double in the bottom of the 9th inning was critical in the famous "Ball on the Wall" victory that marked the Mets' unlikely charge to the pennant.

Staub's move into No. 10 coincided with his best single season as a Met. He hit 19 home runs and 30 doubles and had a .382 on-base percentage while driving in 105 runs, a franchise RBI standard that lasted until Howard Johnson broke it in 1991. Staub was inexplicably traded following the season but reappeared as a free-agent acquisition in 1981 and began a second career as a pinch hitter and local restaurateur.

Willie Randolph's controversial decision to "bring the funk," and Miguel Cabrera's subsequent bases-clearing double all but killed whatever pennant hopes the 2005 Mets might have entertained. **Shingo Takatsu**'s igno-minious Mets debut overshadowed the fact that the side-arming Japanese reliever also ushered in the lowest number in team history for a pitcher.

Dave Magadan sandwiched No. 10 (1989–91) between stints at 29. A slow-footed singles hitter with a poor glove and terrific plate discipline, the Mets seemed reluctant to play Magadan regularly despite obvious skills at reaching base. In 1990 he was second in on-base percentage and third in batting; rarified air indeed for any Met. In 1992 Magadan gave up No. 10 to accommodate new manager **Jeff Torborg** (1992–93), a one-time American League Manager of the Year hired by the Mets on October 10, 1991, and fired nineteen months later with the faltering team he inherited in a shambles.

Endy Chavez (2006–07) capped one of greatest-ever seasons by a Met reserve with a catch that ranks among the best in playoff history. His soaring catch over the left-field fence in Game 7 of the 2006 Championship Series turned what should have been a two-run home run into an inning-ending double play. If he'd been only ten feet taller, Endy might have caught Yadier Molina's decisive blast a few innings later. Endy plays with an urgency and élan that puts him among the pantheon of beloved bench guys like Benny Agbayani and Rod Kanehl.

While they showed promise, **Butch Huskey** (1993) and **David Segui** (1994) topped out as midlevel players for other teams. Of all the tough-luck 10s, Huskey had the worst debut: he struck out his first three times up in the major leagues and made an error as Darryl Kile no-hit the Mets at the Astrodome.

Also in the 10-spot: backup backstops **Greg Goossen** (1966–68), **Joe DePastino** (2003), and **Joe Heitpas** (2004), and clock-punchers **Kevin Collins** (1965), **Mike Jorgensen** (1968), **Ken Henderson** (1978), **Kelvin Chapman** (1979), **Gary Thurman** (1997), **Kevin Morgan** (1997), **Roberto Petagine** (1997), **Jeff Duncan** (2004), and **Brian Buchanan** (2004).

Number of times issued: 25 (22 players, 1 manager, 1 coach)

Longest tenured: Rey Ordoñez (5 seasons, 645 games), Rusty Staub (6 seasons, 573 games), Duffy Dyer (6 seasons, 374 games)

Best single seasons: Staub, 1975 (.282/.371/.448, 19 HR, 105 RBI); Magadan, 1990 (.328/.417/.457, 6 HR, 72 RBI)

Career statistical leaders: Home runs (Staub 32, Dyer 16, Magadan 10), RBI (Staub 207, Ordoñez 197, Magadan 139), batting average (Endy Chavez, .300, Magadan .292, Staub .279)

Teen Idols

Although known in his native Japan as "Mister Zero," Shingo Takatsu was "Mister One-Zero" during his stay with the Mets in 2005. Takatsu succeeded Cory Lidle (No. 11 in 1997) as the pitcher with the lowest uniform number in club history (not counting position players such as Desi Relaford, who pitched a scoreless inning wearing No. 8 in 2001).

Al Jackson, the diminutive left-hander, was the Mets' original teen idol, wearing No. 15 in 1962. Roger Craig donned No. 13 in an attempt to end his bad luck in 1963 and wound up holding a Mets record for lowest number for a pitcher for eighteen years and then sharing it with flaky reliever Neil Allen, who, like Craig, took on 13 seeking a change in fortune.

Ron Darling set a new Mets low in 1985 when he switched from No. 44 to No. 12. Twelve was the best of all three of Darling's Mets uniforms, and it was his suggestion near the end of the 1986 season that Mets starters Rick Aguilera (38) and Sid Fernandez (50) join him, Dwight Gooden (16), and Bob Ojeda (19) in what would be an all-teen starting five.

The Mets reported for spring training in 1987 to find that equipment manager Charlie Samuels had followed through on the suggestion, issuing Aguilera No. 15 and Sid Fernandez No. 10. But the plan went awry when Fernandez couldn't get comfortable in No. 10, preferring the 50 he wore not only for his home state of Hawaii but for the cop show set there, also his favorite. Book 'em, Bobby O.

Following is a list of the lowest uniforms in Mets pitching history through 2007:

10: Shingo Takatsu, 2005
11: Cory Lidle, 1997
12: Ron Darling, 1985–89
13: Roger Craig, 1963; Neil Allen, 1981–83; Jeff Musselman, 1989–90; Jonathan
    Hurst, 1994; Matt Ginter, 2004; Billy Wagner, 2006–07
15: Al Jackson, 1962–65; Dave Roberts, 1981; Rick Aguilera, 1987–88; Ron Darling,
    1989–91
16: Dwight Gooden, 1984–94; Hideo Nomo, 1998; David Cone, 2003

#11: MAGNIFICENT TRANSIENCE

Like that reliever who scares fans to death, or a rough West Coast trip, a No. 11 is one of those things that seems a part of every Mets season. It's not always pleasant, but it's always there.

Despite just a handful of longtime occupants, the Mets have had a No. 11 on the field in all but three of their seasons (1967, 1968, and 2002). The Mets experienced a decade of magnificent transience between 1991 (Tim Teufel) and 2001 (Jorge Velandia) when the jersey was worn by thirteen different men, none for more than a single year. No other number has appeared as consistently—if not so reliably—through the Mets' first forty-five seasons.

The most prominent No. 11 was probably redheaded infielder **Wayne Garrett**, who lasted eight seasons in New York despite the team's best efforts to find someone else to do his job. Garrett (1969–76) arrived as a 21-year-old Rule 5 selection from the Braves in 1969 and surprised observers by making the team and staying with it as a platoon mate for Ed Charles. In the 1969 NLCS, the first scheduled playoff in league history, Garrett's double in Game 1 and home run in Game 3 helped bury his former organization. Although Charles retired following the 1969 season, Garrett did not inherit third base but rather waited to step in while over the next three years the team tried (and failed miserably) to fill third base with Joe Foy, Bob Aspromonte, and Jim Fregosi. Gritting their teeth and sticking with Garrett might have kept Amos Otis and Nolan Ryan in blue and orange . . . at least until the next troubled third sacker was made available by another team.

Garrett finally got a regular opportunity in 1973 and responded with what arguably was his best year. His 16 home runs and 20 doubles included several clutch hits as the Mets visited the postseason again. And on a team devoid of speed, Garrett served as leadoff hitter and led the pennant winners with 6 steals. Yup, 6.

Garrett had a fine glove, an excellent batting eye, but only adequate power for a third baseman. He was traded to Montreal with Del Unser midway through the 1976 season for outfielders Jim Dwyer and **Pepe Mangual**, who immediately inherited the vacant No. 11 jersey. Mangual made virtually no impact whatsoever on the Mets, totaling just 20 hits in 109 at bats in the uniform.

Connecticut native **Tim Teufel** (the name means "devil" in German) was brought in from Minnesota prior to the 1986 season to platoon at second base

with Wally Backman. Never a great fielder, Teufel (1986–91) could swing the bat, hitting .308 with 14 homers doing part-time work in 1987. Teufel inherited the No. 11 jersey from **Kelvin Chapman**, who was Backman's platoon mate in 1984 and 1985. Chapman made his first appearance in 1979 (wearing 10) but disappeared into the minors for five long years before resurfacing in Davey Johnson's offense-first configuration.

Ancient ex-Yankee **Gene Woodling** turned out to be one of the best performers of the 1962 Mets, hitting .274 in 81 games. A deal to return as a player-coach in 1963 was scuttled, however, after Woodling went to bat for teammate Marv Throneberry in contract negotiations. Woodling, it was decided, wasn't management material.

Roy McMillan (1964–66) spent the final years of his long and distinguished playing career as a defensive specialist for a Mets team that had never had one. McMillan, who could still play a mean short-stop and still couldn't hit (.226 and only 44 extra-base hits in 1,127 at-bats over three years) helped groom a successor in his own image: Bud Harrelson. McMillan later served as a Mets coach (1973–76) and as a mediocre interim manager who went 27-28 following the firing of Yogi Berra in 1975.

Len Randle was one of the few things that went right for the Mets in 1977, but even that had an ugly side. Randle was available only after having been released by the Rangers when a spring-training con-frontation with Texas manager

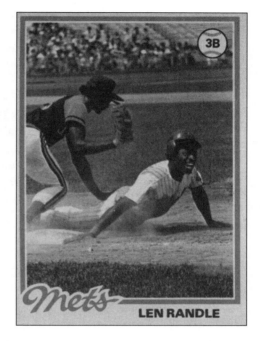

LEN RANDLE

Frank Lucchesi turned violent. But Randle settled in without incident in an otherwise chaotic year, bringing some stability to third base and leading Met regulars with a .304 batting average and 33 stolen bases (as well as 21 times caught stealing). Randle explained he wore No. 11 as a tribute to deposed Ranger manager Billy Martin (No. 1) and to God.

A singles-hitting shortstop with good speed and poor on-base per-centage, **Frank Taveras** served three years' hard time with the 1979–81 Mets. His 42 stolen bases in 1979 broke the club's single-season record set by Randle two years earlier. **Vince Coleman** led the team with 38 steals in 1993, which would be his last and worst season with the Mets, and the only one in which he wore No. 11.

Meaty backup catcher **Ramon Castro** (2005–07) became a Shea fixture after slamming 8 home runs and driving in 41 in just 209 at-bats in 2005. Castro got the call as reserve catcher after his competitors (Vance Wilson and Jason Phillps) were traded away. He missed the last two months of the 2006 season and was still added to the playoff roster when he caught a couple of games during the final week of the season. He was slugging away and battling back pain again in 2007.

Former Brooklyn standout **Duke Snider** (1963) wore 11 while waiting for the Mets to trade Charlie Neal so he could reacquire his familiar No. 4. Bulletproof utility man **Joe McEwing** took No. 11 after Tom Glavine arrived to swipe his old No. 47 in 2003. McEwing (2003–04) settled on 11 by adding the digits on his old jersey.

Cory Lidle held the distinction of wearing the loneliest number for a Mets pitcher until Shingo Takatsu took No. 10 in 2005.

Others (and there's a lot): **Ed Bouchee** (1962); **Tom Veryzer** (1982); **Mike Bishop** (1983); **Tucker Ashford** (1983); shortstop **Garry Templeton** (1991), who arrived in a trade for Teufel; **Dick Schofield** (1992); **Rick Parker** (1994); **Aaron Ledesma** (1995); **Tim Bogar** (1996); Mookie's nephew, **Preston Wilson** (1998); **Wayne Kirby** (1998); utility man **Shane Halter** (1999); leadoff hopeful **Jason Tyner** (2000); and backup infielder **Jorge Velandia** (2000–01).

Number of times issued: 27 (all to players)

Longest tenured: Wayne Garrett (8 seasons, 883 games), Tim Teufel (6 seasons, 463 games)

Best single seasons: Garrett, 1973 (.256/.348/.403, 16 HR, 58 RBI); Lenny Randle, 1977 (.304/.383/.404, 33 stolen bases); Teufel, 1987 (.308/.398/.545, 14 HR, 61 RBI)

Career statistical leaders: Home runs (Garrett 55, Teufel 35), RBI (Garrett 295, Teufel 164), batting average (Vince Coleman .279, Randle .272, Kelvin Chapman .272)

Hot Corner Roll Call

Over their forty-five seasons the Mets have churned through third basemen at the rate of three per year, 137 in all (and counting), from Abbott to Zimmer, or more precisely, from Zimmer in 1962 to Newhan in 2007. Ageless Julio Franco also appeared at third base for the Mets in 2006 and 2007. For the record, he was three years old—and probably already lashing line drives—the day the Mets first took the field in 1962.

Although third base was a running joke for the first twenty-five years of the team's existence, it has become a position of strength over the past two decades: Knight, Johnson, Alfonzo, Ventura, and Wright have been among the team's best players in that span. The following is a list of every Met to man the hot corner, when they first played there (with doubleheader games in parentheses), and the number they wore for their hot-corner debut. The most popular number for third sackers in their debut? It's 6, with thirteen members of that fraternity subset.

Third Baseman	Met 3B Debut	Uniform Number
1. Don Zimmer	April 11, 1962	17
2. Rod Kanehl	April 21, 1962	10
3. Felix Mantilla	April 23, 1962	18
4. Elio Chacon	May 5, 1962+	7
5. Cliff Cook	May 8, 1962	6
6. Frank Thomas	June 17, 1962	25
7. Rick Herrscher	August 2, 1962*	6
8. Sammy Drake	August 10, 1962	12
9. Charlie Neal	August 29, 1962	4
10. Ted Schreiber	April 14, 1963*	43
11. Chico Fernandez	May 12, 1963 (1st game)	7
12. Al Moran	May 12, 1963 (2nd game)	40
13. Larry Burright	May 12, 1963 (2nd game)	6
14. Ron Hunt	May 13, 1963	33
15. Jim Hickman	June 19, 1963	9
16. Pumpsie Green	September 5, 1963	18
17. John Stephenson	April 26, 1964*	49
18. Amado Samuel	May 8, 1964	7
19. Charley Smith	May 24, 1964	1
20. Wayne Graham	August 8, 1964	4
21. Bobby Klaus	August 15, 1964	6
22. Dan Napoleon	April 24, 1965*	16
23. Chuck Hiller	August 22, 1965	2
24. Gary Kolb	September 1, 1965 (2nd game)	18
25. Kevin Collins	September 11, 1965	10
26. Ken Boyer	April 15, 1966	14
27. Eddie Bressoud	May 14, 1966	1
28. Jerry Grote	August 3, 1966	15
29. Sandy Alomar Sr.	April 15, 1967	5
30. Jerry Bucheck	April 23, 1967 (2nd game)	1
31. Tom Reynolds	April 29, 1967	16
32. Ed Charles	May 12, 1967	24
33. Bob Johnson	June 4, 1967 (1st game)	6
34. Phil Linz	July 19, 1967 (1st game)	2
35. Joe Moock	September 1, 1967 (1st game)*	18
36. Amos Otis	September 7, 1967*	28
37. Ken Boswell	September 18, 1967*	24
38. Bob Heise	September 25, 1967	23

Third Baseman	Met 3B Debut	Uniform Number
39. Al Weis	May 1, 1968	6
40. Wayne Garrett	May 4, 1969 (2nd game)	11
41. Bobby Pfeil	June 26, 1969*	1
42. Joe Foy	April 7, 1970	5
43. Tim Foli	September 12, 1970	19
44. Bob Aspromonte	April 6, 1971	2
45. Ted Martinez	July 6, 1971	17
46. Jim Fregosi	April 15, 1972	2
47. Rich Puig	September 13, 1974 (2nd game)*⁺	6
48. Joe Torre	April 8, 1975	9
49. Jack Heidemann	May 7, 1975	12
50. Roy Staiger	September 12, 1975	35
51. Dave Kingman	September 15, 1975	26
52. Mike Phillips	May 16, 1976 (1st game)	5
53. Leo Foster	September 6, 1976	1
54. Len Randle	May 8, 1977 (1st game)	11
55. Doug Flynn	June 22, 1977	23
56. Joel Youngblood	June 24, 1977	18
57. Bobby Valentine	July 6, 1977	1
58. Sergio Ferrer	April 30, 1978	3
59. Elliott Maddox	May 26, 1978	21
60. John Stearns	June 28, 1978	12
61. Alex Treviño	October 1, 1978	29
62. Richie Hebner	April 5, 1979	3
63. Kelvin Chapman	May 10, 1979	10
64. Phil Mankowski	April 15, 1980	2
65. Mario Ramirez	May 22, 1980	3
66. Jose Moreno	June 18, 1980	4
67. Bill Almon	July 27, 1980	25
68. Hubie Brooks	September 4, 1980	39
69. Wally Backman	April 18, 1981	6
70. Mike Cubbage	April 26, 1981 (2nd game)	3
71. Bob Bailor	September 24, 1981	4
72. Ron Gardenhire	September 27, 1981	19
73. Tucker Ashford	May 6, 1983	11
74. Clint Hurdle	September 12, 1983	33
75. Ross Jones	July 28, 1984	21
76. Ray Knight	August 29, 1984	22

Third Baseman	Met 3B Debut	Uniform Number
77. Kevin Mitchell	September 13, 1984	32
78. Howard Johnson	April 9, 1985	20
79. Tim Teufel	April 12, 1986	11
80. Gary Carter	July 22, 1986	8
81. Dave Magadan	April 18, 1987	29
82. Mackey Sasser	May 11, 1988	2
83. Keith Miller	June 18, 1988	25
84. Gregg Jefferies	August 28, 1988*	9
85. Jeff McKnight	June 10, 1989	15
86. Craig Shipley	September 7, 1989	35
87. Tom O'Malley	September 7, 1989	27
88. Chris Donnels	May 7, 1991*	23
89. Garry Templeton	June 7, 1991	11
90. Bill Pecota	April 6, 1992	32
91. Junior Noboa	April 15, 1992	3
92. Chico Walker	May 11, 1992	34
93. Steve Springer	August 20, 1992	13
94. Jeff Kent	September 26, 1992	39
95. Tim Bogar	May 29, 1993	23
96. Bobby Bonilla	June 25, 1993	25
97. Butch Huskey	September 8, 1993*	10
98. Doug Saunders	September 24, 1993	2
99. Fernando Viña	April 10, 1994	1
100. Edgardo Alfonzo	May 2, 1995	13
101. Aaron Ledesma	July 6, 1995	11
102. Bill Spiers	July 23, 1995	19
103. Carlos Baerga	July 30, 1996 (1st game)	6
104. Alvaro Espinoza	August 2, 1996	12
105. Matt Franco	September 8, 1996	15
106. Kevin Morgan	June 15, 1997*+	10
107. Jason Hardtke	June 21, 1997	19
108. Luis Lopez	July 12, 1997	17
109. Manny Alexander	July 13, 1997	6
110. Shawn Gilbert	September 24, 1997	12
111. Craig Paquette	May 3, 1998	18
112. Jim Tatum	May 16, 1998	19
113. Lenny Harris	July 12, 1998	19
114. Mike Kinkade	September 8, 1998	33

Third Baseman	Met 3B Debut	Uniform Number
115. Robin Ventura	April 5, 1999	4
116. Melvin Mora	July 6, 1999	6
117. Shawon Dunston	August 8, 1999	12
118. Kurt Abbott	April 26, 2000	20
119. Joe McEwing	May 20, 2000	47
120. David Lamb	July 14, 2000	26
121. Jorge Velandia	September 8, 2000	11
122. Desi Relaford	April 22, 2001	8
123. John Valentin	April 14, 2002	4
124. Ty Wiggington	May 17, 2002*	9
125. Marco Scutaro	July 28, 2002	26
126. Jay Bell	April 10, 2003	44
127. Todd Zeile	April 11, 2004	27
128. Ricky Gutierrez	April 22, 2004	6
129. David Wright	July 21, 2004*	5
130. Chris Woodward	April 13, 2005	4
131. Miguel Cairo	April 21, 2005	3
132. Jose Valentin	May 26, 2006	18
133. Eli Marrero	July 2, 2006	32
134. Julio Franco	September 10, 2006	23
135. Damion Easley	April 19, 2007	3
136. Ruben Gotay	September 7, 2007	6
137. David Newhan	September 29, 2007	17

* Major league debut in the field
+ Only career appearance at 3B

#12: "IT'S A NICE NUMBER"

Although a long playing, coaching, and captaining career aligned **Willie Randolph** most closely with that other team in New York, a symbolic gesture at the beginning of his first spring training as Mets manager revealed he was one of us all along.

"I'm gonna wear No. 12. Why? You remember Ken Boswell? Second baseman on the '69 team? He was my favorite player growing up," Randolph told Bill Madden of the *Daily News*. "No. 12. It's a nice number."

While fans can drown in the empty platitudes spouting from athletes these days, there is something authentic about a **Ken Boswell** name check. Boswell indeed wore No. 12 (at least after shedding 24 for Art Shamsky in 1968), played the lefty-hitting second baseman in the strict Gil Hodges platoon system, and had a flair for the dramatic. Boswell clubbed home runs in two straight '69 NLCS games, and although the arrival of Felix Millan in 1972 made Boswell a full-time backup, he excelled in that role. Boswell batted 1.000 (3-for-3, all in pinch-hit duty) in the 1973 World Series.

Randolph, by the way, also wore No. 12 in his last-gasp appearance as a player with the ill-fated 1992 Mets. The customary No. 30 he wore with the Yankees was unavailable then due to pitching coach Mel Stottlemyre. In 2005, Cliff Floyd held title to 30. As a manager, Randolph appears to command the respect of the players while possessing a certain gruff charm. He's esteemed if not embraced. After 2007, he's thankful for his job.

Jeff Kent was never much for uniforms, baseball or otherwise. As a Mets rookie in 1992, he petulantly refused to engage in the customary freshman ritual of wearing an outlandish costume for a Mets road trip. The joke was ultimately on the Mets, who paid too much to get Kent (David Cone) and took too little in return for him four years later (Carlos Baerga and forgettable No. 12 **Alvaro Espinosa**). In between, Kent (1993–96) showed traces of the skill that would one day make him a National League MVP, hitting 21 home runs and driving in 80 in 1993. His attitude never improved quite like his baseball did. Some around the league believe it still hasn't.

Fans looking for a counterpoint to Kent might find one in **Tommy Davis**, who was acquired prior to the 1967 season for longtime Mets Jim Hickman and Ron Hunt and flipped afterward for in a deal that brought the Mets 1969 mainstays Tommie Agee and Al Weis. Davis made the most of his short stay, leading the '67 Mets in virtually every statistical category.

With four All-Star appearances in a ten-year Mets career, **John Stearns** makes a good case as the Mets' all-time No. 12 for his hard-nosed tenure. Nicknamed "Bad Dude," Stearns (1977–84) was a star defensive back at the University of Colorado who brought the same hard-hitting intensity to the baseball field. Acquired from Philadelphia in the Tug McGraw deal, Stearns in time would prove to be a stronger offensive contributor

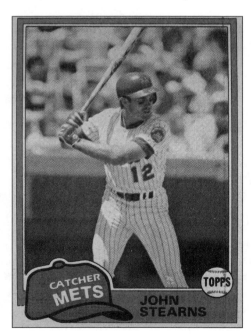

than predecessor Jerry Grote ever was, including a .264-15-73 performance in 1978 that included a National League record for stolen bases by a catcher, 25. The mark stood until Jason Kendall broke it for the 1998 Pirates.

Pittsburgh's Dave Parker once left a collision with Stearns with a broken jaw; Atlanta's Chief Nok-a-Homa absorbed an open-field tackle from Stearns and thought better about dancing too close to the Mets' side of Fulton County Stadium ever again; and when an Expo threw a pitch near Mike Jorgensen's head in the wake of a long home run, there was Stearns dashing from dugout to mound faster than you can say, "Ralphie the Buffalo." Stearns would eventually discover he was not indestructible, spending much of his final years with the Mets on the sidelines.

Stearns wore No. 16 for his maiden appearances with the Mets in 1975 and 1976. He and **Lee Mazzilli**, who wore 12 for his first 24 games of his career, switched jerseys prior to the 1977 season.

When he was informed of the principals in the 2001 trade that made **Roberto Alomar** a Met, manager Bobby Valentine had one question. "What's wrong with him?" he reportedly asked. The answer, Mets fans would learn, was a sudden and irreversible decline in skills that made the trade for the Cooperstown-bound second baseman one of the most disappointing in recent club history. The twelve-time All-Star spent a listless season and a half in New York, and the Mets seemed eager to erase his memory after his trade to the White Sox by issuing his No. 12 to rookie second baseman **Danny Garcia** later in the same 2003 season.

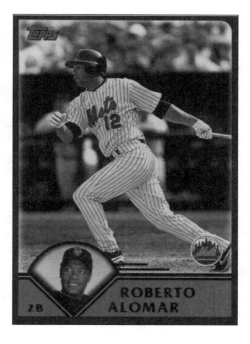

Garcia, the first Met who was also a Brooklyn Cyclone, was a marginal talent, but his hustle got him through the following season.

In the middle of this family of second basemen and catchers was pitcher **Ron Darling**, who decided in 1985 that he preferred 12 to the No. 44 he'd worn the first few years of his career. Darling was the first and still is the only Mets pitcher to wear No. 12 and at the time set the mark for the lowest number worn by a hurler in club history.

Of the three uniform numbers Darling wore (15 was the third, which he changed to in August 1989), he was most successful in No. 12, going 68-38 with a 3.38 ERA. Darling was a first-round draft choice of the Texas Rangers out of Yale and was acquired along with Walt Terrell for Lee Mazzili in one of the most lopsided trades in team history. Darling not only had a brighter future than Mazzilli, but he filled out his uniform every bit as well, succeeding Mazzilli as a new favorite of Shea's female fans and copping the cover of *GQ*, too. Darling also fielded better than most of the second basemen.

The Mets debuted No. 12 on the back of veteran catcher **Joe Ginsberg**, who would appear in just two games with the '62 Mets. Expansion draftee **Sammy Drake** also wore 12 that year. Neither played in the majors ever again. Power-hitting catcher **Jesse Gonder** (1963–65) had a fine year offensively as the regular backstop in 1964. **Cleon Jones** appeared in No. 12 in 1965 and then it went to backup catcher **John Stephenson** in 1966.

Others: mutton-chopped reserve infielder **Jack Heidemann** (1975–76); just-passing-through outfielder **Keith Hughes** (1990); **Shawn Gilbert** (1997–98), a Bobby V. special who made the Mets as a 32-year-rookie reservist; catcher **Jorge Fabregas** (1998); and **Shawon Dunston,** the free-swinging, late-season, bench-strength acquiree who made the most of a short stay in 1999.

Number of times issued: 22 (20 players, 1 coach, 1 manager)

Longest tenured: John Stearns (8 seasons, 718 games), Ken Boswell (7 seasons, 670 games), Ron Darling (5 seasons, 158 games)

Best single seasons: Jeff Kent, 1994 (.292/.341/.475, 14 HR, 68 RBI); Stearns, 1978 (.264/.364/.413,15 HR, 73 RBI, 25 stolen bases); Darling, 1986 (15-6, 2.81, 184 strikeouts); Tommy Davis, 1967 (.302/.342/.440, 16 HR, 73 RBI)

Career statistical leaders: Home runs (Kent 64, Stearns 41, Boswell 30), RBI (Stearns 302, Kent 264, Boswell 189), batting average (Kent .281, Stearns .265, Roberto Alomar .265)

Shea: It Ain't So

The Mets have been notoriously stingy in retiring uniform numbers. Since 1962 they've so honored only Casey Stengel (37), Gil Hodges (14), and Tom Seaver (41). Major League Baseball retired number 42 for every franchise in tribute to Jackie Robinson on the fiftieth anniversary of his landmark debut. Bud Selig made this pronouncement at Shea Stadium on April 15, 1997.

Other teams have been far more generous in retiring numbers. Almost 150 men have had their numbers retired throughout baseball, including six players whose careers ended before uniform numbers (those names are honored similarly to their club's other retired numbers), plus an owner in St. Louis and an executive in Florida who had numbers capriciously selected and retired for them after their deaths. Twenty-one former residents of Shea Stadium—or the Polo Grounds the two years the Mets called it home—have had their numbers retired by other clubs. The list below includes the retired numbers of everyone who shared the same home as the Mets, including the New York Jets (1964–83) and New York Yankees (1974–75). Most men had the same number they wore at Shea retired by the other clubs (when this is not the case, the number they wore at Shea is listed in parentheses). Rogers Hornsby, Mel Harder, and Bob Gibson, who served as Mets coaches but never played or managed for the club, are not listed.

Number	Player	Team That Retired His Number	Year(s) in Uniform at Shea/Polo Grounds
1	Richie Ashburn	Philadelphia Phillies	1962
1	Billy Martin	New York Yankees	1975
4[1]	Ralph Kiner	Pittsburgh Pirates	1962–2007 (announcer)
4 (4, 11)	Duke Snider	Brooklyn/Los Angeles Dodgers	1963
8	Yogi Berra	New York Yankees	1965 (player), 1965–71 (coach), 1972–75 (manager)
8	Gary Carter	Montreal Expos	1985–89
10 (4, 10)	Rusty Staub	Montreal Expos	1972–75, 1981–85
11 (2)	Jim Fregosi	LA/California/Anaheim Angels	1972–73
12	Joe Namath	New York Jets	1965–76
13[2]	Don Maynard	New York Jets	1962–72
14	Ken Boyer	St. Louis Cardinals	1966–67
15	Thurman Munson	New York Yankees	1974–75

Number	Player	Team That Retired His Number	Year(s) in Uniform at Shea/Polo Grounds
21	Warren Spahn	Boston/Milwaukee/ Atlanta Braves	1965 (player-coach)
24	Willie Mays	New York/San Francisco Giants	1972–73 (player), 1974–79 (coach)
27[3] (29)	Catfish Hunter	Oakland A's	1975
30, 34 (30)[4]	Nolan Ryan	Angels/Houston Astros/ Texas Rangers	1966, 1968–71
33	Eddie Murray	Baltimore Orioles	1992–93
33 (30)	Mike Scott	Houston Astros	1979–82
35 (25, 35)	Randy Jones	San Diego Padres	1981–82
37	Casey Stengel	New York Yankees	1962–65 (manager)
Weeb[5]	Weeb Ewbank	New York Jets	1963–73 (head coach)

1. Announcer Ralph Kiner is included because Detroit included announcer Ernie Harwell with its immortals, so the Mets could conceivably do the same thing.
2. Only Don Maynard's years playing football at the Polo Grounds (and later Shea) after the Mets came into existence are included.
3. Catfish Hunter played at Shea for the Yankees in 1975, but shockingly the Hall of Famer's 29 is not one of the sixteen numbers retired by the Yankees. The Oakland A's retired 27 in his honor.
4. Nolan Ryan—remember him?—has numbers retired by three different teams: 30 by the Angels and 34 by Houston and Texas. The Mets are the only team he played for that hasn't retired his number.
5. The Jets list Weeb Ewbanks among retired numbers, but the extent of the honor is a jacket facsimile that reads "Weeb" and is posted on the stadium wall at the Meadowlands during Jets games.

#13: LUCKY US

Traditionally considered bad luck, the Mets rarely issue No. 13 unless requested, which usually—but not always—indicates a flake of some kind was doing the asking. As of 2007, the number has been issued to only fourteen Mets players and to one coach.

The most prominent of these wasn't a flake at all. It was **Edgardo Alfonzo**, who, like many of his Venezuelan countrymen, preferred to wear No. 13 in honor of Reds great Dave Concepción.

Alfonzo (1995–2002) began his career as a twenty-year-old fill-in infielder with the Mets in 1995 but didn't truly arrive until he was inserted as the everyday third baseman in 1997 and revealed himself to be among the best all-around players the team had ever developed. He hit well and ran the bases smartly and was an exceptional fielder at third base and second base, where he moved to accommodate Robin Ventura when he arrived in 1999. Alfonzo shifted back to third again in 2002 to make room for Roberto Alomar.

In 1999 the Fonz hit .304-27-108, not to mention a scorching 6-6-6 night in the closing days of the Astrodome, going 6-for-6 and crossing the plate half a dozen times to set club records in each category. He launched some of the biggest hits that October—a two-run home run in the 1st inning of the loser-goes-home Wild Card play-in game with the Reds and a pair of home runs in Game 1 of the Division Series against Arizona, including a tie-breaking grand slam in the 9th. Several all-time career standards were in reach for Alfonzo when the Mets abruptly let him go as a free agent in 2002. At the time, he ranked third in doubles, runs, and hits, fourth in total bases, and seventh in RBI, but Fonzie had faded from being a great player to a merely good one. Alfonzo's subsequent performance—if not the performance of those who replaced him on the Mets—indicated this unpopular decision was also a prudent one.

After establishing himself as a budding relief ace wearing No. 46, **Neil Allen** sought to distinguish himself by changing to the No. 13 jersey as the 1981 season began. He was the first to boldly wear 13 since the **Roger Craig** exorcism of late 1963 (see sidebar). In time, Allen's role would be usurped by a succession of more reliable men, including the maligned Doug Sisk and revered Jesse Orosco. Allen eventually brought good luck on the trade market, being the principal guy shipped to St. Louis in the 1983 Keith Hernandez heist.

Bad luck arrived via trade in 1989 when the Mets foolishly sent Mookie Wilson to Toronto for left-handed reliever **Jeff Musselman**, a Harvard grad who'd be ineffective for the Mets and out of professional baseball in a little more than a year.

Lee Mazzilli went to the Blue Jays the same day as Mookie, only Maz went over the waiver wire and was on his last legs. Mazzilli had gotten three more years out of a career that seemed over in July 1986, when he was let go by the last-place Pittsburgh Pirates. The Mets reacquired him and dressed him in No. 13 (his familiar 16 belonging at the time to Dwight Gooden). Mazzilli (1986-89) brought the Mets luck in winning the World Series that year, and he was the only Met to see both the '77 Seaver trade and the '86 parade.

In a move indicating the Mets were no longer in a position to tolerate bullpen uncertainty, they signed veteran fireballer **Billy Wagner** to a contract prior to 2006. Wagner, despite a few hiccups, was most everything they wanted a $10 million closer to be, collecting 74 saves with a 2.43 ERA over his first two seasons.

Other 13s: **Clint Hurdle** (1985), last seen wearing 13 as manager of the World Series–bound Colorado Rockies; **Rick Cerone** (1991); **Rodney McCray** (1992), still crashing through a minor-league outfield fence on a highlight reel somewhere; **Steve Springer** (1992); **Jonathan Hurst** (1994); **Jorge Velandia** (2003); **Matt Ginter** (2004); and **Brian Daubach** (2005).

Number of times issued: 15 (14 players, 1 coach)

Longest tenured: Edgardo Alfonzo (8 seasons, 1,086 games), Lee Mazzilli (4 seasons, 243 games), Billy Wagner (2 seasons, 136 games), Neil Allen (3 seasons, 114 games)

Best single seasons: Alfonzo, 2000 (.324/.425/.542, 25 HR, 94 RBI); Alfonzo, 1999 (.304/.385/.502, 27 HR, 108 RBI,); Wagner, 2006 (3-2, 40 saves, 2.24 ERA)

Career statistical leaders: Home runs (Alfonzo 120), RBI (Alfonzo 538), batting average (Alfonzo .292), ERA (Wagner 2.24), wins (Allen 12)

Very Superstitious, Nothin' More to Say

The de facto ace of the early Mets, Roger Craig, did nothing so well as lose. He lost close games and he lost blowouts. He lost because his team didn't support him with their gloves, and he lost because they didn't support them with their bats. Often, he lost because of both. Frequently, he lost because of his own mistakes. He lost as a starter, and because Casey Stengel trusted him most, he lost as a reliever. He lost and lost.

After fashioning a record of 10 wins and a league-leading 24 losses for the 1962 Mets, Craig got off to a 2-2 start in 1963 before a loss May 4 to the Giants started a mind-bogglingly luckless streak. Between May 4 and August 4 he lost 18 decisions in a row. (It was the kind of streak only another Met could break: Craig Anderson topped it in 1964 (19), and Anthony Young shattered both marks three decades later with 27 straight.)

At Wrigley Field on July 4, 1963, Craig was working the bottom of the 9th of a 1-1 game when Ernie Banks reached second on a throwing error by shortstop Chico Fernandez. Craig proceeded to throw a wild pitch to the following batter that catcher Norm Sherry collected only to throw into left field in an attempt to catch Banks advancing to third. He trotted home for consecutive loss No. 11.

The streak reached fourteen games when Craig began to think about unconventional ways to change his luck. It began with borrowing teammate Tracy Stallard's No. 36 jersey for his July 19 start against the Phillies at Connie Mack Stadium (Stallard, a starter who did not appear in the game, presumably wore the No. 38 formerly belonging to Craig and caused no clubhouse fuss because there were no names on the back to sew).

Craig was riding No. 36 to a three-hit shutout when with one out in the bottom of the 9th and the Mets ahead 1-0, Tony Gonzalez tripled and Roy Sievers followed with a game-ending two-run home run.

No. 36 went back to Stallard and Craig lost four more times before, on August 9, he wore a 2-20 record and the No. 13 jersey to the Polo Grounds mound to face the Cubs. Tied at 3 in the bottom of the 9th, and with two men on base, Stengel pinch hit Tim Harkness for Craig, and Harkness was intentionally walked. "I wouldn't care if he was my uncle," Stengel said, "he was out of the game."

Jim Hickman followed with a fly ball to left field that ticked off the overhanging bleachers for a grand slam that could only have been hit in the odd dimensions of the Polo Grounds. An excited Craig left the dugout to make sure the runners touched the bases. Craig spent the rest of the season—two more wins and two more losses—wearing No. 13. In an act of mercy, over the offseason the Mets traded him to St. Louis, where he won a World Series ring while wearing No. 41.

Changing the number on the shirt doesn't always accompany a change in luck. Howard Johnson got more than he bargained for when he impulsively grabbed the No.

44 jersey David Cone left in May of 1991. Although Johnson thought the number change might put a charge into a slumbering bat, he admitted after a few days he felt "uncomfortable" in 44 and that his wife didn't like it either. The Mets were on the road by the time Johnson came to this realization, so the team had a No. 20 jersey shipped out to San Diego for Johnson to wear.

Ron Darling twice changed his number for the Mets: once from 44 to 12, then from 12 to 15. The switch paid immediate dividends for Darling, who threw a complete-game victory over the Expos in his first appearance wearing 15.

"I'm not a superstitious guy," Darling protested after the second change, "but I thought I'd try something different. No. 12 hasn't been showing up this year."

#14: GOOD OLD GIL

The story of No. 14 literally begins and ends with the first and last man to wear the jersey for the Mets, **Gil Hodges**.

Hodges was nearing the end of his playing career when selected by the Mets in the expansion draft in 1961. A seven-time All-Star first baseman who to that point had spent his entire sixteen-year career with the Dodgers, Hodges was a beloved figure in New York, remarkable even among the bevy of ex–New York players who populated the Mets' roster in their early years. Although an Indiana native, Hodges had married a local girl and lived year-round in Flatbush. His steadying influence and quiet power on the field and in the clubhouse had already begun speculation that he could someday manage the fledgling Mets.

His playing highlights with the Mets included the franchise's first-ever home run, one of 9 home runs contributed in just 127 at-bats in '62. But aching knees were putting an end to Hodges' career, so early in the 1963 season the Mets traded him to Washington, where he was immediately installed as the manager of the expansion Senators.

When Mets manager Wes Westrum resigned late in the 1967 season, the Mets' board of directors was strongly in favor of retrieving Hodges from Washington, where he'd begun to turn around that team's fortunes. The Senators eventually took pitching prospect Bill Denehy and a reported $100,000 for Hodges.

Hodges helped improve the Mets by 12 wins in his first year at the helm and in 1969 did what many felt was impossible, leading a team that had never before played at .500 to a 100-win season and the world championship. To a man, players on those late 1960s teams speak reverently of Hodges' influence, and the results of 1969 are evidence of magnificent managerial maneuverings. Deploying limited resources skillfully, Hodges used platoons at several positions to complement an outstanding pitching staff en route to winning 41 games by a single run.

The Mets had disappointing 83-win seasons in 1970 and 1971. While players were striking during spring training of 1972, Hodges finished an afternoon of golf with his coaches and promptly collapsed dead of a heart attack at age 48. The Mets formally retired his number 14 in 1973.

Between Hodges' departure in 1963 and his 1968 return, two men wore No. 14 for the Mets: **Ron Swoboda** (1965) and **Ken Boyer** (1966–67).

Swoboda was a 21-year-old rookie in 1965 when he led the team with 19 home runs. Boyer, a veteran third baseman, requested his familiar No. 14 when he arrived in a trade from the Cardinals prior to the 1966 season, and Swoboda switched, eventually, to No. 4.

Number of times issued: 4 (3 players, 1 manager)

Longest tenured: Ken Boyer (2 seasons, 192 games), Gil Hodges (as manager, 4 seasons, 648 games).

Best single season: Ron Swoboda, 1965 (19 HR, 50 RBI)

Career statistical leaders: Home runs (Swoboda 19), RBI (Boyer 74), batting average (Boyer .258)

Retired: June 9, 1973

In Tribute

Over their forty-five years, many people with ties to the Mets have died suddenly. None, perhaps, has been as much of a shock as the death of Gil Hodges in 1972. In honor of their fallen skipper, the Mets wore black armbands just below the team logo on the left sleeve for that 1972 season, the first time a deceased Met had been so honored. His number was retired a year later. Eddie Yost, third-base coach and close friend, still looked stunned in his 1973 yearbook photo.

Yost and the Mets wore black armbands again in 1976 after the franchise's matriarch and patriarch—owner Joan Payson and original manager Casey Stengel—died within a week of each other the previous autumn. The Mets have subsequently honored the passing of William Shea, who helped create the franchise and for whom the stadium was named; umpire John McSherry, who died of a heart attack on the field during a game in Cincinnati; Tommie Agee, beloved hero of the 1969 Miracle Mets; Brian Cole, a 22-year-old prospect killed in an accident at the end of spring training 2001; Tug McGraw, rally maker for the 1973 club and coiner of the catchphrase "Ya Gotta Believe"; and Bob Murphy, adored announcer and voice of two-plus generations of Mets fans.

In Honor of	Season	Tribute
Gil Hodges	1972	Black armband on left sleeve
Casey Stengel, Joan Payson	1976	Black armband on left sleeve
William Shea	1992	S in pinstriped circle on left sleeve (the Mets wore no logo on the sleeve at the time)
John McSherry	1996	Home plate with crossed bats and "JM/NL Umpire/10" on right sleeve
Tommie Agee, Brian Cole	2001 (Opening Day only)	A patch resembling a baseball on the right sleeve with the two players' numbers: 20 (Agee) and 60 (Cole)
Tug McGraw	2004	"Ya Gotta Believe" signed "Tug" under Shea fortieth anniversary patch on right sleeve
Bob Murphy	2004 (August to October)	"Bob Murphy" embroidered under Mets logo on left sleeve

#15: METSMERIZED

The first in what has become a Mets tradition of acquiring catchers in lopsided trades was the 1965 deal that sent pitcher Tom Parsons and cash to Houston for **Jerry Grote.**

Just twenty-three years old at the time, Grote was seen as something of a failed prospect for the Astros. He had struggled mightily in limited appearances as a hitter and fallen below catching prospects John Bateman and Ron Brand on Houston's depth chart. Above all, however, Grote had a reputation as a "red ass." That is, he had an irascible personality the Astros feared might negatively affect relationships with teammates or management. He rarely had much more than a growl for the writers following the Mets.

Yet it was Grote's gruff demeanor that made him the valuable backstop he became with the Mets. His bat would come around only enough to turn him into a passable singles hitter: he reached career highs of 6 home runs and 40 RBI in 1969. Grote (1966–77) blocked the plate and threw out runners with the very best of them, but he truly earned his keep by

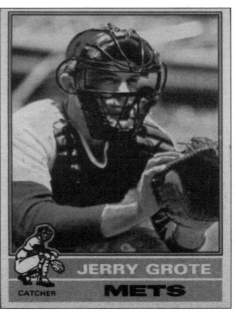

JERRY GROTE
CATCHER METS

helping to develop an emerging group of young pitchers, including Koosman, Seaver, Gentry, McGraw, and Ryan. Teammates note Grote did this by force when necessary: he had a low tolerance for pitches that didn't go where he wanted them to go and often delivered that message with a hellacious return throw to the pitcher.

The tough love obviously had some effect. Seaver and Ryan thought enough of Grote to thank him by name at their respective Hall of Fame inductions.

Grote's acquisition may have flown under the radar at the time, but that was hardly the case with the Mets' two other most prominent 15s: **George Foster** and **Carlos Beltran**.

Foster had all the bona fides to perhaps become the last-ever 15 when the Mets traded for him in the winter of 1981 and subsequently signed him to a five-year contract, the richest the team had ever given to that point. But Foster didn't have the kind of Mets career anyone had in mind.

The menacing black bat that once swatted 52 home runs for the Reds was only good for 13 in 1982, Foster's first season as a Met. Foster cautioned pilots approaching LaGuardia not to fly too low, but that remark turned into a joke about pop-ups. Foster rebounded some in subsequent years—he knocked in 98 runs on 28 homers in 1983—and if nothing else served as a first step toward the future glories of the team.

Unfortunately for him, Foster wasn't around to taste champagne in 1986—he only rapped about it in the "Get Metsmerized" single—his unlistenable but lasting contribution to Mets lore. ("I live to play and that's my thing/This year we're gonna win the Series ring" rapped Foster in one of the song's better couplets). Struggling with a reduced role and hearing increasing boos, Foster was released midseason. So was "Get Metsmerized."

The "largest contract ever" label belongs currently to Carlos Beltran. Like Foster, Beltran's first year in New York did not live up to its advance billing. Healthier and more comfortable since, Beltran is earning every dollar. In 2006, he turned in one of the best seasons any Met has ever had, tying the franchise record with 41 home runs, driving in 116 runs (tied for fourth all-time), and adding 38 doubles. He added 33 home runs and 112 RBI in 2007. A few more years like that and 15 truly will disappear from circulation.

The first No. 15 in franchise history was diminutive lefty **Al Jackson** (1962–65), who lost 20 games twice but was probably the best young pitcher on the early Mets. Jackson held the franchise mark for most victories (43) until that record was broken by 24-year-old Tom Seaver. Jackson was liberated to St. Louis for the 1966–67 season but returned in 1968 and 1969 for the last years of his playing career (wearing No. 38). Since then, Jackson has spent many years in the Mets' employ as a roving (or stationary) pitching instructor and is virtually the only remaining connection to the club's 1962 origins besides Ralph Kiner.

Ron Darling (1989–91) tried 15 after 44 and 12. It is the only number in which he had a losing record (18-20, 3.79 in 61 games). Shortstop **Kevin Elster,** who was close to Darling, requested he take over 15 after Darling was traded in 1991 but was convinced to wait until 1992, when he only got into six games before undergoing season-ending shoulder surgery.

One of the more underappreciated Mets of recent vintage was **Jose Vizcaino** (1994–96), the goggle-wearing middle infielder acquired from the Cubs for Anthony Young in 1994. Vizcaino in 1995 had perhaps the best offensive season by a Mets shortstop until Jose Reyes came along, but that season was forgotten amid the eye-opening arrival of Rey Ordoñez in 1996. Vizcaino is probably better remembered for ending the nightmarish Game 1 of the 2000 World Series with a game-winning, 12th-inning single for the Yankees than he was for his contributions as a Met.

Shortly after Vizcaino was traded to Cleveland in 1996—a throw-in to "even out" the Carlos Baerga and Alvaro Espinoza for Jeff Kent fiasco—No. 15 went to minor league journeyman **Matt Franco** (1996–2000). Franco, nephew of actor Kurt Russell and a Bobby Valentine favorite, subsequently became one of the franchise's all-time pinch-hitting specialists, remembered still for the game-winning hit off Mariano Rivera in a 1999 interleague game.

Two short-burning, enigmatic outfielders arrived in June trades, wore No. 15, and quietly left town afterward. **Claudell Washington** (1980), who shortly after arriving hit three of his ten Met home runs in a single game against the Dodgers, ran away from the troubled Mets after the season. The arrival of **Richard Hidalgo** (2004) invigorated the franchise for as long as he was hot, which was one month and one month only (although it did help fuel the Mets' first-ever sweep of the Yankees).

Others: reserve catcher **Butch Benton** (1979–80); free-agent lefty **Dave Roberts** (1981); **Brian Giles** (1981; no, not that Brian Giles); pitcher **Rick Aguilera** (1987–88); the everpresent **Jeff McKnight** (1989); first in your alphabetical charts, Don Aase (1989); and hastily discarded outfielder **Brady Clark** (2002).

Number of times issued: 19 (17 players, 2 coaches)

Longest tenured: Jerry Grote (12 seasons, 1,235 games), George Foster (5 seasons, 655 games)

Best single seasons: Carlos Beltran, 2006 (.275/.388/.594, 41 HR, 116 RBI); Beltran, 2007 (.276/.353/.525, 33 HR, 112 RBI); Foster, 1984 (.269/.311/.443, 24 HR, 86 RBI); Jose Vizcaino, 1995 (.287, 21 doubles)

Career statistical leaders: Home runs (Foster 99, Beltran 90), RBI (Foster 361, Grote 357), batting average (Vizcaino .282, Claudell Washington .275), wins (Al Jackson 40), ERA (Ron Darling 3.79)

Catch Them if You Can

Catchers once all looked the same: shin guards, chest protector, glove, mask, and cap on backwards. Many catchers flipped up the bill on their cap to help keep the mask in place. That was about as stylish as it got. They all looked a lot like Jerry Grote and batted somewhere around seventh or eighth in the order, depending on how weak the weakest-hitting infielder was. Grote played 1,235 games as a Met, third-most in club history; it wasn't his fashion, his personality, or his hitting that got his name on the lineup card.

Grote was the antithesis of Cincinnati slugger Johnny Bench. While both were excellent receivers, Bench popularized the style of catching with one hand, using a hinged glove like Randy Hundley of the Cubs. Bench wore a helmet under his mask, an idea that resounded with catchers who didn't deem it a badge of courage to get a foul ball off the coconut with only a cloth cap for protection (helmets for catchers became mandatory in 1987). Grote still caught with both hands and without a helmet—there's even a yearbook photo of his young son in catching gear with a cloth cap—but Grote's backups kept their noggins protected.

J. C. Martin and Duffy Dyer were Mets trailblazers with batting helmets underneath their masks. Ron Hodges spent a dozen seasons at Shea wearing a catching helmet with no brim, resembling a bowl that might be used to cut an unkempt child's hair. Alex Treviño wore one just like it. John Stearns, always his own man, sometimes wore a brimmed helmet and sometimes not. (Stearns graced the cover of the 1978 Mets yearbook—the last edition that cost a buck—diving and missing a tag in his cloth-capped glory.) Dude's catching helmet—he wore one with an earflap while batting—sported his number 12 in orange on the back. Bruce Bochy's head was so large that he had to have a custom-made helmet that never seemed the right shade of blue (he arrived at camp in 1981 with a size 8 helmet in Astros orange: officials had to paint it blue).

Gary Carter provided stability and style at the position. The Kid used a mask with a built-in throat protector, and he wore the same headgear to both hit and catch. Todd

Hundley, Mike Piazza, and Paul Lo Duca succeeded him as All-Stars at the position. Piazza made New Yorkers proud with his homemade "NYPD" batting helmet in the team colors in 2001. Piazza was an early advocate of Knee Savers, padding that fits over the back of the calves to help relieve some stress on the knees while crouching. If only Piazza, perhaps the best-hitting catcher ever, could have worn a full suit of armor to protect him from the dings and tips that constantly riddled him . . . it couldn't have hurt his throwing.

Backup backstops are often innovators of the tools of ignorance. Sourpuss Charlie O'Brien donned the first "hockey mask" in the majors with Toronto in 1997, four years after leaving the Mets. Alberto Castillo, a classic catch-and-throw guy—because he certainly wasn't a hit or run guy—first brought hockey to Shea. In late '97 he donned this newfangled tool of ignorance, complete with oversized baseball stitches painted white on blue and a big orange "NY" over the skull, perhaps half a foot of padding more than Jerry Grote ever had, or wanted. Kelly Stinnett, who'd replaced Charlie O. as backup catcher back in 1994, returned to the Mets briefly in 2006 and donned the hockey mask seven times. His .083 average made both him and the mask expendable; a somewhat healthy Ramon Castro replaced him on the postseason roster. The most interesting part-timer of late, however, was Jason Phillips. Not only did he wear those funky Bono-like glasses every game, day or night, but he wore his helmet forward, with the mask fitting over the brim. On your knees, boy.

The Mets through 2007 have employed 72 catchers, more than half of whom played fewer than 100 games. Following are the uniform numbers appearing most frequently on their catchers' backs:

Number	Catchers Appearing	Notes
5	5	The first four 5s in Met history were catchers (Hobie Landrith, Joe Pignatano, Norm Sherry, Chris Cannizzaro).
9	5	Neither Joe Torre nor Todd Zeile count (Zeile's two catching appearances came while wearing No. 27)
20	5	Mike Fitzgerald (1983–84) was the only regular catcher in 20.
33	5	All hail the obscure backstops of 33: Chuck Estrada, Barry Lyons, Kelly Stinnett, Tim Spehr, and Mike DiFelice.
7	4	Digit of Jeff McKnight's lone inning behind the dish, 1993.
35	4	Orlando Mercado, with 40 games at catcher, leads the pack.

#16: OH, DOCTOR

Almost as soon as **Dwight Gooden** arrived in 1984, there was little doubt the Mets would win a World Series again.

Everything about the young hurler was distinctive, including his age (nineteen) and his uniform number (he was the first Met pitcher ever to wear No. 16), but what set him apart from mere mortal Mets was what happened when he unleashed his electric right arm on the unsuspecting National League.

DWIGHT GOODEN

Gooden was something of a secret weapon when Davey Johnson took over as manager in 1984. Johnson had gotten a taste of Gooden's stuff during the 1983 Class AAA playoffs after Gooden was recalled to Tidewater from Class A Lynchburg, where all he'd done was whiff 300 batters in 191 innings. A strong proponent of promoting Gooden all the way to the big leagues in 1984, Johnson won a brief battle of wills with general manager Frank Cashen to get it done. It was a fight worth winning.

Gooden turned in a spectacular Rookie of the Year campaign and an even better season in 1985, when he went 24-4 with a club-record 1.53 ERA, 8 shutouts, and a Cy Young Award. The following year was not quite as dominant (17-6, 2.84), but the promise of a world championship was realized.

Although he reached mind-boggling heights in these early years, injuries and a recurring drug problem would assure that Gooden would spend much of his remaining days as a Met hiking the hills and valleys along the comeback trail. Struggling with an ERA of 6.31 in June 1994, Gooden was suspended by the league for violating his drug treatment program, a move that ultimately ended his Mets career in shame. He later compounded his sins by joining the Yankees, becoming a member of a world championship team there and throwing the no-hitter in the Bronx that every Met fan who saw him in '84 and '85 assumed he would get in Flushing.

Gooden was a bit of uni number experimenter. He wore No. 64 in spring training of 1993 as a means of recapturing the focus of the 1984 training camp when he first won a job. He also spent some time wearing No. 00 as a means to cut the tension during the uptight spring training of 1989 (Roger McDowell joined Doc, wearing No. 0). At the same time, Gooden could be fiercely protective of his No. 16, swiftly squashing speculation that he might surrender it to Frank Viola when the latter pitcher was acquired in 1989. Viola had worn 16 in Minnesota for eight seasons, including a Cy Young year.

"I don't care how much money he makes. He can have my locker. I'll take him to the best restaurants and show him New York. He can even have my wife," Doc told *Newsday*. "But he can't have my number, no way."

Viola took another number, but that wasn't the case when the Mets acquired another one-time pitching sensation, **Hideo Nomo**, in 1998. Nomo was the first player to wear 16 since Gooden's departure but didn't do it much justice, going 4-5 and showing none of his Dodger flash. Nomo's final appearance wearing 16 with the Mets was the last day of the season, a fine relief effort in a doomed game that dashed the club's blundered hopes of postseasonhood. By the time Nomo got his career straightened out he was long gone from Shea.

While Gooden was reportedly unhappy with the Mets issuing his number to Nomo, the next two wearers of the jersey asked for and received Doc's blessing.

Seafaring outfielder **Derek Bell**, the booby prize in the Mike Hampton trade, had long worn No. 16 in other locales as a tribute to Gooden, who preceded him from Tampa to the big leagues and whom Bell (2000) considered a hero. Bell's most distinctive uniform characteristic belonged not his shirt, however, but to his pants, which were wide enough to serve as an auxiliary sail on the Hudson River–docked houseboat Bell lived on during his stay with the Mets.

Bell had a fine start to his Mets career, as his hip-hop-inspired charisma and style won over fans and writers, but he slumped badly in the second half of the year, finally limping off the field in Game 1 of the Divisional Playoffs and into Mets history.

Gooden's former teammate **David Cone** paid him tribute by wearing No. 16 during what proved to be the final days of his career in 2003.

Lee Mazzilli was a different kind of teen idol. The Brooklyn-born outfielder, who wore No. 16 for the majority of his time as a Mets regular, was about the best thing the Mets had during the disco era, and they never let their fans forget it.

The handsome, 14th overall pick in the 1973 draft—literally made a poster boy in a 1978 Shea giveaway—was a capable, switch-hitting outfielder with some power, speed, and a good batting eye at a time when it was difficult to find a Met possessing any of those qualities. To show how badly the Mets had corroded from the inside out, Maz was the only Met first-round pick between 1969 and 1976 to make more than a token appearance in the major leagues. Beaten-up Mets fans of 1979 fondly recall Mazzilli's smashing performance in the All-Star Game at the Kingdome that year. He went 1-for-1 with a game-winning, bases-loaded walk against Ron Guidry, and a pop-fly of a home run to the left field corner that to Met fans looked like a 500-footer.

Mazzilli's trade to Texas following the 1981 season helped launch the Mets' mid-1980s glory years by bringing Ron Darling and Walt Terrell to New York, but Maz returned for a victory lap in 1986 (wearing No. 13 now that Gooden commanded 16). His current gig as an SNY studio analyst may help fans begin to forgive Mazzilli for various acts of treachery as a Yankee coach under Joe Torre.

When the Mets failed to lure free agent Carlos Delgado in 2005, they settled instead for strong glove/weak bat **Doug Meintkiewicz**. His discount performance prompted the Mets to bench him and then trade for Delgado the following year.

Brooklyn-born like Mazzilli, and a childhood fan of the Gooden-era Mets of the 1980s, **Paul Lo Duca** is perhaps the ideal No. 16. Acquired in a trade with the Marlins following the 2005 season, Lo Duca made the unenviable task of succeeding Mike Piazza look like a breeze. The catcher hit .318 with 39 doubles in his first season with the Mets and provided "red ass" intensity that fans appreciated and opponents didn't. He had trouble repeating the trick in 2007.

The first wearer of the No. 16 jersey was reserve outfielder **Bobby Gene Smith**, who also holds the distinction of being the first active player the Mets ever traded. The guy they received for him, catcher **Sammy Taylor**, inherited his No. 16 jersey.

Catcher **Jesse Gonder** wore 16 briefly in 1963 but turned it over to **Dick Smith** in midseason. Smith (1963–64) and the man who followed him in the 16 jersey, **Danny Napoleon** (1965–66), were typical of the early Mets: free-swinging minor league sluggers whose power didn't translate to the big leagues. Following Napoleon were reserves **Tommy Reynolds** (1967), **Kevin Collins** (1968), and Queens native **Mike Jorgensen** (1969–71).

Crouching, choked-up slap-hitter **Felix Millan** wore No. 16 for 1973, his first year with the Mets. Millan switched to 17 a year later while reserve outfielder **Dave Schneck** switched into 16. Catcher **John Stearns** began his Mets career wearing No. 16 in 1975 and 1976.

Number of times issued: 18 (18 players)
Longest tenured: Dwight Gooden (11 seasons, 305 games), Lee Mazzilli (5 seasons, 702 games)
Best single seasons: Dwight Gooden, 1985 (24-4, 1.53 ERA, 268 strikeouts in 278.1 innings, Cy Young Award); Lee Mazzilli, 1979 (.305/.395/.449, 15 HR, 79 RBI)
Career statistical leaders: Home runs (Mazzilli 59, Derek Bell 18), RBI (Mazzilli 296, Paul Lo Duca 103), batting average (Lo Duca .297, Felix Millan .290, Mazzilli .271), wins (Gooden 157), saves (Gooden 1) ERA (Gooden 3.10)

Strikeouts by the Numbers

On May 18, 2005, soon-to-be-released Mets relief pitcher Manny Aybar faced the Cincinnati Reds in the top of the 9th inning and the Mets leading 10-3. And though Aybar would surrender a double, a single, and a two-run homer during the inning, when he caught Ryan Freel looking at strike three for the first out, it marked a momentous occasion in team history: That was the moment that 36 surpassed 41 as the uniform number to produce the most strikeouts in Mets history.

That nobody had occupied the 41 jersey for twenty-three years speaks well of the greatness of Tom Seaver, who provided 2,541 strikeouts—roughly 96 percent of the strikeouts of all Mets to wear No. 41 (or close to the same number as his record-setting percentage of votes for Hall of Fame induction). Seaver by himself, in fact, struck out more batters than all the combined wearers of all numbers but for 36, which draws most of its power from Jerry Koosman's 1,799 whiffs. Number 36 also has the advantage of nineteen other guys on the job, including Tracy Stallard (228 K's), Ed Lynch (223) and Greg McMichael (143). Thanks to retiring the 41 jersey in 1988, it is stuck at five wearers and 2,651 K's forever.

Following is a list of the most strikeouts by a Mets uniform number through 2007.

No.	Strikeouts	Notes
36	2,674	Koosman with 1,799; Tracy Stallard 228; Ed Lynch 223
41	2,651	All but 110 K's by Seaver (2,541)
16	2,018	Doc Gooden 1,875; three others 143
29	1,891	Steve Trachsel 580; Frank Viola 314
32	1,888	Jon Matlack with 1,023
38	1,807	28 contributors, including Dave Mlicki with 402 K's and reliever Skip Lockwood with 368
45	1,771	Tug McGraw leads with 618; Pedro Martinez second with 377
22	1,763	Al Leiter with 1,106; Fat Jack Fisher with 475
47	1,592	Tom Glavine (516) overcame Jesse Orosco (506) in what looks to be the final indignity
39	1,574	Gary Gentry 563; Nino Espinosa 213
27	1,539	Craig Swan 671; Dennis Cook 234
50	1,529	All but 80 K's belong to Sid Fernandez (1,449)

#17: "I'M KEITH HERNANDEZ"

Fourteen Mets wore the No. 17 jersey before **Keith Hernandez.** Fourteen men have worn it after him (through 2007). That Keith Hernandez is right in the middle of any discussion of Mets who wore No. 17 only makes sense.

Acquired from St. Louis in June 1983 at the bargain price of Neil Allen and Rick Ownbey, Hernandez was not unlike a lot of new arrivals to New York: he needed to fight it for a bit to see how he fit in. He was dealing with cocaine allegations that hastened his departure from St. Louis and struggling with the question of whether the Mets were the kind of team he would want to sign with again when his contract expired following the season.

For another thing, the uniform number he'd worn to a co-MVP award in 1979 (37) was unavailable, as it had been retired for Casey Stengel in 1966. And since the '83 Mets already employed a 7 (Hubie Brooks), a 27 (Craig Swan), and a 47 (Jesse Orosco), Hernandez had to adjust to 17.

Although the 1983 Mets were far from a success, Hernandez hit .306 in his new environs and found just enough talent on the horizon—and excitement in the city—to commit to a five-year engagement in what he'd once considered a "baseball Siberia." What the Mets got in return was one of the team's all-time performers: a revolutionary defensive player, a skilled hitter slotted comfortably in the No. 3 slot in the lineup, and the headstrong, urbane, chatty, on-field general who'd see the team through its best era.

Photo by Dan Carubia

Batting averages over his first four Mets seasons—.306, .311, .309, and .310—illustrate just how consistent Hernandez could be offensively, while Gold Glove awards in eleven consecutive seasons (seven as a Met) only begin to describe the swashbuckling style with which Mex played first base. His aggressive, daring defense could change the opposition's strategy.

Although injuries brought a sudden decline to his productivity and eventually his career, his fame as an ex-Met was only beginning, thanks to post-career *Seinfeld* appearances and a current gig as New York's most acerbic and honest sportscaster.

Mets teammates found Hernandez unforgettable as well. Pitcher **David Cone** switched from 44 to 17 midway through the 1991 season as a tribute to his departed teammate and brought the number to the All-Star Game in 1992. Ex-teammates Ron Darling (Oakland A's), Bobby Ojeda (Los Angeles Dodgers), and Roger McDowell (Dodgers, following Ojeda) all wore their respect for Hernandez on their backs for teams they played for after leaving the Mets. Cone wore 17 again with the Royals in 1993.

While Hernandez has used the bully pulpit of the broadcast booth to lament the parade of lesser-lights the Mets have trotted out in the 17 jersey recently, it should be noted that short-lived and insignificant players wearing 17 had been a Mets tradition long before Mex arrived.

The lone exception might be slap-hitting second baseman **Felix Millan**, who, like Hernandez, led his team in hits multiple times, played outstanding defense, and wore one of the more memorable mustaches in team history.

Millan (1974–77) rarely struck out and rarely walked. Choking up on the bat as if it were a dumbbell—nobody else held their hands so high—Millan slapped 191 hits in 1975, a team record that

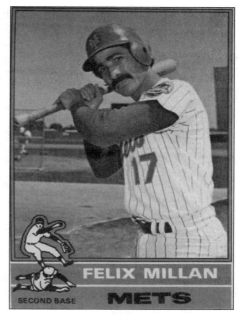

stood for twenty-one years. All but 40 of those hits were singles. Millan that season also became the first Met to play 162 games in a single year, a team record he shares today with John Olerud, who accomplished the feat in 1999.

Millan had a fiery temper that inadvertently brought an end to his major league career: he foolishly threw a punch at massive Pirates catcher Ed Ott, who summarily body-slammed Millan to the Three Rivers Stadium turf, dislocating Millan's shoulder.

That 17 was going to be a frequently issued number was evident all the way back in 1962, when it debuted on the back of **Don Zimmer** and went next to infamous catcher **Choo Choo Coleman**. Zimmer, the first third baseman in team history, suffered through an 0-for-34 slump but rallied all the way to 4-for-52 before being released in early May.

Coleman (1962–63) was a speedy, left-handed hitting, defensively challenged catcher whose peculiarities made him a legend on the scale of a minor Marv Throneberry. Coleman made uniform number history when he reportedly welcomed roommate Charlie Neal back after the 1962 season by saying, "I know you. You're No. 4."

Veteran pitcher **Frank Lary** was the first two-time Met in team history and a curious one at that. Purchased from the Detroit Tigers in May 1964,

Lary made thirteen forgettable appearances and was sent away to the Milwaukee Braves that August (in exchange for pitcher **Dennis Ribant**, who wore the 17 jersey the rest of the year). Lary, however, reported to Mets camp the following spring, leading to speculation there were under-the-table conditions to the deal the previous summer: was Lary only loaned to the Braves, or was he, like original Met Harry Chiti, traded for himself? The Mets explained, vaguely, that Lary was payment for certain debts the Braves owed the Mets in the aftermath of one or more of the fifteen "conditional" deals the Mets and Braves had engaged in over the past three seasons. Whatever, the first two-time Met in team history was more effective the second time around, going 1-3, 2.98 in fourteen appearances, including seven starts. But he'd be on the move again—for good this time—to the White Sox in July.

Dick Stuart (1966) wanted Ed Kranepool's number (7) and job (first base), but didn't get either. A prodigious slugger with an ego to match, Stuart had hit 28 home runs in 1965 with the Phillies but accounted for only 4 by the time the Mets released him in June of '66. Stuart wasn't a complete disappointment: With 6 errors in 23 games at first base, he lived up to his nickname, "Dr. Strangeglove."

Mets fans were titillated at glowing reports of the speedy switch-hitting minor league center fielder they'd acquired from Pittsburgh over the 1967 offseason and could hardly believe their eyes when he turned out to be slight, balding **Don Bosch** (1967–68), who in parts of two seasons hit only .157 and, needless to say, failed to solve the club's longstanding center field problem.

Rod Gaspar (1969–70) and **Ted Martinez** (1970–73) were modest but useful role players for the '69 and '73 pennant-winning Mets. Modest reserves **Gil Flores** (1978–79) and **Jerry Morales** (1980) weren't so lucky. **Ellis Valentine** (1981–82) was a one-time fearsome power hitter and possessor of the strongest right-field cannon arm in baseball, but by the time he got to the Mets (from Montreal in a poor trade for fireballing reliever Jeff Reardon), aftereffects of a beaning rendered him harmless with a bat in his hands.

The Mets also paid full retail—exciting young Melvin Mora—for summer rental **Mike Bordick** when they needed an experienced short-stop for 2000's pennant run. Bordick thrilled fans by hitting a home run in his first New York at-bat before things went downhill. An injury prevented him from doing much in the World Series that year, and he re-signed with Baltimore after the season.

When the Mets also failed to retain Mike Hampton following 2000, Steve Phillips made sure he didn't miss the next-best free agent, **Kevin Appier** (2001). The one-time Kansas City phenom got a great contract but only had a so-so season. Correctly sensing that the four-year deal would momentarily become an albatross, Phillips sent Appier to Anaheim for Mo Vaughn and a whole new set of expensive problems.

Talented but unlikable pitcher **Bret Saberhagen** wore 17 for two of his four years with the Mets, including an excellent 1994 (14-4, 2.74 ERA, and a stunning 143:13 strikeout to walk ratio). Explaining that his name was difficult to pronounce, Korean-born relief pitcher **Dae Sung Koo** (2005) informed media and teammates he'd prefer to be referred to as "Mr. Koo." Mr. Koo's one and only career highlight was shocking the Yankees' Randy Johnson with a double to deep center field and then brazenly scoring from second with a swanlike, full-Met-jacketed dive on a subsequent sacrifice bunt. Clownish veteran **Jose Lima** (2006) took what appeared to be the final gasps of his career as an ineffective injury replacement.

Luis Lopez (1997–99) filled in for Rey Ordoñez at shortstop, out-hit Rey-Rey as a Met (.250 to .245), and punched the Gold Glover on the team bus, which was something everyone wished they'd done when Ordoñez later called the Shea fans "stupid." Lopez was part of two shocking developments on September 14, 1997. First, he started the game wearing 17 on "Keith Hernandez Day" when many fans hoped the number might be put in storage to honor Mex (it was the same year Jackie Robinson's 42 was retired at a Shea ceremony). Second, the banjo-hitting Lopez socked a homer for the only run in a 1-0 win that afternoon.

Others: backup catchers **Jim Schaffer** (1965) and **Brent Mayne** (1996); whiff-prone outfielder **Larry Elliot** (1966); utility man **Jeff McKnight** (1993); ineffective relief pitchers **Satoru Komiyama** (2002), **Graeme Lloyd** (2003), and **Jason Anderson** (2003); reserve infielder **Wilson Delgado** (2004); and **David Newhan** (2007), who had an interesting pedigree as the son of a famed sportswriter but failed off the Mets bench under deadline pressure.

Number of times issued: 29 (19 position players, 10 pitchers)

Longest tenured: Keith Hernandez (7 seasons, 880 games), Felix Millan (4 seasons, 528 games)

Best single seasons: Hernandez, 1984 (.311/.409/.449, 15 HR, 94 RBI); Bret Saberhagen, 1994 (14-4, 2.74 ERA); David Cone, 1991 (14-14, 3.29, 241 strikeouts in 232.2 innings)

Career statistical leaders: Home runs (Hernandez 80, Choo-Choo Coleman 9), RBI (Hernandez 468, Millan 167), batting average (Hernandez .297, Millan .273), wins (Cone 24), saves (Frank Lary 2) ERA (Saberhagen 2.98)

This One Goes Out

As noted above, Keith Hernandez left a strong enough impression on teammates like David Cone, Ron Darling, and Roger McDowell that they went on to honor him by wearing his number elsewhere. Worth noting is McDowell, who switched to 17 in 1993, leaving behind his old Dodgers number, 31, to be picked up by a young catcher named Piazza. That the Mets may one day retire No. 31 therefore can be traced almost directly to Hernandez, who, of course, is an indirect numerical descendent of Casey Stengel.

From the obscure (Tito Fuentes, Ken Boswell, John Mabry) to the legendary (Ted Williams, Roberto Clemente, Jackie Robinson), following is a list of some Mets and the men they honored with their choice of uniform number:

No.	Player	In honor of
9	George Theodore	Ted Williams
12	Willie Randolph	Ken Boswell
13	Edgardo Alfonzo	Dave Concepción
13	Jorge Velandia	Edgardo Alfonzo
17	David Cone	Keith Hernandez
21	Carlos Delgado	Roberto Clemente
23	Ted Martinez	Tito Fuentes
42	Butch Huskey	Jackie Robinson
42	Mo Vaughn	Jackie Robinson
45	John Franco	Tug McGraw
47	Joe McEwing	John Mabry

#18: DAR-RYL!

Darryl Strawberry is always going to be 18.

That was his age when the Mets drafted him, first in the nation, out of Crenshaw High in Los Angeles in 1980. At 18, all things were possible. "Best tools I've seen in thirty years," one scout gushed. "The black Ted Williams," others suggested.

That was just the beginning of the expectations heaped upon a kid who, just as expected, would become the greatest offensive player the organization had ever developed. At the same time, this Rookie of the Year, this shoulda-been '88 MVP, this seven-time Mets All-Star, this Game 7 homering right fielder would always fall under the classification of unfulfilled promise.

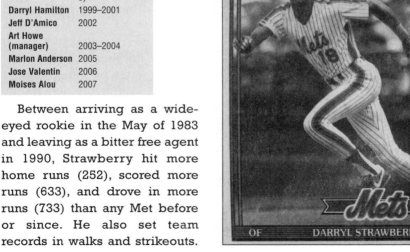

Between arriving as a wide-eyed rookie in the May of 1983 and leaving as a bitter free agent in 1990, Strawberry hit more home runs (252), scored more runs (633), and drove in more runs (733) than any Met before or since. He also set team records in walks and strikeouts.

Somehow he did all of that while appearing at times that he wasn't trying very hard. Part of that was the illusion of his gracefulness—Strawberry took long, easy strides in the field and on the base paths and unfolded long, powerful arms when he swung—and part unreasonable expectations to meet. Strawberry, like no other Met, seemed to grasp that fan sentiment and through comments to the media, he fed it, always promising to have "a monster season" while providing only very good ones. He knew how to hurt fans, too, saying "now you'll see the *real* Darryl Strawberry," while displaying a new uniform number—44—on a Dodger jersey after signing with his hometown team as a free agent.

If that were so, we'd take the unreal Strawberry. Over the next nine seasons Strawberry would encounter legal troubles, health scares, and drug scandals while toiling in 44 (Dodgers), 17 (Giants), and 26 and 39 (Yankees) and hitting only 83 home runs. He was 18 no longer.

Felix Mantilla (1962) was the opening-day shortstop for the 1962 Mets, even though he spent most of the year as a third baseman. The Mets got three players for Mantilla in a trade with the Red Sox after the season, but the deal still blew up in their faces. One of the returnees was **Pumpsie Green** (1963), remembered as the first player to break the color barrier for the last team to integrate. Green was a switch-hitting, versatile infielder who reached base at a pretty good clip, but he arrived at Mets camp overweight and spent most of the year in AAA.

JOEL YOUNGBLOOD
OF-2B

Lost in the twin tragedies of the Seaver and Kingman trades of June 15, 1977, was a third trade that sent reserve infielder Mike Phillips to St. Louis for **Joel Youngblood** (1977–82). That one turned out to be a good deal, even though it became the Shea equivalent of "Apart from that Mrs. Lincoln, how did you enjoy the play?"

Youngblood played some third base, second base, and all three outfield positions for the Mets, although his versatility might also have been a curse in that Joe Torre never found him a regular position. His strong arm was suited best for right field, but the Mets couldn't resist the temptation of trying power bats there. Youngblood didn't like third base and vice-versa but for his part hit nearly everywhere he was asked to play. He led the team in home runs (16) and doubles (37) in 1979 and was challenging for the league batting crown in 1981—his only All-Star season—when he got injured.

Youngblood is destined to be remembered for becoming the first man to get hits for two different teams in the same day: He singled for the Mets in a day game at Wrigley Field, was informed he was traded to Montreal, and joined the Expos that night in Philadelphia, where he singled off Steve Carlton (wearing No. 25, by the way). The circumstances overshadowed the fact that the second Youngblood trade also turned out pretty well for the Mets, bringing pitcher Tom Gorman.

Youngblood was the last player to wear 18 before Strawberry; **Bret Saberhagen** (1992–93) was the first to receive No. 18 after him. Saberhagen had worn No. 18 to stardom (and two Cy Young Awards) in Kansas City, but the Mets didn't get a good season from him until he changed to No. 17 in 1994.

Moises Alou came to the Mets in 2007 with a reputation for a strong bat, a weak glove, and shaky health, and he didn't disappoint on any count. Injured early in the season, Alou returned and safely hit in 30 straight games (a club record), carrying the ball club on his back down the stretch. Alou couldn't handle all that dead weight alone.

His arrival in New York forced **Jose Valentin** to switch to No. 22. Wearing 18 in 2006, Valentin sat on the bench while two other men tried and failed to nail down the second base job: When he finally got his chance, he socked 18 home runs (including two grand slams) and hit .271 in a comeback year.

In what seemed like a deliberate attempt to sedate the manager's office after the frenzy of the Bobby Valentine era, the Mets hired low-key skipper **Art Howe** in 2003 and subsequently put fans to sleep. Probably remembered best for Mike Piazza's botched transition to first base, Howe appeared to be a quiet observer while a front-office leadership crisis (and to be sure, poor results on the field) led to his own firing late in 2004—an event the tabloid readers knew sooner than Howe did. Howe met this fate the way he always did, with quiet dignity, staying on as a lame duck until the end of the season.

The remaining 18s are almost entirely reserves of various skill. Pitcher **Dennis Ribant** wore 18 for the first part of 1965, was sent to the minors, and returned in September to see the jersey on the back of recently acquired utility man **Gary Kolb.** Ribant switched to No. 30, and Kolb, who hit just .167, was traded following the season. Diminutive outfielder **Al Luplow** (1966–67) had a respectable campaign as a part-timer in '66; infielder **Joe Moock** (1967) joined in late 1967 when the Mets were giving anyone a chance. **Duffy Dyer** (1968) got the only one of his 440 Met hits while not wearing No. 10 during his major league debut as 18.

Reserve outfielders **Jim Gosger** (1969), **Dave Marshall** (1970–72), **George Theodore** (1973), and **Benny Ayala** (1974) followed. Gosger saw more action in 5 and 19 later in his career, Marshall was a fine pinch hitter with just enough power to be dangerous, Theodore shortly changed to No. 9, and Ayala's Met career peaked with a home run in his first turn at-bat.

Jeff McKnight (1994) took 18 when Saberhagen switched to 17. It would be McKnight's fifth and final number with the Mets. More short-lived scrubeenos followed in 18, including **Jeff Barry** (1995), **Kevin Roberson** (1996), **Craig Paquette** (1998), and **Todd Haney** (1998).

In Japan, 18 is the number traditionally assigned to ace pitchers: that was the number given the Mets' first Japanese player, left-handed relief pitcher **Takashi Kashiwada**, in 1997. He was no ace, but he debuted two months before Hideki Irabu's first appearance in another borough, making Kashiwada New York's first Japanese import. Gangly starter **Jeff D'Amico** (2002) pitched some wonderful games early in the year but was out of the rotation by August and out of New York for good soon after.

Another Darryl, 1999 stretch-run pickup **Darryl Hamilton** (1999–2001), hit .339 as the Mets held off the Reds to reach the postseason. Hamilton eventually lost a starting job to injuries and his backup job to whining. **Marlon Anderson** (2005) had a fine year as a pinch hitter, highlighted by a 9th-inning pinch-hit, inside-the-park home run to tie what became the club's signature win of 2005. Anderson returned in 2007 wearing 23 and still hitting.

Number of times issued: 26 (25 players, 1 manager)

Longest tenured: Darryl Strawberry (8 seasons, 1,109 games), Joel Youngblood (6 seasons, 610 games)

Best single seasons: Strawberry, 1987 (.284/.398/.583, 39 HR, 104 RBI, 36 stolen bases); Strawberry, 1988 (.269/.366/.545, 39 HR, 101 RBI); Moises Alou, 2007 (.341/.392/.524, 13 HR, 49 RBI)

Career statistical leaders: Home runs (Strawberry 252, Youngblood 38), RBI (Strawberry 733, Youngblood 216), batting average (Alou, .341, Felix Mantilla .275, Jose Valentin .271), wins (Bret Saberhagen 10), saves (Dennis Ribant 3), ERA (Saberhagen 3.38)

Great Runs

Someday the Mets may find a young player good enough to wear the No. 6 uniform for more than a few months at a time, and by doing so bridge the gap between their young stars wearing No. 5 (David Wright) and No. 7 (Jose Reyes).

Until then, the most devastating straights in Mets uniform history are the late teens of the late '80s. Following are lists of notable Mets teammates who wore consecutive numbers.

6 numbers:
1986: Foster 15, Gooden 16, Hernandez 17, Strawberry 18, Ojeda 19, Johnson 20

1987–88: Aguilera 15, Gooden 16, Hernandez 17, Strawberry 18, Ojeda 19, Johnson 20

1989: Darling 15, Gooden 16, Hernandez 17, Strawberry 18, Ojeda 19, Johnson 20

5 numbers:
1989: Gooden 16, Hernandez 17, Strawberry 18, Ojeda 19, Johnson 20

3 numbers:
1968–71: Seaver 41, Taylor 42, McAndrew 43

1969–71: Agee 20, Jones 21, Clendenon 22

1975–77: Kingman 26, Swan 27, Milner 28

1986: Backman 6, Mitchell 7, Carter 8

1992: Gooden 16, Cone 17, Saberhagen 18

#19: HE'S CRAFTY

The 1985 season ended about as painfully as it could for the Mets, who won 98 games only to see the NL East title flag fly over St. Louis and their left-handed junkballing ace, John Tudor, who in six assignments versus the 1985 Mets pitched to an eye-popping, soul-crushing, pennant-deciding ERA of 0.93.

The Mets were still smarting that offseason when they surrendered four prospects to Boston for **Bob Ojeda**, thereby securing a crafty soft-tossing lefty of their own.

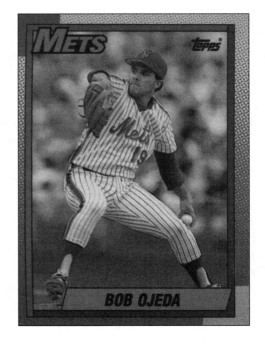

BOB OJEDA

Early reviews of the trade, which sent the Red Sox highly regarded pitching prospects Wes Gardner and Calvin Schiraldi, suggested the Mets paid too high a price for Ojeda, whose career record was just over .500 and who was viewed merely as a candidate to crack the '86 rotation. But Ojeda became perhaps the steadiest, if least spectacular, of the Mets' starters that year. He led the team with 18 wins and a 2.57 ERA, finished fourth in Cy Young voting, and was at his best in critical games during the postseason. He started and won Game 2 of the NLCS and Game 3 of the World Series with the Mets trailing in each case. He was also the starter in Game 6 of both the NLCS and World Series. The loser of the latter was Schiraldi, who also lost Game 7 for Boston.

Ojeda found it difficult to replicate his success in the coming years. He was injured in 1987 and a rebounding year in 1988 ended when, on the same day the Mets clinched a tie for the NL East title, Ojeda severed a portion of his middle finger with a hedge clipper in an accident at home. He bounced back from that to win 13 games in 1989 before finishing his Mets career as a reliever in 1990.

Ojeda's body of work with the Mets—51 wins and a 3.12 ERA over five seasons—qualifies him for the rather dubious honor of being the best of the twenty-seven men who wore No. 19 for the Mets. Ojeda brought No. 19 with him from Boston: It is unlikely he'd want to be among those presented with the uniform by the Mets.

Like **Anthony Young**, for instance. Nobody ever doubted that the hard-throwing Young had plenty of ability, but in three years with the Mets nobody had worse luck. In two years wearing No. 19 (he wore No. 33 in his rookie year of 1991), Young won three games and lost 30—including an excruciating 27 straight losing decisions to break Craig Anderson's club and major league record 19, set over three seasons—amid racking up 18 saves and fashioning a none-too-poor ERA of 3.98.

Balancing bad luck and bad decisions brought three players back to the 19 jersey after leaving the Mets.

Infielder **Tim Foli** was the first overall selection in the 1968 amateur draft: he spent parts of the 1970 and '71 seasons with the Mets but was traded to Montreal in the Rusty Staub deal. The Mets reacquired Foli to be Bud Harrelson's successor in 1978 and then shipped him off again for shortstop Frank Taveras in a 1979 challenge trade won by the soon-to-be-world-champion Pirates.

Lenny Harris was a premier Mets pinch hitter in 1998, but while the Mets' front office was busy dealing with the extramarital office affairs of general manager Steve Phillips, Harris signed as a free agent with the Rockies. Phillips subsequently tried to right his mistake by reacquiring

Harris in 2000: this time he cost a young pitcher, Bill Pulsipher, once a prized possession of the Mets organization.

In between Harris's two stays with the Mets, the No. 19 jersey went to **Roger Cedeño.** His 66 steals in 1999 set a then-team record and gathered enough value for him to be a key figure in the Mike Hampton trade the following winter. Mets fans who witnessed Cedeño's misadventures in the outfield and his poor second half in '99 felt they dodged a bullet, only to be shot down when Phillips, wildly overestimating Cedeño's abilities as a leadoff hitter and outfielder, signed him to a four-year deal starting in 2001.

That announcement came just days after Harris was included in a typically convoluted Phillips trade involving three teams, eleven players, and a suitcase of cash: what was important was that it left 19 open again for Cedeño, who subsequently had two of the most awful seasons a Mets outfielder has ever had. As of the writing of this book, he is out of professional baseball.

Left-handed reliever **Ken MacKenzie** (1962–63) was the first wearer of the 19 jersey for the Mets, and with a 5-4 record in 1962, the first Mets pitcher to have a winning record. He was traded to St. Louis for right-handed reliever **Ed Bauta** (1963) in a deal that helped neither team.

Hawk Taylor (1964–67) was among the bonus-baby rejects that populated the early Mets. A rugged catcher who signed with the Braves for a reported six-figure bonus in 1957, Taylor carved out a living as a light-hitting reserve over parts of four years with the Mets. Taylor briefly lost No. 19 in 1964 to utility man **John Stephenson**, who would later return in other numbers.

Tom "The Blade" Hall (1975–76) was one of the Mets' smallest pitchers ever; **Heath "Rollerblade" Bell** (2004–06) one of the largest. Both were capable at times of quality relief, and both were at their best in uniforms that didn't say "Mets." Veteran sinkerballer **Scott Erickson** (2004) made the opening-day roster against just about every fan's wishes, but he injured himself while warming for his first start. He finally joined the team in July, had one good and then one bad start for the Mets, and was traded to Texas for a player to be named later named Josh Hoffpauir, who was later never heard from again.

Infielder **Ron Gardenhire** (1981–85) the only Met ever born in Germany, was the regular shortstop in 1982 and had a chance to play under four managers in a five-season career (Joe Torre, George Bamberger, Frank Howard, and Davey Johnson). Injuries and a weak bat eventually did him in, but Gardenhire learned from the many different managing styles he experienced and put his heart to work in a successful run as the skipper of the Minnesota Twins.

That journeyman long shot reliever **Lino Urdaneta** (2007) made it all the way back from the Mexican League became easier to explain when it was revealed he'd failed a test for performance-enhancing drugs. Veteran catcher **Sandy Alomar Jr.** surfaced in 2007 while his namesake dad coached third. Alomar surrendered No. 19 to **Jeff Conine**, as the erstwhile Mr. Marlin who played the last weeks of his career as a wannabe Mr. Met.

Other products of 19: blue-collar reservists **Kevin Collins** (1967), **Brian Ostrosser** (1973), **Jim Gosger** (1973–74), **Leo Foster** (1977), **Luis Alvarado** (1977), **Butch Benton** (1978), **Jeff Gardner** (1991), **Shawn Hare** (1994), **Bill Spiers** (1995), **Jason Hardtke** (1996–97), and **Jim Tatum** (1998).

Number of times issued: 32 (28 players)

Longest tenured: Roger Cedeño (3 seasons, 453 games), Lenny Harris (3 seasons, 261 games), Bobby Ojeda (5 seasons, 140 games)

Best single seasons: Ojeda, 1986 (18-5, 2.57 ERA); Cedeño, 1999 (.313/.396/.408, 66 stolen bases, 23 doubles)

Career statistical leaders: Home runs (Cedeño 18, Hawk Taylor 11), RBI (Cedeño 114, Tim Foli 52), batting average (Cedeño .279), wins (Ojeda 51), saves (Anthony Young, 18), ERA (Ojeda 3.12)

Why Don't We Steal Away

Roger Cedeño did one thing pretty well. In 1999, under the tutelage of Rickey Henderson, while being used judiciously enough to reach base at a .400 clip, and not yet fat, Cedeño stole Mookie Wilson's name out of the Mets record books with 66 stolen bases—a single-year standard that stood until 2007, when it was broken by Jose Reyes (78).

Although Cedeño, in two subsequent seasons with the Mets, would amass just 39 more steals, it was enough to get No. 19 into the discussion of the stealingest Mets uniform numbers ever.

No.	Steals	Notes
1	461	Mookie Wilson with 281; Lance Johnson with 65; and Vince Coleman with 61
7	378	Jose Reyes, with 234 steals through 2007, is on pace to out-steal every uniform number
20	331	Howard Johnson with 202; Tommie Agee 92
11	266	Team effort of Frank Taveras (90), Len Randle (47), Vince Coleman (38), and Wayne Garrett (33)
18	255	Darryl Strawberry with 191
6	211	Wally Backman with 104; Darryl Boston 33
16	172	Lee Mazzilli with 144
12	171	John Stearns with 86; Ken Boswell with 26
3	168	Bud Harrelson with 115
19	146	Roger Cedeño with 105

#20: THUNDER AND LIGHTNING

Two of the most notable Mets to combine power and speed have worn No. 20. For a franchise that often has often struggled to get it all together, **Tommie Agee** and **Howard Johnson** were standouts.

When Agee first arrived at Shea in 1968, he looked a lot like all the other candidates to become the team's first great center fielder. He was a bust.

The 1966 American League Rookie of the Year with the White Sox, Agee was acquired by the Mets in a trade for Tommy Davis in 1968 (Al Weis came, too). His great athleticism and strength had some observers comparing him to Willie Mays, but the newly dubbed "Shea Hey Kid" struggled badly. In his first at-bat as a Met in spring training, he was struck by a Bob Gibson fastball, and the hurting didn't go away. He encountered an 0-for-34 slump en route to hitting a paltry .217 with 5 home runs and 13 stolen bases on the year, and he may have been the least popular athlete in New York.

Observers credit manager Gil Hodges with helping Agee orchestrate one of the most dramatic reversals of fortune in team history. Displaying a new confidence steeled in lengthy talks with his skipper, Agee led the '69 Mets with 26 home runs and 76 RBI, numbers that don't begin to describe his contributions. Agee's home run in Game 3 of the '69 World Series was all but forgotten by the time the game ended, as the center fielder saved five runs with two amazin' catches: the first reaching to rob Elrod Hendricks with two on in the fourth and the second a sprawling catch of Paul Blair's drive to right-center with the bases loaded in the 7th.

Agee twice more led the Mets in home runs, but his game deteriorated following the death of Hodges. Agee was traded to Houston after 1972,

ironically making room for the "real" Willie Mays. Although his number wasn't retired, it's displayed prominently at Shea Stadium, provided one looks to deep left field and up several dozen feet. On the facing of the concourse entryway near upper deck section 48 marks the spot where, on April 10, 1969, Agee hit what was believed to be the only fair ball ever hit into the upper deck at Shea.

Howard Johnson had a familiar name but was otherwise an unknown quantity when he arrived from Detroit in a trade for pitcher Walt Terrell in 1985. In time it looked like one of the great steals the Mets ever made.

One of the top switch-hitting power hitters in baseball history, Johnson had some great seasons as a Met. He had an alarmingly good 1991, in

which he led the league and set the Mets' all-time mark in RBI (117), with 38 homers and 30 steals (one of three 30-30 seasons he had for the club). Johnson had a tendency to alternate great years with so-so ones. HoJo finished in the top ten in NL MVP voting in 1987, '89, and '91, but his respective averages in '88, '90, and '92 were .230, .244, and .223. But when the year was odd and HoJo was smoking the ball, few players were better. When he finished his Mets career in 1993, HoJo ranked second all-time in home runs (192), RBI (629), stolen bases (202), doubles (214), and runs (627) and third in total bases (1,823).

Expansion draftee **Craig Anderson** (1962–64) was the first player to wear No. 20 for the Mets. The tall right-handed reliever got off to a 3-1 start, including winning both games of a doubleheader against the Braves. He then lost his next nineteen decisions in a row (sixteen in 1962, two in 1963—including the last major league game ever played at the Polo Grounds—and one in 1964) to break original Met Roger Craig's record for most consecutive losses and set a standard that would last until it was bested three decades later by another unlucky Met hurler, Anthony Young.

John Pacella (1977, 1979–80) is better remembered for what he didn't wear—his hat—which flew off his head with nearly every pitch he threw. Pacella's violent delivery brought the Mets three wins over parts of three seasons.

All-or-nothing slugger **Jeromy Burnitz** (2002–03) returned to the Mets in 2002 and had a year even worse than his .219 batting average and 19 home runs suggested. Burnitz had a good enough comeback in 2003 to earn some value at the midseason trade deadline, when he brought back, among others, **Victor Diaz** (2005–06). Diaz, like Burnitz, wore No. 20, swung violently, and had impressive power. His most distinguishing characteristic, however, was an iron glove that made every ball hit his way an adventure.

When **Kurt Abbott** (2000) arrived at camp as a non-roster veteran, nobody imagined he'd be starting in the World Series that year. Unfortunately, he did.

In a deflationary market and in need of a right fielder, the Mets somehow allowed free agent Vladimir Guererro to sign with Anaheim while settling unsatisfyingly for ex-Yankees troublemaker **Karim Garcia** (2004), who made bigger news in the police column than the sports pages and within months was swapped to Baltimore. Garcia's brief reign surpassed in disappointment the short Mets career of **Ken Henderson** (1978), the veteran right fielder who, seven games into his Mets tenure, ran into a wall and never appeared in a game for them again. If only fans could have escaped the '78 Mets so easily.

The Mets were searching for a right fielder again in 2006 when they arranged a deal for veteran slugger **Shawn Green** (2006–07), whom they hoped would rebound from a string of subpar seasons. Like Ken Henderson, Green was not the same player he'd once been; like Victor Diaz, he made fans wince every time a ball was hit near him; and like John Pacella, he just couldn't keep that hat on.

Other 20s: nineteen-year-old catcher **Greg Goossen** (1965), waning superstar **Bob Friend** (1966), the second coming of **Choo Choo Coleman** (1966), utility man **John Sullivan** (1967), briefly visiting catchers **Jerry May** (1973) and **Ike Hampton** (1974), ambidextrous pitcher **Greg Harris** (1981), pitcher/surfer/Frisbetarian **Rick Ownbey** (1982–83), catcher **Mike Fitzgerald** (1983–84), potentially cursed outfielder **Ryan Thompson** (1994–95), sabermetric heartthrob **Roberto Petagine** (1996), pinch hitter **Mark Johnson** (2001), outfielder **Prentice Redman** (2003), and resurrected reliever **Ricky Bottalico** (2004).

Number of times issued: 24 (23 players, 1 coach)

Longest tenured: Howard Johnson (9 seasons, 1,154 games), Tommie Agee (5 seasons, 661 games)

Best single seasons: Johnson, 1991 (.259/.369/.559, 38 HR, 117 RBI, 30 stolen bases) Johnson, 1989 (.287/.369/.559, 36 HR, 101 RBI, 41 stolen bases); Agee, 1969 (.271/.342/.464, 26 HR, 76 RBI)

Career statistical leaders: Home runs (Johnson 190, Agee 82), RBI (Johnson 626, Agee 265), batting average (Shawn Green .284, Agee .262), wins (Bob Friend 5), ERA (John Pacella 4.83)

I Got the Power

From Howard Johnson's 190 dingers to Prentice Redman's one and only, fourteen men in Mets history through 2007 have combined to hit 384 home runs while wearing the No. 20 jersey. Eighteen off the bat of Jeromy Burnitz in 2003 helped 20 surpass 18 as the most powerful jersey in team history, though give Moises Alou another crack versus Shawn Green and we're back to 18 on top.

Following is a list of combined home runs by uniform number, updated through 2007:

No.	HRs	Notes
20	384	HoJo's 190 home runs, Agee's 82, and 37 from Burnitz lead the way.
18	377	Darryl Strawberry (252 HRs) accounts for 69 percent; Joel Youngblood (38) contributes 10 percent.
9	314	Todd Hundley (116), Jim Hickman (56), Gregg Jefferies (42), Todd Zeile (32), and Ty Wigginton (29) lead a relatively balanced attack.
5	281	Sure to climb as David Wright (97 HRs through 2007) ascends the all-time ranks; John Olerud provides 63 dingers.
15	275	Carlos Beltran (90) is poised to surpass George Foster (99) in 2008 for numerical supremacy.
7	245	Compiler Ed Kranepool (106 HRs) leads, but Jose Reyes (45) is coming.
4	243	Robin Ventura (77), Ron Swoboda (50), Rusty Staub (43), Len Dykstra (30).
25	242	Bobby Bonilla leads with 95 home runs.
22	234	Maligned Kevin McReynolds (122 HRs) leads the way.
31	228	96.5 percent of these belong to Mike Piazza. Were you expecting Mike Vail?

#21: CLEON AND ON

The Mets never seemed shy about making an example of **Cleon Jones**, their talented and occasionally defiant outfielder.

There was the time in 1969 when Jones was led off the field by manager Gil Hodges after a fly ball fell in front of him for a hit. There was the awkward public apology the Mets had Jones give after an extramarital affair made the headlines. Finally there was a battle of wills between Jones and manager Yogi Berra over Jones's allegedly refusing Berra's order to pinch hit, an incident that hastened the end of both men's respective tenures with the Mets.

CLEON JONES

But Jones, who wore 21 for the last ten of his twelve years with the Mets, ought to be best remembered as an example of the kind of player the Mets developed far too few of in their formative years. The kind that could hit, catch, and run. Signed out of Alabama A&M in 1963, Jones was the first farm-developed everyday Mets player to approach superstar status and until Darryl Strawberry came along, was probably the best hitter in team history.

When he walked away from New York in 1975 (he spent a month with the hideously garbed White Sox in '76), Jones was the Mets' all-time leader in hits, home runs, and RBI and the first Met to collect 1,000 hits. Although all those records have since been broken, his .340 average in 1969 (third in the NL that year) stood as the Mets standard for twenty-nine years, until it was broken by John Olerud. And his shoe-polish-on-the-baseball, kneel-down catch to end the 1969 World Series remains as unforgettable as his team was amazin'.

Even today, Jones provides an example for Met 21s to aspire to. His successors have shown promise, and often quirks.

There was **Kevin Elster**, the handsome farm-raised shortstop, who added 10-homer-a-year power to the Mets' traditional all-glove, no-hit shortstop model. A solid fielder who made everything look easy, Elster (1987–91) may have been too smooth for his own good. When he switched his uniform from No. 21 to 15 in 1992 he remarked to *Newsday* that he felt 21 was "a sissy number." He proceeded almost immediately to require

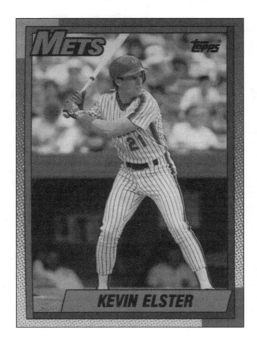

KEVIN ELSTER

major surgery on an injured shoulder and never played for the Mets again. Elster's best year as a Met was probably 1989, when he hit 10 home runs and drove in 55. During that season he ended his major league record 88 consecutive games without an error at shortstop.

Bill Pulsipher (1995, 1998) began his Mets career promisingly as the left-handed representative of the doomed pitching trio (alongside Jason Isringhausen and Paul Wilson) known as "Generation K." Pulsipher was the first of the three to reach the majors, the first to go down to injury, and probably endured the weirdest trip back, overcoming elbow woes as well as anxiety issues to reappear briefly in 1998. The Mets traded Pulsipher away twice: once in 1998 and again in 2000 after they'd reacquired him (and dressed him in 25). But he never won more than the 5 he got out of the chute in 1995.

Shortly after Pulsipher was traded in 1998, right-handed junkball artist **Masato Yoshii** (1998–99) slipped into his discarded No. 21 jersey. The first successful Mets import from Japan, Yoshii overcame first-half struggles to be a key contributor down the stretch in 1999, when he finished a respectable 12-8. Yoshii was traded to the Rockies following the season for pitcher **Bobby M. Jones** (2000, 2002), whose frequent injuries averted a lot of potential confusion with a teammate of the same name. Jones was one of three men to wear 21 in 2002: **Mark Little** arrived in a deadline trade just in time to play a small but crucial role in the doubleheader sweep by the Diamondbacks that killed all hopes of postseason play that year and set off a string of crushing defeats (Little interrupted a rally by reaching on a force play and immediately was picked off first). Little was traded away days later, and light-hitting reserve outfielder **Raul Gonzalez** (2002–03) took over No. 21.

Like Yoshii, first baseman/outfielder **David Segui** (1994–95) switched to 21 at his first opportunity. Segui's beloved No. 21 belonged to backup catcher candidate Joe Kmak, who was cut as the team broke camp. A well-traveled but nonetheless decent player most days, Segui's stint with the Mets (10-42-.241 in '94) was probably the worst of his eight major league stops.

Slugging first baseman **Carlos Delgado** famously rejected a contract offer from the Mets in 2005 to sign instead with Florida, but the tables turned when the Marlins traded him to the Mets the following season. Delgado, whose customary No. 25 belonged at the time to Kaz Matsui, proudly donned No. 21 instead as a tribute to Puerto Rican great Roberto Clemente. Delgado fit right in, hitting 38 home runs and driving in 114 in 2006. A series of injuries limited his productivity in 2007, and he just never managed to get it going offensively.

Elliot Maddox (1978–80) wound down his career as a middling outfielder/third baseman for the Mets and a plaintiff in a suit against Shea Stadium and the city of New York. Maddox claimed sloppy field conditions caused him to slip in the outfield as a member of the Yankees when they shared Shea in 1975, nuking his career. Maddox lost. That's what Mets did then.

He spent the vast majority of his Mets career wearing No. 7, but **Ed Kranepool** (1962–63) debuted in No. 21—the first Met to wear it—and might never have changed had the Mets not acquired legendary lefty **Warren Spahn** (1965) in what was to be Spahn's final year. Hired as a pitcher/pitching coach and viewed as a possible successor to manager Casey Stengel, Spahn neither pitched nor coached with much effectiveness or enthusiasm. He was released midseason and finished his career as a Giant.

Others: reliever **Bob Moorhead** (1965), outfield reserves **Billy Baldwin** (1976) and **Pepe Mangual** (1977), power prospect **Gary Rajsich** (1982–83), utility man **Ross Jones** (1984), outfield prospects **Herm Winningham** (1984) and **Terry Blocker** (1985), veteran enemy **Kevin Bass** (1992), and ex-Yankees reserve **Gerald Williams** (2004–05). Mysterious, fictional Met Sidd Finch wore 21 also.

No. of times issued: 23 (21 players, 2 DNPs)

Longest tenured: Cleon Jones (10 seasons, 1,165 games), Kevin Elster (5 seasons, 512 games)

Best single seasons: Jones, 1969 (.340/.422/.482, 12 HR, 75 RBI); Carlos Delgado, 2006 (.265/.361/.548, 38 HR, 114 RBI)

Career statistical leaders: Home runs (Jones 92, Delgado 62, Elster 34), RBI (Jones 513, Delgado 201, Elster 174), batting average (Jones .284, Gary Rajsich .273), wins (Masato Yoshii 14), ERA (Warren Spahn, 4.36)

Big in Japan

About five minutes after the Mets traded Bill Pulsipher to the Brewers in 1998, Masato Yoshii claimed Pulsipher's No. 21 jersey. Notoriously superstitious, Yoshii said he made the switch for "good luck."

Japanese generally associate No. 4 with bad luck. Four is a homonym of *shi*, which means "death," and as a result is often issued to unknowing U.S. *gaijin* playing in Japan.

When Takashi Kashiwada became the first Met from Japan in 1997, he was issued No. 18, which in Japan is the jersey usually reserved for superstar pitchers (as evidenced by Daisuke Matusaka, 18 for his clubs in Japan and the United States).

Pitchers in Japan tend to wear numbers between 11 and 19. But since Japan's major and lone minor league clubs share numbers, it's not unusual to see numbers over 50, with bullpen catchers and coaching staffs frequently appearing in triple digits. Field staff typically wear numbers in the 70s: in Bobby Valentine's first stint managing the Chiba Lotte Marines, he wore No. 81.

The Marines, by the way, never issue No. 26 to a player. That number belongs to the 26th man—their fans.

#22: WE COULD BE HEROES

The Mets have had two World Series MVPs in their history and both have worn No. 22. If a few things—OK, a lot of things—broke differently, they might have had three.

Donn Clendenon, **Ray Knight**, and **Al Leiter** each did the Mets proud in their post-season history. Somehow, the Mets made the 1973 World Series without a 22 to lead them.

Clendenon was the only significant in-season addition the Mets made in 1969. They were nine games behind the Cubs on the day they made the trade and eight games up by the time the season ended. Credit for the turn-around goes beyond what Clendenon was able to provide in 200-plus at-bats as a platoon first baseman, but teammates would later say the veteran's presence helped the team develop the character to win.

Statistics made Clendenon's case for World Series MVP: He hit .357 against Baltimore, with 3 home runs and 15 total bases—the latter two figures were records for a five-game Series, and Clendenon only played four games against Baltimore. Amazingly, he did not bat even once in the Mets' NLCS sweep of Atlanta. (Gil Hodges was strict with his platoons!) Clendenon stuck around for another two seasons in New York, setting what was then a team record with 97 RBI in 1970.

Like Clendenon, Knight (1984–86) was a right-handed-hitting veteran corner infielder whose best years were with other clubs but whose signature moment came leading the Mets to postseason glory. But where the '69ers benefited from Clendenon's cool professionalism, the '86ers would absorb the emotional and at times bloodthirsty style of Knight.

The Mets thought enough of Knight when he arrived in a trade with Houston in 1984 that Bobby Valentine, then serving as third-base coach, gave up No. 22 for him. But Knight nearly played his way out of a Mets

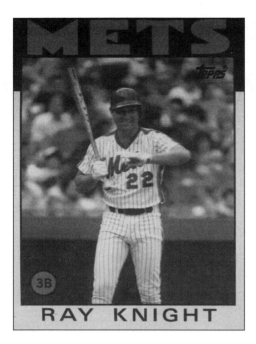

RAY KNIGHT

jersey in 1985, hitting just .218 with 6 home runs amid injuries and boos. Knight fought his way back, bare knuckled, in 1986. With new acquisition Howard Johnson poised to take over third base, Knight blasted off to a furious start with 6 April home runs. His brawls with the Dodgers' Tom Niedenfuer and the Reds' Eric Davis served as rallying points for the '86 team.

Knight finished off the year just as furiously. He hit .391 in the World Series, including the third of the three two-out singles to spark the miraculous Game 6 rally, scoring the winning run on Mookie Wilson's famous trickling ground ball. And his home run in the 7th inning of Game 7 provided the Mets with the last lead they'd need.

Yet Knight gracing the cover of *Sports Illustrated* with his foot crossing home plate was to be the last fans would see of him in a Mets uniform. Heartbroken, he finished his career quietly with two final seasons in the American League.

Al Leiter never won a sports car for being the World Series MVP. He didn't even win a World Series game for the Mets. But at the turn of the century, the hardworking lefty was the team's soul and the closest thing it had to a big-game pitcher. Leiter shut down Cincinnati to win the 163rd game of the season in 1999. His performance in the 2000 World Series—particularly the doomed final-game effort—should be remembered as one of the most courageous in team history.

Despite his Yankee pedigree, Leiter was one of those guys who just looked right in a Mets uniform. Over seven years wearing one, Leiter went 95-67 with a 3.42 ERA, though by the end fans found his outings as strenuous for them as for Leiter: They required maximum effort and grunts just to get through.

Kevin McReynolds (1987–91, 1994) was a true Catch-22: Despite numbers that might indicate greatness (27 home runs, 99 RBI, and 21 steals without getting caught in 1988) the droll country slugger lacked the charisma to be a true superstar. Fans never forgave the indignity of McReynolds's remarks comparing playing in the postseason with fishing, but then they probably didn't understand how much he loved casting a line. Reacquiring McReynolds in 1994 after he'd demonstrated his laconic blandness was a curious decision, but it did rid the team of Vince Coleman.

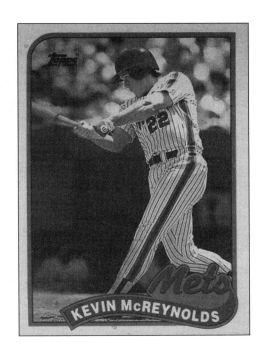

Workhorse **Jack Fisher** (1964–67) won 38 games and lost 73 over four long seasons with the Mets but was the team's de facto ace until Tom Seaver came along. Although "Fat Jack" was best known as the Baltimore pitcher who allowed a home run to Ted Williams in his last turn at-bat, that was a better legacy than equaling Roger Craig's Mets record of 24 losses—despite a 3.94 ERA—during the 1965 season. Fisher was acquired by the Mets from San Francisco in the 1963 "make-good" draft the National League offered to the hapless New York and Houston franchises. He'd be traded to the White Sox in the Tommie Agee deal.

Maybe all the losing by Casey's club wasn't that much fun after all. While exiting the playing field following an ineffective outing, right-handed reliever **Bob Moorhead** (1962) punched a dugout door at St. Louis' Sportsman's Park, breaking two knuckles and ending his season without a win or a save in 105.1 innings. Moorhead did not resurface until three years later in a different number (21).

The Mets owe **Xavier Nady** a beer. Not only were the 2006 Mets indebted to the right fielder's sizzling hot start, but they were still thanking him a year later for bringing back Oliver Perez in a midseason trade from Pittsburgh. Nady used a Kingman-like cut to slam 14 home runs in a half-season with the Mets. That was despite missing time with an emergency appendectomy.

The Mets won a bidding war with the Dodgers for veteran free agent leadoff man **Brett Butler** (1995) only to trade him to Los Angeles late in the season.

Others: outfield reserves **Joe Hicks** (1963) and **Bob Gallagher** (1975); would-be phenoms **Hank Webb** (1972–73), **Alex Ochoa** (1995–97), and **Royce Ring** (2005); journeymen hurlers **Jack Aker** (1974), **Doc Medich** (1977), and **Dale Murray** (1978–79); briefly appearing catcher **Jay Kleven** (1976); returning prodigy **Mike Jorgensen** (1980–83); backup catcher **Charlie O'Brien** (1992–93); bench bat **Michael Tucker** (2006); and second baseman **Jose Valentin** (2007).

Number of times issued: 23 (20 players, 1 coach, 1 DNP)

Longest tenured: Al Leiter (7 seasons, 213 games), Kevin McReynolds (6 seasons, 787 games), Mike Jorgensen (4 seasons, 363 games)

Best single seasons: McReynolds, 1988 (.288/.336/.496, 27 HR, 99 RBI); Leiter, 1998 (17-6, 2.47 ERA, 174 strikeouts in 193 innings)

Career statistical leaders: Home runs (McReynolds 122, Clendenon 45), RBI (McReynolds 456, Clendenon 171), batting average (Brett Butler .311, Alex Ochoa .273), wins (Leiter 95, Jack Fisher 38), saves (Dale Murray 9), ERA (Leiter 3.42)

Teamwork (to Make the Dream Work)

Position for position, there may not be a better number than 22, at least as Mets go. It provides a speedy leadoff center fielder and a strong defensive catcher. A couple of power hitters, a five-tool prospect, and hardworking left-right combinations in the rotation and the bullpen.

Following are a few representative "teams" staffed only by players who wore the same number as Mets. In some cases, players have been placed in positions they hadn't necessarily played, and certain players, due to number switches, appear for more than one team (Jose Valentin, adept at several positions and strategically dressed in two numbers, fits both categories). The teams listed consist of only those numbers that qualified without massive or unimaginable switches (for example Teams 21 and 25 couldn't take the field without a catcher; Team 27 hadn't enough middle infielders even to fake it).

TEAM 22

Scouting report: Considerable power and strong defense, although Hicks is in unfamiliar territory at second base with Valentin moving over to shortstop. Leiter and Fisher need to go deep into games because the bullpen is shaky.

C: Charlie O'Brien
1B: Donn Clendenon
2B: Joe Hicks
SS: Jose Valentin
3B: Ray Knight
LF: Kevin McReynolds
CF: Brett Butler
RF: Alex Ochoa
SP: Al Leiter, Jack Fisher
RP: Royce Ring, Dale Murray

TEAM 17

Scouting report: Tough to beat the right side of the infield, but the outfield could use a few hitters. Starting pitching a plus.

C: Choo-Choo Coleman
1B: Keith Hernandez
2B: Felix Millan
SS: Mike Bordick
3B: Don Zimmer

LF: Jerry Morales
CF: Rod Gaspar
RF: Ellis Valentine
SP: David Cone, Bret Saberhagen
RP: Graeme Lloyd, Dae Sung Koo

TEAM 18
Scouting report: Cleanup man Strawberry gives the 18s a puncher's chance.

C: Duffy Dyer
1B: George Theodore
2B: Jose Valentin
SS: Felix Mantilla
3B: Joel Youngblood
LF: Al Luplow
CF: Darryl Hamilton
RF: Darryl Strawberry
SP: Bret Saberhagen, Jeff D'Amico
RP: Takashi Kashiwada, Dennis Ribant

TEAM 20
Scouting report: Short a few infielders but stacked in the outfield. The 20s will score runs but allow plenty, too.

C: Mike Fitzgerald
1B: Roberto Petagine
2B: Greg Goossen
SS: Kurt Abbott
3B: Howard Johnson
LF: Jeromy Burnitz
CF: Tommie Agee
RF: Shawn Green
SP: Craig Anderson, John Pacella
RP: Ricky Bottalico, Greg Harris

TEAM 23
Scouting Report: Pat Mahomes is the long man, and they're going to need him.

C: Jason Phillips
1B: Julio Franco
2B: Doug Flynn
SS: Tim Bogar
3B: Chris Donnels
LF: Bernard Gilkey
CF: Joe Christopher
RF: Dave Schneck
SP: Kaz Ishii, Brian Rose
RP: Pat Mahomes

TEAM 26
Scouting Report: Weak outfield production and Kingman at third base. Good thing the pitching looks strong.

C: Jason Phillips
1B: Rico Brogna
2B: Marco Scutaro
SS: David Lamb
3B: Dave Kingman
LF: Bruce Boisclair
CF: Terrence Long
RF: Jon Nunnaly
SP: Frank Viola, Orlando Hernandez
RP: Terry Leach, Alejandro Peña

TEAM 33
Scouting Report: aka Eddie and the Losers.

C: Barry Lyons
1B: Eddie Murray
2B: Mike Kinkade
SS: Ron Hunt
3B: Clint Hurdle

LF: Andy Tomberlin
CF: Dan Norman
RF: Bubba Trammell
SP: John Maine, Ray Sadecki
RP: Ken Sanders, Anthony Young

TEAM 16
Scouting Report: Doc and Dude and somewhat crude. Derek Bell is also the long reliever.

C: Paul Lo Duca
1B: Doug Meintkiewicz
2B: Felix Millan
SS: Kevin Collins
3B: John Stearns
LF: Dick Smith
CF: Lee Mazzilli
RF: Derek Bell
SP: Dwight Gooden, David Cone
RP: Hideo Nomo

#23: SKIDOO

Bernard Gilkey brought No. 23 and a contract the Cardinals could no longer bear to pay from St. Louis in 1996. He summarily delivered what easily was the most impressive accomplishment of any Mets player ever to wear the No. 23 uniform and what might have been the best single season to that point in club history.

Without so much as a warning, the wide-eyed, right-handed slugger hit .317 with 30 home runs, 117 RBI, and 44 doubles. The RBI total tied Howard Johnson's team record (which has since been broken by Mike Piazza), but the 44 doubles are still the all-time club standard. Gilkey added 17 stolen bases and 18 assists from left field.

The Mets were quick to reward Gilkey with a four-year contract only to see him transform back into an unwanted commodity. He slipped to 18 home runs in 1997 and just 4 in 1998 by the time the Mets finally unloaded him on the Arizona Diamondbacks.

One surprisingly strong season in otherwise mediocre tenures is a characteristic of several Met 23s. Call it the 23 Skidoo.

Original Met **Joe Christopher** (1962–65) turned in a 16-76-.300/.360/.466 performance in 1964; numbers that looked unimaginable for the smiling Virgin Islander, considering his first two seasons with the Mets. They were distant memories again in 1965.

Well-traveled mop-up man **Pat Mahomes** (1999–2000) fashioned an unexpected 8-0 record in 1999 out of an uncanny ability to hold the fort while the offense fought back deficits, often massive ones, and was a key ingredient in the playoff push. Mahomes even singled in the go-ahead run in the top of the 13th and then held off the Cubs in the bottom of the inning in his most memorable Mets moment. Alas, 1999 would be the best year by far of his career: despite having earned some starts in 2000, Mahomes struggled through them.

While bouncing between New York and the minor leagues, catcher **Jason Phillips** wore four different numbers for the Mets, but it was while wearing No. 23 in 2003 that Phillips surfaced to stay. He made the opening roster thanks only to Mike Piazza's suspension (for fighting with nemesis Guillermo Mota), but thanks to some pop in his bat and Mo Vaughn's career-ending injuries, Phillips took over at first base despite having no experience at the position. Phillips promptly whacked 11 home runs, hit 25 doubles, and went .298/.373/.442 in 403 at-bats. That performance earned him a full-time gig in 2004, which turned into a total flop (7-34-.218/.298/.326 in 362 at-bats). Just prior to the 2005 season, Phillips turned over his jersey in a trade for **Kaz Ishii** (2005), a one-time Dodger phenom who never found his stuff again, despite ample opportunity with the Mets.

It would have been nice to have gotten just one great year from **Doug Flynn** (1977–81), but a Gold Glove award in 1980—and splendid defense generally—was about as good as it ever got. Flynn arrived in the Tom Seaver trade in 1977, in time to take over for injured and/or departing middle infielders Felix Millan and Bud Harrelson. He eventually settled in at second base but never hit any better than .255 or reached base at a .300 clip, and he didn't steal much and rarely hit for power. His offensive signature was connecting for three triples in a single game on August 5, 1980: one each to left, center, and right at Montreal's Olympic Stadium. Did we mention he could really pick it?

After Flynn departed, the Mets were optimistic that **Brian Giles** (1982–83) would also be a Gold Glover at second base. But a lack of a bat scorched his career when Davey Johnson took over in 1984 and reinstalled Wally Backman at second base.

Reserve outfielder **Dave Schneck** hit .187 and .194 in abbreviated appearances with the 1972 and '73 clubs, respectively. Schneck was the pivot man in a three-way number swap prior to 1974 that saw Felix Millan switch from 16 to 17, **Ted Martinez** switch from 17 to 23, and Schneck switch from 23 to 16. Martinez selected 23 because it was the number worn by his contemporary and hero, Tito Fuentes.

That ancient pinch hitter **Julio Franco** was still playing in 2006 was nearly as big a shock as the fact he was playing fairly effectively, and in the first year of a two-year contract. Franco, whose big-league career pre-dated the birth of many his teammates—and four franchises—by 2007 appeared to finally be reaching his limits, though he set or extended any number of "oldest player to" marks, including oldest Met ever and oldest Met ever to be released. His role as a pinch hitter for the 2007 Mets would be given to **Marlon Anderson**, who made a triumphant return in a new number.

Others: reserve outfielders **Bill Murphy** (1966); **Leroy Stanton** (1970–71); **Jesus Alou** (1975); **Leon Brown** (1976); **Jermaine Allensworth** (1998); **Matt Lawton** (2001); **McKay Christensen** (2002) and **Esix Snead** (2002); back-up infielders **Bob Heise** (1967–68), **Chris Donnels** (1991–92), and **Tim Bogar** (1993–95); and pitcher **Brian Rose** (2001). **Bob G. Miller** (1962) suited up in 23, but did not play until switching to No. 36.

Number of times issued: 26 (23 players, 2 coaches, 1 DNP)

Longest Tenured: Doug Flynn (5 seasons, 636 games), Joe Christopher (4 seasons, 485 games), Bernard Gilkey (3 seasons, 380 games)

Best single seasons: Gilkey, 1996 (.317/.393/.562, 30 HR, 117 RBI); Christopher, 1964 (.300/.360/.466, 16 HR, 76 RBI); Jason Phillips, 2003 (.298/.373/.442, 11 HR, 58 RBI); Pat Mahomes, 1999 (8-0, 3.68 ERA)

Career statistical leaders: Home runs (Gilkey 52, Christopher 28), RBI (Gilkey 223, Christopher 156, Flynn 155), wins (Mahomes 13, Kaz Ishii 3), ERA (Mahomes 4.74)

Chain, Chain, Chain

Reserve infielder and former No. 23 Tim Bogar was traded away by the Mets more than a decade ago and has been retired since 2001, but Bogar DNA is still part of the Mets' ecosystem. Barely.

As of 2007, Bogar was the patriarch of the Mets' longest active "trade chain" connecting players in the organization via transactions. In 1997 Bogar was traded to Houston for Luis Lopez, who was traded in 2000 to Milwaukee for Bill Pulsipher, who was traded to Arizona later that year for Lenny Harris, who was swapped in 2001 to Milwaukee for Jeromy Burnitz, whose 2003 trade to Los Angeles yielded Victor Diaz, who in 2006 was traded for catcher Mike Nickeas, who in 2007 was hanging around the Mets' minor leagues with at least an outside shot of a promotion or chain-extending trade.

Follow a Mets trade chain and you'll find both diminishing returns and surprising successes. Roger Craig was turned into George Altman who became Billy Cowan who became Lou Klimchock. In three years and four trades, the Mets—Presto!—turned Len Dykstra and Roger McDowell into Paul Gibson. Yet an amazing roster of talent and twenty-year returns churned out of 1986 reserves Ed Hearn and Rick Anderson. They were traded to Kansas City for David Cone; Cone was later traded for Ryan Thompson. Thompson went to Cleveland for Mark Clark, who went to the Cubs in the six-player deal that brought the Mets Brian McRae and Turk Wendell. Wendell went to Philadelphia for Bruce Chen, who went to Montreal in 2002 for Scott Strickland, who broke the chain when he was released by the organization in 2005.

A related chain begins with 1984 debut of Kevin Mitchell, who went to San Diego for Kevin McReynolds, who went to Kansas City for Bret Saberhagen, who went to Colorado for Juan Acevedo, who went to St. Louis for Rigo Beltran, who (along with McRae), went to Colorado for Chuck McElroy, who went to Baltimore for Jesse Orosco, who went to St. Louis for Joe McEwing. That chain was also snapped when McEwing was released in 2005.

Should Nickeas not make it, the title of Trade Godfather will go to Ty Wigginton, whose 2004 trade to Pittsburgh has blossomed into separate branches bearing Orlando Hernandez (from Jorge Julio, from Kris Benson, from Wigginton), John Maine (from Benson), and Ruben Gotay (from Jeff Keppinger, who came along with Benson in the same trade). While El Duque, as seemingly ageless as a sturdy oak, may be here for the duration, Maine and Gotay are leafy saplings of the Wigginton Trade Tree.

#24: SAY HEY

While the fan base, and to a certain extent the character of the early Mets, can be traced most directly to their predecessors in Brooklyn, it should not be forgotten that the team's first owners were fans of the team in Upper Manhattan.

Joan Payson, the wealthy society matron who bankrolled the Mets, was a former minority owner of the New York Giants and the most prominent shareholder to oppose the baseball team's move to San Francisco. Payson would eventually own around 80 percent of the Mets but left running the franchise to an appointed board of directors. The most influential of these was her stockbroker, M. Donald Grant.

With Payson a Giants diehard and Grant doing her bidding, it came as no surprise the young Mets openly coveted the Giants' star center fielder, **Willie Mays.** Speculation circulated throughout the 1960s regarding what it might take to corral Mays—a million dollars?—and how prepared Payson and Grant might be to part with such a sum. Obtaining the best player in the game by trade back then was, quite simply, impossible. The Mets hadn't enough talent to give up.

Finally in May of 1972, the Mets traded a young pitcher, Charlie Williams, and $100,000 to San Francisco for Mays in a deal many considered a Mother's Day gift from Grant to Payson. **Jim Beauchamp** was invited to surrender his No. 24 jersey at once as the Say Hey Kid returned. Mays hit a home run in his first game—against San Francisco to boot—to provide the margin of victory.

It was understood the Mets weren't getting the same Willie Mays who last played in New York in 1957. Though even at the age of 41, Mays was still effective as a part-time first baseman/outfielder, pinch hitter, and clubhouse presence whose legendary instincts and hustle inspired his teammates. He was popular at the gate, too. Mays looked considerably creakier by the time he'd announced his retirement in 1973, but his victory-lap season continued when the Mets and Mays found themselves in the postseason.

Mays occupied 24 as a coach from 1974 to 1979, at which point the jersey went into a kind of limbo. While Mays never achieved the impact of a player whose number would be retired by the club, the Mets seemed to acquiesce to Payson's wishes that the number not be issued again (Payson died in 1975).

So quietly into mothballs 24 went, and there it slumbered for more than ten years until the Mets issued it again to minor league journeyman **Kelvin Torve** upon his recall from AAA in August of 1990. While no official explanation for the screw-up ever emerged, fan and media outcry was swift. Seventeen years later, Torve confesses to being unaware of any controversy until asked to wear a different jersey.

"When I got to New York, I saw a locker with my uni in it, No. 24. I didn't give a second thought to it," Torve said in an interview from Davidson, North Carolina, where he works as a salesman for a packaging company and as a guest instructor at youth baseball camps. "I was just happy to be there. I'd have worn 2.4 if they asked me to.

"When we were on the road in California was the first I heard of any controversy," Torve added. "Charlie [Samuels] came up to me and said, 'Listen, we made a mistake with your number. People have been calling. It was Willie Mays's number. So we'd like to change your number.' I said, 'Shoot, that's fine with me.' I didn't want to be a pain about it. And I guess they wanted to keep it low-key, not make a big deal about it. So I just started wearing No. 39 from that point on."

That he was issued No. 24 by accident is virtually all that is recalled of Torve, a left-handed-hitting first baseman/outfielder who wasn't even the Mets' most memorable Kelvin. He came to the Mets as a free agent following stints in the Giants and Twins organizations and played two seasons with the Orix Blue Wave in Japan following his release by the Mets in 1991.

It should be noted that Torve hit .545/.615/.727 in 11 at-bats while wearing No. 24, with two doubles, including a game-winner. "I know Willie Mays did it proud, too," he said. Over parts of the 1990 and '91 seasons wearing No. 39, Torve hit a modest .263.

Until Mays came along, 24 was most closely associated with **Art Shamsky** (1968–71), the power-hitting outfielder and hero to countless fans who identified with a Jewish star. Shamsky was swiped from Cincinnati after 1967 in a trade for utility man Bob Johnson. He overcame an early-season injury to post the best season of his career in 1969, providing 14 home runs and 47 RBI in 303 at-bats as the left-handed-swinging member of three-way outfield rotation with Ron Swoboda (the righty) and Rod Gaspar (the switch-hitter who backed up both men).

Shamsky was part of the outgoing freight in an ultimately poor trade with St. Louis following the 1971 season; beefy pinch hitter Beauchamp was among the returnees. (Also going away were Jim Bibby, who would be a fine pitcher before long, and Rich Folkers, a decent reliever. In addition to Beauchamp, the Mets got back relievers Chuck Taylor and Harry Parker.) Beauchamp skedaddled from 24 to 5 when Mays arrived.

Bob L. Miller (1962)—the L. distinguished him from teammate Bob G. Miller and also indicated his box score specialty—was the first wearer of the 24 jersey. Miller scuffled through a 1-12 season that belied his true ability: He'd be traded by the Mets following the season but last another 12 years in the majors, many of them as an effective reliever. He rejoined the Mets in 1973, wearing No. 30.

Johnny Lewis (1965–67) was something of a discount Willie Mays: he had speed, a strong arm, power, and wore No. 24. Lewis just didn't do those things as well or as consistently as his Giants contemporary. That said, his 15-home run, .331 on-base percentage season in 1965 made him that year's most accomplished player. His greatest moment came that year when he broke up Jim Maloney's no-hitter in the 11th inning on June 14, homering to account for the only run of New York's win in Cincinnati.

Jerry Hinsley, one of the many early Mets without a career win, wore 24 in '64. **Ed Charles** wore it early in his Met career in '67, and **Ken Boswell** debuted in 24 later that year.

Although the Mets survived the Torve Insurrection, some were up in arms again in 1999 when another future Hall of Fame outfielder, **Rickey Henderson**, was acquired and insisted upon receiving his customary No. 24. (Henderson was serious about No. 24. He once purchased it from Blue Jays teammate Turner Ward for $25,000.) Henderson informed the Mets that he wanted 24 but would accept No. 35—his number as an A's rookie—in the event he would be denied 24 (though Rick Reed may have had something to say about that). In the end, Henderson received Mays's blessing and then went out and had the last great year of his great career, hitting .315, reaching base at a .423 clip, and stealing 37 bases. Sulking over the Mets' refusal to renegotiate his contract, and smarting over his implication in the previous season's card-playing fiasco during the NLCS (stories emerged after the Mets' heartbreaking elimination that he and '99 villain Bobby Bonilla spent the final innings of the elimination game not suffering with comrades in the dugout but enjoying a round of hearts in the clubhouse), Henderson was released in 2000. He worked his way back post-retirement, serving as a base-running instructor in spring training, then as first-base coach in 2007.

Number of times issued: 11 (10 players, 2 coaches)

Longest tenured: Art Shamsky (4 seasons, 404 games), Johnny Lewis (3 seasons, 226 games)

Best single seasons: Shamsky, 1969 (.300/.375/.488, 14 HR, 47 RBI); Rickey Henderson, 1999 (.315/.423/.466, 12 HR, 42 RBI, 30 doubles, 37 stolen bases); Lewis, 1965 (.245/.331/.384, 15 HR, 45 RBI)

Career statistical leaders: Home runs (Shamsky 42, Lewis 20), RBI (Shamsky 162, Lewis 67), batting average (Henderson .298)

Future Schlock

"Leading off . . . playing left quadrant . . . Rickey Henderson."

When Henderson dug into the plate to lead off the Mets' first inning on July 27, 1999, he looked up to the Diamond Vision screen to see a portrait of himself looking back, albeit one with three eyes and the long pointy ears of a Vulcan. Turning now to the evening's opposing pitcher, Pittsburgh's Kris Benson, revealed Benson wearing a shiny sleeveless jersey adorned with an oversize Pirates logo that made him look as if he were wearing a beach towel.

Henderson in his long career no doubt had seen some dumb things; he'd come up with Oakland when Charlie Finley still owned the team. "Turn Ahead the Clock" night had to be near—or over—the top.

A league-wide promotion that dressed teams in futuristic uniforms, "Turn Ahead the Clock" asked fans to imagine the games were taking place in the year 2021—a ham-handed reference to its sponsor, the real estate company Century 21. Similar events took place that year at thirteen other parks. Eight clubs, including the traditionalist Yankees, Dodgers, and Cubs, wisely chose not to participate. The Mets were not only enthusiastic hosts but provided its signature moment of garish inelegance, the Mercury Mets.

For the Mets it wasn't enough to update their logo; they'd relocated the team to planet Mercury. (Perhaps the city, not to mention the planet, got to be too much to share with the Yankees.) Their uniform was a black, sleeveless v-neck with silver graphics depicting a symbol casting its shadow onto the surface of a cratered planet.

The same symbol—imagine the Prince logo if it were designed by a preschooler—appeared on black Mets hats. On the uniform backs, names appeared vertically alongside numbers in a futuristic font. And this was the year the team had taken the names off their here-and-now home jerseys.

The doctored stadium graphics, renamed position, and other details completed the very picture of future schlock; like a 1950s-era science fiction film so gloriously bad it was campy good. But that's only in retrospect. At the time it was just embarrassing.

"If we can't sell the product as it is, maybe we should give it a

Photo by Dave Murray

rest," the Mets' starting pitcher, Orel Hershiser, told reporters after the game (under a barrage of similar criticisms, Century 21 quietly dropped the promotion for 2000). The Mercury Mets lost their only game, 5-1, victims of a complete-game effort by Benson, or perhaps something worse, Mike Piazza speculated.

"We weren't beamed up to the proper coordinates," he deadpanned.

#25: BOBBY BOO

When the Mets introduced **Bobby Bonilla** after having signed him to what was then the richest contract in baseball history, they presented him with jersey No. 25.

It was, perhaps, a sign that things wouldn't turn out as exactly as expected.

While Bonilla (1992–95, 1999) had some good seasons for the Mets, they weren't at the level that fans or the press demanded. And Bonilla's handling of criticism while the team struggled wrote an odd, and at times ugly, story of his years with his hometown team. Then again, signing Bonilla for considerably more money than they were willing to pay Darryl Strawberry a year before didn't exactly invite reasonable expectations.

Bonilla led the Mets in home runs, on-base percentage, and slugging percentage for three straight seasons beginning in 1992, but he was best remembered for having a thin skin. He offered to fight beat writers who wrote critical articles, he motioned to official scorers when charged with an error, and he tried to tune out boo-birds by playing with earplugs. The volume was always tuned to high when Bobby Boo stepped up.

Bonilla's ascension to the most reviled player in team history wasn't complete until the Mets curiously reacquired him in 1999. Unhappy with a reserve role, Bonilla feuded with manager Bobby Valentine, complained of injuries, and was exposed for playing cards in the clubhouse as the Mets lost in excruciating fashion in the National League Championship Series.

Met fans booed themselves hoarse over another 25, **Kaz Matsui**, though Matsui was more of a patsy than a criminal, and he hadn't an ounce of Bonilla's contempt or arrogance. Like Bonilla though, Matsui was an expensive mistake and out of position in more ways than one.

Seemingly lusting after the same new marketing revenue streams the Yankees had tapped into with Hideki Matsui in 2003, the Mets outbid several suitors for the services of Kaz Matsui that offseason, despite already having a terrific young shortstop in Jose Reyes. The Mets wound up giving Matsui Reyes's position (shortstop) and lineup slot (leadoff) but stopped short of taking the shirt off Reyes's back. Matsui wore No. 7 in Japan and would have favored it with the Mets.

Matsui hit the first pitch he saw in the majors over the fence in right-center field at Turner Field. Then things started getting weird. By the end of his first season in New York, the Mets knew Matsui was miscast as a shortstop, probably needed eyeglasses, apparently had a recurring back problem, and almost certainly struggled with language barriers and general dislocation. Yet, they also knew he could hit some. Attempts at second base in 2005 and 2006 started promisingly when Matsui, remarkably, hit home runs in his first plate appearances those two years as well (his 2006 lid-lifter was an inside-the-park job). But recurring injuries slowed his progress, frustrated management, and brought out a meanness in fans normally reserved for Bonilla. He was traded away in 2006 for his own good and has been surprisingly effective in his new environs, playing a key role in leading the Rockies all the way to the 2007 World Series.

For all the futility of the 1962 Mets, it certainly took a while for anyone to match the power production that year of **Frank Thomas** (1962–64). His 34 home runs stood as the team record until Dave Kingman bashed his way to 36 in 1975; his 94 RBI was the standard until Donn Clendenon knocked in 97 in 1970. Acquired for Gus Bell and $125,000 worth of George Weiss's post–expansion draft "mad money" in the first big trade the Mets ever made, Thomas had a swing tailor-made for the Polo Grounds and its inviting short deck in left field. Thomas slumped to 15 home runs in 1963 as age and competitors for an outfield job began catching up with him.

When Thomas was traded to Philadelphia and their doomed pennant drive late in the 1964 season, one of the players that came in return, 6-foot-6 pitcher **Gary Kroll**, could fit only into the No. 25 jerseys Thomas left behind. One in a string of strapping young project pitchers of the early Mets, Kroll (1964–65) never got his act together despite having what observers agreed was outstanding raw material. He threatened to retire upon a 1965 demotion and eventually would be surrendered to Houston as a fallen star.

Flashy first baseman **Willie Montañez** (1978–79) was always fun to watch, even when the Mets weren't. Montañez brought style to acts as mundane as catching a pop fly, holding a runner on base, taking a warm-up swing, and famously circling the bases after a home run. He drove in 96 runs for an awful 1978 Mets team but had little to style about in 1979. Montañez was one of the lucky ones: he was traded away in August. One of the returnees was Ed Lynch, who'd go on to have a fine career as a Met.

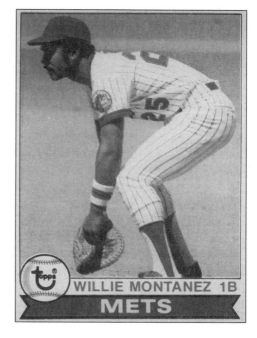

WILLIE MONTANEZ 1B
METS

In May of 1967, the Mets purchased the contract of journeyman reserve infielder **Bob W. Johnson** from Baltimore; after the season they'd trade him straight-up for Art Shamsky. In between, Johnson (1967) had the best four months of his career, batting .348/.377/.474 in 230 at-bats.

Center fielder **Don Hahn** (1971–74) came to the Mets with a great reputation for his glove, perhaps because the Mets feared his bat wouldn't ever make much of an impression. Hahn's triple in Game 5 of the 1973 World Series chased Vida Blue from the game and drove in the insurance run in a 2-0 win. The heart of a Mets reserve squadron, known as the "Scum Bunch," **Danny Heep** (1983–86) provided a dangerous left-handed bat off the bench and proved to be a capable, if slow, everyday player in case of injury. Heep was acquired in exchange for future Mets enemy Mike Scott.

Del Unser became an excellent pinch hitter later in his career, but he was yet another short-term center-field solution. A first-round pick in Washington when Gil Hodges managed the Senators, Unser landed in New York—along with John Stearns and Mac Scarce—in the Tug McGraw deal. Unser batted .294 with 10 home runs, mostly out of the leadoff spot in his one full season at Shea in 1975, but he was sent to Montreal at the trading deadline the next year in one of the many bad Met trades involving center fielders (and third basemen). **Jim Dwyer** (1976), another future bench specialist, was part of the paltry return from the Expos that also cost Wayne Garrett; Dwyer was later traded for a handful of beans a mere fourteen seasons before he played his last game.

Young outfielder **Amos Otis** (1969) got on Gil Hodges's bad side while moping though a trial at third base and was subsequently traded to Kansas City in a move the Mets would regret for years and years and years. By contrast, nobody ever questioned the desire of **Keith Miller** (1987–91) even if his talent wasn't up there with the best. Miller is now a player agent representing, among others, David Wright.

Others: outfielders **Larry Stahl** (1967–68), **Jay Payton** (1998), **Alex Escobar** (2001), and **Gary Matthews Jr.** (2002); infielders **Bill Almon** (1980) and **Al Pedrique** (1987); and pitchers **Randy Jones** (1981), **Charlie Puleo** (1981–82), **Yorkis Perez** (1997), **Bill Pulsipher** (2000), **Scott Strickland** (2002), and **Pedro Feliciano** (2006–07).

Number of times issued: 27 (24 players, 1 coach)

Longest tenured: Bobby Bonilla (5 seasons, 515 games), Danny Heep (4 seasons, 395 games), Frank Thomas (2 seasons, 342 games)

Best single seasons: Thomas, 1962 (.266/.329/.496, 34 HR, 94 RBI); Bonilla, 1993 (.265/.352/.522, 34 HR, 87 RBI); Willie Montañez, 1978 (.256/.320/.392, 16 HR, 96 RBI)

Career statistical leaders: Home runs (Bonilla 95, Thomas 52, Montañez 22), RBI (Bonilla 295, Thomas 173, Montañez 143), batting average (Del Unser .271, Bobby Bonilla .270), wins (Charlie Puleo 9), saves (Scott Strickland 2), ERA (Pedro Feliciano 1.89)

Uni Swaps

Uniform numbers and transactions are practically blood relatives. Following is a list of Mets trades in which the acquiree took the place—and uniform number—of the guy he was traded for. Some of these trades were multiplayer deals, but this list includes only those whose unis were swapped, and only those in which the new player took over the number at the first available opportunity. We might also call these Del Unser Deals, in honor of the former No. 25 who arrived, and departed, via the uni swap.

Date	Met Traded	Team	In exchange for	Number
April 26, 1962	B. G. Smith	Cubs	Sammy Taylor	16
Aug. 5, 1963	Ken MacKenzie	Cardinals	Ed Bauta	19
Aug. 7 1964	Frank Thomas	Phillies	Gary Kroll	25
Aug. 8, 1964	Frank Lary	Braves	Dennis Ribant	17
Oct. 15, 1964	Dick Smith	Dodgers	Larry Miller	16
April 1, 1967	Ed Bressoud	Cardinals	Jerry Buchek	1
July 11, 1967	Chuck Hiller	Phillies	Phil Linz	2
Oct. 18, 1971	Art Shamsky	Cardinals	Jim Beauchamp	24
Dec. 3, 1974	Don Hahn	Phillies	Del Unser	25
July 21, 1976	Del Unser	Expos	Jim Dwyer	25
July 21, 1976	Wayne Garrett	Expos	Pepe Mangual	11
Sept. 10, 1982	Tom Hausman	Braves	Carlos Diaz	32
July 31, 1989	Kevin Tapani	Twins	Frank Viola	26
May 31, 1991	Tim Teufel	Padres	Garry Templeton	11
Jan. 22, 1992	Mark Carreon	Tigers	Paul Gibson	45
July 29, 1996	Jeff Kent	Indians	Alvaro Espinosa	12
Sept. 14, 1999	Dan Murray	Royals	Glendon Rusch	48
Dec. 11, 2000	Bubba Trammell	Padres	Donne Wall	33
July 23, 2001	Todd Pratt	Phillies	Gary Bennett	7
Aug. 15, 2002	Shawn Estes	Reds	Pedro Feliciano	55
March 20, 2005	Jason Phillips	Dodgers	Kaz Ishii	23
Jan. 21, 2006	Kris Benson	Orioles	Jorge Julio	34
Dec. 5, 2006	Brian Bannister	Royals	Ambiorix Burgos	40

#26: KONG

On July 19, 1976, in the top of third inning, Phil Niekro of the Atlanta Braves hit a soft, sinking liner to left field off Craig Swan of the Mets. **Dave Kingman**, playing left field instead of his usual right, hustled in toward it, stuck out his glove, and went into a slide.

Kingman wore No. 26 on his back but the significant numbers on this night were 91 (the number of games Kingman had appeared in of the 93 the Mets had thus far played), 32 (the number of home runs Kingman had registered in those 91 games), and 56 (both the number of home runs Kingman was on pace to hit for the season and Hack Wilson's then National League record).

Niekro would wind up on second base as Kingman's lanky frame rattled to the ground without the ball, landing awkwardly on his glove hand. Kingman would wind up on an operating table having torn thumb ligaments repaired, and the most serious threat any Mets hitter had ever made on the all-time record books was over.

With the Mets a safe distance from the pennant race, Kingman's injury also effectively eliminated the best reason anyone would show up at Shea, hastened the eventual departure of manager Joe Frazier, and inspired, forty-eight hours later, the insipid Unser/Garrett for Mangual/Dwyer trade. Before you knew it, it was 1977 and things were really falling apart.

Over two rocky tenures with the Mets (1975–77 and 1981–83), Kingman was at once impossible to ignore and maddeningly flawed. He was a strapping power hitter who might send the next pitch through a bus window in the parking lot but more likely would swing ferociously and miss by a lot. He couldn't field at four positions. Described as aloof with teammates and often icy to the press, Kingman had a kind of stardom that looked good only from a distance. He left the Mets for good following the 1983 season as their leading career home run hitter (he has since fallen to fourth all time). Kong never batted higher than .238 (1976) and reached base at a .300 clip only once (1981) as a Met.

Kingman returned to the '76 lineup in late August and gave Mike Schmidt a challenge for the National League home run title, but he lost that one by a single dinger, 38-37. He'd settle instead for a new club record that he'd tie in 1982, and Darryl Strawberry would break five years after that. To Mets fans who grew up in the 1970s, though, Kingman was a guilty pleasure in a decade filled with disappointment.

Side-arming swing man **Terry Leach** (1985–89) fulfilled Kingman's legacy of the one freaky season when, in 1987, he started the year 10-0 and finished 11-1. Never given a full-time shot, Leach hung around the fringes of the organization for seven seasons (the last five wearing No. 26), amassing a career record of 24-9, 3.11. His book about the experience, called *Things Happen for a Reason*, is among the best ever authored by a Met (sorry, Tom Seaver; your mystery novel doesn't make the list).

Any list of poorly timed Mets injuries should include the right calf strain suffered by **Orlando Hernandez** prior to his scheduled start of Game 1 of the National League Division Series in 2006. El Duque injured himself while jogging, a testament to his advanced age—a number no one may ever know—when he joined the Mets. But surprising success while healthy (9-7, 4.09) earned him a return engagement in 2007 . . . when he got hurt at the worst possible time.

Lefty **Frank Viola** wore 26 upon his arrival from Minnesota in 1989; **Rico Brogna** (1994–96) had a respectable .289-22-76 campaign in 1995 but was traded when John Olerud arrived as a free agent. **Alejandro Peña** (1990–91) was John Franco's first setup man and not a bad one at that. Journeyman right-hander **Bob Shaw** (1966–67) was one of three 11-game winners on the 1966 Mets. Enigmatic fifth starter **Jae Seo** (2004–05) and his array of good and bad spent two seasons in 26. Only the bad seemed to follow him upon being sent away.

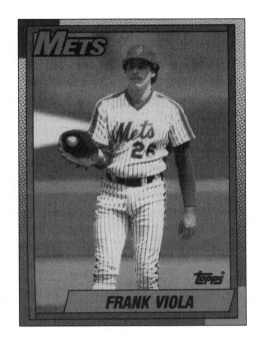

FRANK VIOLA

Galen Cisco (1962–65) took a sound beating along with the rest of the early Mets. His 3.62 ERA led the 1964 Mets even though he lost 19 games, second most in the league to teammate Tracy Stallard. Cisco was the third man to wear 26 on the 1962 Mets: the first two, **Herb Moford** and **Wilmer "Vinegar Bend" Mizell**, threw the last pitches of their respective careers in the jersey. Combined, they were 0-3 with a 7.30 ERA.

A Queens native and son-in-law of Gil Hodges, **Mike Bruhert** (1978) might have been born to be Met, but his 4-11 record assured his stay was brief. Relievers **Barry Manuel** (1997) and **Billy Taylor** (1999) became familiar with Shea boo-birds in their respective short-lived tenures with the club.

The remainders all made brief appearances: pitchers **Bill Graham** (1967), **Ray Burris** (1979), **Scott Holman** (1980), and **Kevin Tapani** (1989); the debuting **Bruce Boisclair** (1974); and reserves **Ced Landrum** (1993), **Ralph Milliard** (1998), **Terrence Long** (1999), **Jon Nunnally** (2000), **David Lamb** (2000), **Jason Phillips** (2001), and **Marco Scutaro** (2002–03).

Number of times issued: 28 (26 players, 1 coach)

Longest tenured: Dave Kingman (6 seasons, 664 games), Galen Cisco (4 seasons, 126 games)

Best single seasons: Terry Leach, 1987 (11-1, 3.22 ERA); Kingman, 1976 (.238/.286/.506, 37 HR, 86 RBI)

Career statistical leaders: Home runs (Kingman 154, Rico Brogna 34), RBI (Kingman 389, Brogna 126), batting average (Brogna, .291), wins (Leach 21, Cisco 18), saves (Alejandro Peña 9), ERA (Peña 2.98)

Spring Training and Other Untrustworthy Things

Not including Viagra-related spam, the most common e-mail received over seven-plus years at MBTN.net headquarters (aka metsbythenumbers.com) comes from fans who recall Dwight Gooden wearing No. 64 and wondering why it isn't listed.

That happened all right, just not during a regular-season or postseason game: it was during spring training. And rules of the project state that what happens in St. Lucie stays in St. Lucie (or St. Petersburg, as the case may be).

That yearbook and baseball-card photographers for years made spring training sites their home helped spread the confusion. This was especially true as Gooden became a sensation in 1984 and pictures of the phenom wearing 64 from 1984's spring training were widely distributed.

For some players spring training offers the opportunity to work on a new stance or learn a new pitch. Others give new uniforms a tryout. Gooden donned No. 00 (along with Roger McDowell, who wore 0) in an attempt to lighten the mood in 1989, but both were back in their respective 16 and 42 when the games started counting. John Franco wore No. 00 during some 1993 workouts (along with 76, 77, and 92).

Seeing players wearing uniform numbers usually suited for linemen or wide receivers is a sure sign that spring has arrived. Although as chaotic as it looks, the Mets appear to apply some logic to their spring assignments, using uniform numbers to group their invitees into certain loosely defined categories.

Which is why you'll often see players newly arrived from other organizations wearing numbers in the high 50s. This group includes minor-league free agents, trade throw-ins, and Rule 5ers (players picked from other teams and given a chance to either make the big-league club or be returned from whence they came). Young prospects who have earned invitations to big-league camp through promising play in the minors follow with numbers in the 60s. The most promising members of this group could find themselves upgraded to a lower number.

Organizational prospects—or the likely denizens of that season's AA and AAA rosters—populate the 70s. Catchers are as essential to spring training as sunblock, floppy caps, and loud shirts. Backstops are put to good use with all the arms in camp, and they tend to get their own designation in the 90s. But their specialized skill may earn them a future spring training invite while low-numbered flashes in the pan may get burned from too much exposure too soon.

#27: SWANNIE AND COOKIE

Craig Swan probably deserved better. He made his debut appearance just as the Mets were winning a division and his last one just as they became contenders again. The decade between might be called the Craig Swan Era, a period that bridged the gap between the Mets of Seaver, Harrelson, and Kranepool and those of Mookie, Darryl, and Gooden and featured all of two winning seasons: 1975 and 1976.

Swan (1973–84) would be the last in long line of successful farm-raised starters of the '60s and '70s. On his best days Swan was a worthy successor to Tom Seaver, but injuries cost him consistency, and a poor supporting cast cost him victories.

CRAIG SWAN

With Seaver gone in 1978, Swan won the National League ERA title at 2.43 to go along with a so-so 9-6 record (the low-octane Mets lost the majority of his starts in ten of his twelve seasons). He won a team-high 14 games for the putrid 1979 Mets—the next closest finisher had 6—and finished 11-7 for a 1982 squad that lost 97 games.

If Swan provides a lesson for Met 27s, it is, perhaps, that the numbers just don't matter. Writing in the *New York Times* in 1976, Murray Chass relayed how Swan miserably failed a pop quiz regarding uniform numbers administered by equipment manager Herb Norman. Swan, Chass reported, whiffed when asked to identify No. 17 (Felix Millan) and No. 6 (Mike Vail), guessing that neither number was occupied. No. 55? "Don't be silly. There is no 55," Swan remarked, forgetting that the digits belonged to his manager, Joe Frazier.

Pete Harnisch (1995–97) briefly assumed No. 1 starter duties, but he was no Tom Seaver. He was no Craig Swan, even. The Long Island native battled depression and tobacco withdrawal while clashing badly with manager Bobby Valentine.

At age thirty-three and in his thirteenth professional season, **Don Cardwell** (1967–70) was the oldest pitcher on the 1969 pitching staff and was looked to as something of its leader. Cardwell in '69 redeemed some early-season shakiness by winning five consecutive decisions starting in August as the Mets caught, then surpassed, the Cubs to clinch the Eastern Division. The streak, which included six straight starts allowing two runs or fewer, lowered Cardwell's season ERA by nearly an entire run.

An intense competitor who wanted the ball in the worst way, **Dennis Cook** (1998–2001) teamed with Turk Wendell to give the Mets one of the league's best lefty-righty setup tandems in the Bobby Valentine era. Cook won 10 games and saved 3 in relief in 1999 and didn't allow a run over 10 appearances in postseason play (although Cookie was less stingy in letting others pitchers' runs score in those situations).

Rookie call-up **Mike Jacobs** was ticketed to return to AAA in 2005 when he walloped a pinch-hit, three-run home run in his first major league at-bat, which led to more at-bats and more home runs: a torrid pace of 11 in his first 100 at-bats. The homeriest season of any Met 27 boosted Jacobs's value high enough to summarily be included in a trade for Carlos Delgado.

Jacobs is the fourth man to homer in his first plate appearance for the Mets. The uniform numbers of the players go in ascending order: Benny Ayala 18, Mike Fitzgerald 20, Kaz Matsui 25, and Jacobs 27. Never living up to the promise of their first at-bats in blue and orange, the Mets traded away all four players.

Others to wear 27 are notable in strange ways. Pitcher **Tom Parsons** (1964–65) went 1-10 in 1965, but Houston deemed him acceptable trade fodder for Jerry Grote. Reliever **Mark Corey** (2001–02) is best remembered for a pot-related freakout that ended his Mets career and would be cited by critics as justification for manager Bobby Valentine's firing after the season. Utility man **Tom O'Malley** (1989–90) was no great shakes as a Met but was a future MVP in Japan. **Dallas Green** (1966) spent two weeks as a reliever for the Mets but would return as the team's manager twenty-seven years later. Overmatched infielder **Mike Glavine** (2003) had better connections (yes, he's Tom's brother) than skill.

Others: pitchers **Larry Foss** (1962), **Wes Gardner** (1984–85), **Bob McClure** (1988), **Jason Middlebrook** (2002–03), **Mike Matthews** (2005), and **Darren Oliver** (2006). Also, reserves **Stan Jefferson** (1986), **Randy "Moose" Milligan** (1987), **Chuck Carr** (1991), and **Ced Landrum** (1993). The future may or may not reside in the development of five-tooled outfielder **Carlos Gomez** (2007).

Jim Hickman (1966), **Bruce Berenyi** (1984), and **Todd Zeile** (2004) did their most memorable work in other uniform numbers. Although Zeile homered in his final career at-bat to send out 27 in style.

Number of times issued: 25 (24 players, 1 coach)

Longest tenured: Craig Swan (12 seasons, 229 games), Dennis Cook (4 seasons, 225 games), Don Cardwell (4 seasons, 101 games)

Best single seasons: Swan, 1978 (9-6, 2.43 ERA); Swan, 1979 (14-13, 3.29 ERA); Cook, 1999 (10-5, 3 saves, 3.68 ERA, 68 strikeouts in 63 innings)

Career statistical leaders: Home runs (Mike Jacobs 11), RBI (Todd Zeile 35), batting average (Jacobs, .310), Wins (Swan 59, Cook 25), saves (Cook 6), ERA (Swan 3.72)

Out of the Blue and into the Black

Mets uniforms got a lot more complicated in the 1990s. In 1998, a year after the introduction of the "snow white" home uniform—and the failed white cap experiment—the Mets made black the new blue. New alternate hats were black with blue brims. Black became the primary shading color on both home and away uniforms as well as the skyline patch (now minus an "NY"). A black alternate jersey that read "Mets" was worn at home and on the road. The plot darkened.

The next year an all-black third alternate hat was introduced, as was a new black road uniform that read "New York." These changes were made without abandoning the old uniforms, so the Mets, who'd never worn more than one uniform at Shea Stadium in any of their first thirty-five seasons, now had three different uniforms and three different hats for home games, not to mention two road uniforms plus a new batting practice jersey and hat. The Mets also removed names from the backs of the home uniforms in 1999, the first time players had gone nameless at Shea in twenty-two seasons. That experiment ended after one year.

But why all the new uniforms? Why black? "The black was added as a style element based on some degree of research of fans in terms of what was popular in the marketplace," Mets VP Dave Howard told the *New York Times* in 2006. The Mets created new inventory—as the Milwaukee Brewers had done repeatedly—and it sold better than the old items. Of course, the Mets had improved dramatically on the field, inter-league play with the Yankees created even more area interest in the team, and there were 1.5 million more fans at Shea in 1999 than there had been five seasons earlier when pinstriping and blue had been the rule. They came, they saw, they bought merchandise.

Equipment manager Charlie Samuels ultimately decides which Mets outfit will be worn each night. He also serves as enforcer to keep the Mets from wearing blue caps on all but the hottest days lest someone wears a black dugout jacket that might make the colors clash. This rule seemed to ease somewhat in 2006, but the Mets still wore black uniforms and hats for significant moments like the NL East clincher and Game 1 of the NLCS.

Critical reaction to the black uniforms has been mixed. While younger fans inclined to spend big money on replica jerseys have bought in—literally—to the new color scheme, fans whose allegiance traces back to prior eras tend be less enthusiastic. Paul Lukas, an ESPN.com columnist and the Tim Gunn of sports uniform criticism, dislikes the Mets black uniforms so much he started an online petition to get the Mets to eliminate the color.

When Mets fan extraordinaire Jerry Seinfeld first saw the uniforms, he used his guest microphone in the booth to comment, "And the black shirts? It's a summer game. . . . I like black, too, but not when I'm at the beach. These guys are in the sun all day."

Better black than puffy pirate shirts.

#28: THE HAMMER

The young team that won the 1969 World Series was a mature one when it contended for the 1973 title, with the notable exceptions of pitcher Jon Matlack and 23-year-old first baseman/outfielder **John Milner**.

One of the club's few exciting young offensive players of the early 1970s, and until Darryl Strawberry the only farm-developed left-handed power hitter in team history, Milner (1971–77) led the Mets in home runs for three straight seasons beginning in 1972 but never hit more than 23 in a year. He played both outfield and first base respectably, and his snare of a soft liner and two-step to the bag clinched the unexpected '73 division title.

Milner cut an impressive figure in the No. 28 jersey. Possessed of a lean, powerful build, he wore menacing sideburns of the style George Foster would imitate, sweatbands of the style Tsuyoshi Shinjo would rock some thirty years later, and stirrups as high as they would go.

Nicknamed "The Hammer" for a resemblance to Hank Aaron, Milner lacked none his namesake's power, just his consistency and good health. Milner pulled everything, and when he got a hold of one it made first basemen nervous or maintenance crew order new scoreboard light bulbs. His five Met grand slams—three in 1976 alone—held up as the club record until Mike Piazza broke it. Milner was also a patient hitter who could take a walk. But injuries—and, some say, attitude—got in the way of consistency for Milner, who was traded to Pittsburgh in the convoluted Willie Montañez deal.

The Mets never had another hitter nearly as accomplished as Milner wear No. 28. **Amos Otis** (1967) and **Wally Backman** (1980) stopped off en route to different numbers. Reserves **Bob Heise** (1969) and **Darren Reed**

(1990) also wore other numbers in their Mets careers. **Tommy Herr** (1990–91) was a veteran of the mid-1980s Cardinals teams that Mets fans had always hated, and their feelings didn't change much as Herr's career sputtered ineffectively toward an end in orange and blue.

Bobby Jones (1993–2000) was never going to be the best Fresno-born pitcher in Mets history, but he was about as far ahead of Fresnonians Jaime Cerda, Dennis Springer, and Rick Baldwin as he was behind Tom Seaver.

Guilty of unglamorousness and, even, at times, dullness, Jones over eight seasons gave his team a chance to win often enough to rack up 74 wins, ninth in team history through 2007. And just when fans expected a struggle, he tossed a one-hit, complete-game shutout to eliminate the Giants in the 2000 Division Series. That game turned out to be Jones's swan song, about as beautiful as one could be written.

Coming out of nowhere to record 9 wins and a team-best 3.10 ERA, lantern-jawed Mainer **Carl Willey** (1963–65) emerged as the Mets' best starting pitcher of 1963. Willey was poised to assume opening-day pitching duties for the Mets in 1964 when a line drive off the bat of Gates Brown in a spring training game broke his jaw. When Willey returned in June he was assigned to the bullpen and never regained effectiveness as a starter.

The Mets most often called on 28 in relief: **Sherman "Roadblock" Jones** (1962) returned in 28 after an earlier stint in 36. Relievers included **Jim Bethke** (1965), hard-throwing but wild **Bill Hepler** (1966), shaggy **Dwight Bernard** (1978–79), maverick philosopher and well-past-his-prime fireman **Mike Marshall** (1981), **Scott Holman** (1982–83), talented but erratic **Scott Strickland** (2003), and goggle-wearing reliever/magician **Juan Padilla** (2005).

In what had to have been the first time in major league history that 41-year-old teammates swapped uniforms, creaky 2007 Mets reserves **Jeff Conine** and **Sandy Alomar** exchanged No. 28 for No. 19, respectively.

The relative paucity of occupants in 28 is explained in part by the number belonging to coach **Bill Robinson** for five seasons in the 1980s. He inherited the number from departing third-base coach **Bobby Valentine**, who left Shea for a managing job in Texas in 1985. Robinson received singles hitters at first base with a finger-swipe congratulatory greeting that oozed urban cool. Meanwhile in Oakland, the A's were developing the forearm smash, foretelling of a louder, more aggressive baseball future.

Number of times issued: 22 (18 players, 3 coaches)

Longest tenured: Bobby Jones (8 seasons, 193 games), John Milner (7 seasons, 741 games)

Best single seasons: Jones, 1997 (15-9, 3.63 ERA); Carl Willey, 1963 (9-14, 3.10 ERA, 4 shutouts); Milner, 1973 (.238/.340/.423, 23 HR, 72 RBI); Milner, 1976 (.271/.362/.447, 15 HR, 78 RBI)

Career statistical leaders: Home runs (Milner 94), RBI (Milner 338), batting average (Wally Backman .323, Milner .245), wins (Jones 74), saves (Juan Padilla 1), ERA (Willey 3.29)

The Namesake Series

Luggage and fan mail may have been another story, but fans rarely had trouble distinguishing Bobby Jones from Bobby Jones when they were Mets teammates in 2000.

Bobby J. Jones was white, right-handed, wore No. 28, and started games; Bobby M. Jones was black, left-handed, wore No. 21, and pitched in relief. Bobby M. Jones relieved Bobby J. Jones three times in 2000. The highlight came on September 28 when the Joneses combined to defeat Greg Maddux and the Braves, 8-2. The Braves, as the saying goes, couldn't keep up.

More difficult to distinguish between were the Bob Millers of 1962, perhaps because they were so undistinguished themselves. Bob L. Miller, a right-handed starter, finished with a 1-12 record. Bob G. Miller, the left-hander reliever acquired from the Reds in midseason, went 2-2 with a gaudy 7.20 ERA. The Millers appeared in the same game on five different occasions, the lone win coming on a 14th-inning home run by Frank Thomas. Bob L. went the first seven innings; Bob G. pitched a scoreless 14th for the win.

The Mets have had three pairs of same-named players who weren't teammates: the Bob Johnsons (one a pinch-hitting whiz of 1967; the other a rookie pitcher who'd be a throw-in in the Otis-Foy deal in 1969), the Mike Marshalls (the legendary reliever, 1981; and the Go-Gos-dating outfielder, 1990, both of whom were washed up by the time they got to Shea), and the Pedro Martinezes (the obscure lefty reliever from 1996 and the other the greatest pitcher of his era). Ike Hampton (obscure catcher of 1974) and Mike Hampton (mercenary lefty of 2000) form the honorary battery of this group.

Pedro A. Martinez (that's the first one) is one of several famous names that weren't. The Mets had the weak-hitting infielder Brian Giles, not the power-hitting All-Star outfielder model. The Kevin Brown who played briefly for the 1990 Mets wasn't the dominant strikeout pitcher of the era but wasn't, that we know at least, a complete jerk either.

The Mets have had several sets of relatives who share a name: the Alomars (Sandy Sr., and sons Roberto and Sandy Jr.), the Alous (Jesus, nephew Moises, and Moises's cousin Mel Rojas), and the Wilsons (Mookie and stepson Preston). Ron Hodges and Gil Hodges were not related, but Gil Hodges and Mike Bruhert were (Bruhert married Gil's daughter).

Related by blood, by marriage, or merely by alphabetical proximity, following are the most populous player surnames in Mets history, through 2007:

No. of Players	Surname	Roster
8	Jones	Barry, Bobby J., Bobby M., Chris, Cleon, Randy, Ross, Sherman
6	Johnson	Ben, Bob D., Bob W., Howard, Lance, Mark
5	Hernandez	Anderson, Keith, Manny, Orlando, Roberto
5	Miller	Bob G., Bob L., Dyar, Keith, Larry
5	Smith	Bobby Gene, Charley, Dick, Joe, Pete
5	Wilson	Mookie, Paul, Preston, Tom, Vance
4	Anderson	Craig, Jason, Marlon, Rick
4	Bell	Derek, Gus, Heath, Jay
4	Marshall	Dave, Jim, Mike A., Mike G.
4	Taylor	Billy, Chuck, Hawk, Ron
3	19 surnames	

#29: SLOW MUSIC

As measured by Pythagorean wins—Bill James's back-of-the-envelope formula to estimate winning percentage based on a team's runs scored and allowed—the 1990 Mets should have won 98 games and not the 91 they ultimately did.

That **Frank Viola** didn't win a few more games that year was also a disappointment—and he won 20. But with 19 wins in mid-September, Viola whiffed in three tries to get No. 20 while the Mets fell from a half-game behind division-leading Pittsburgh to mathematical elimination. Viola reached win No. 20 in the final game of the season. And although Viola is the last Met to win that many games in a year, he's also become a symbol of the talented but dysfunctional teams the Mets fielded as they faded from their mid-1980s glory.

It was reasonable for the Mets to have expected more of Viola (1989–91), a New York native and St. John's grad who was at the top of his game when the Mets acquired him in a blockbuster summer trade in 1989. The Mets surrendered five pitchers, including Rick Aguilera and Kevin Tapani, who'd combine for 198 wins and 311 saves over their careers (including a World Series championship in 1991), to get Viola.

Viola couldn't make the difference in 1989 (as in 1990, the Mets faded near the stretch and settled for second place). In 1991, Viola battled an infected fingernail and lost 10 of his final 12 decisions.

Not exactly chummy with the press, nor with Bud Harrelson, his manager for the majority of his stay in New York, Viola may also have been dissatisfied with his uniform number. With 16 belonging to Dwight Gooden,

Viola wore 26 in 1989 and then tried 29 in deference to his assigned number at St. John's, but he was back in 16 at his earliest opportunity—when he signed with the Red Sox in 1992.

Dave Magadan (1986–89, 1992) gave up his assigned No. 29 for Viola and then claimed it back after "Sweet Music" ceased. Magadan played a bunch of positions, drew a lot of walks, hit some doubles, and always plodded slowly around the bases. Magadan's .292 career batting average as a Met ranked fifth-highest among Mets with 1,000 at-bats (through 2007); his .391 career on-base percentage was second only to another noted slowpoke left-handed hitting first baseman: John Olerud.

Speaking of slow, no Mets player wore No. 29 longer than **Steve Trachsel** (and no, we don't mean in a single game). Trachsel's career as a Met began terribly (he accepted a demotion to AAA after starting 2-10, 6.72 in 2001) and ended ugly (reportedly begging out of NLCS Game 2 in 2006, having surrendered 5 runs in an inning-plus).

Between those extremes, Trachsel was a slow-working model of moderately priced consistency who by 2006 had become the team's longest-serving player. Trachsel led the Mets in earned-run average in 2002 and in 2003, won 16 games in 2003 (one of four times he led or tied for the team lead), and his 66 wins overall rank tenth in team history.

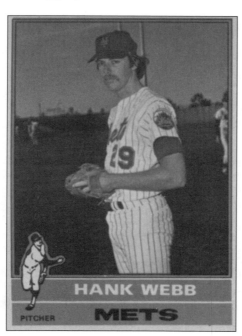

Hank Webb (1974–75) was wearing 29 when he entered in the 25th inning at Shea on September 11, 1974. He allowed a hit to the first Cardinal he faced, Bake McBride, and then chucked a pickoff throw into right field. Ron Hodges, who'd entered after Duffy Dyer caught the first 23 innings, dropped the throw to the plate as McBride scored the first run by anyone in fifteen innings. This is how the longest night game in National League history was decided.

Walrus-sized southpaw **Mickey Lolich** was a two-time 20-game winner and World Series hero for Detroit, but the trade that made him a Met was a jumbo bust. Out went Rusty Staub, who had just set the season RBI mark as a Met and would drive in 318 runs over the next three seasons in the AL. In came the 35-year-old Lolich, who posted a 3.22 ERA in '76, but lacking run support, won only 8 games and retired following his one and only season in New York.

Staub initially arrived in a trade for **Ken Singleton** (1970–71), a young outfielder who'd grow into a player with the offensive skills the Mets could have used for years to come. "Poor trade" is about all that comes to mind with the mention of **Rich Chiles** (1973), who arrived from Houston in the Tommie Agee deal and hit .120 in eight games.

Like Lolich, **Frank Tanana** (1993) was a veteran American League lefty strikeout artist who retired after a year with the Mets. By 1993, however, Tanana had long lost his strikeout stuff. He was traded to the Yankees for Kenny Greer in mid-September, where he absorbed the last two losses of his career.

Junk-throwing lefty swingman **Tom Gorman** (1982–85), whom Keith Hernandez called "Gorfax" in a needling reference to the lefty fireballer of Dodger fame that Gorman clearly was not, posted a 6-0 record in 1984.

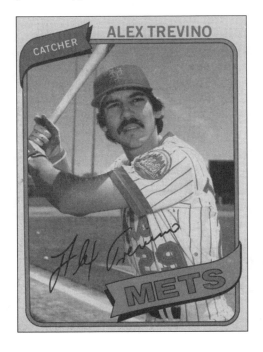

Gorman's claim to fame was being the winning pitcher in the July 4, 1985, marathon with Atlanta despite having allowed a game-tying home run to pitcher Rick Camp in the bottom of the 18th inning (the Mets won in the 19th).

Another lefty, **Rob Gardner** (1965–66), pitched the first 15 innings of a 0-0 game against Philadelphia interrupted by a curfew in 1965. Still more lefties who wore 29: **Willard Hunter** (1962), Rule 5 draftee **Don Rowe** (1963), and **Nick Willhite** (1967).

The Mets had high hopes for catching prospect **Alex Treviño** (1978–81). So did the Reds, who insisted on receiving him in the George Foster trade to succeed Johnny Bench. Treviño got raves for his defense and filled in admirably for an injured John Stearns in 1980, but he holds the team record for most turns at-bat without ever hitting a home run (733). He returned briefly for a nine-game cup of coffee with the Mets in 1990 (wearing No. 6), his final major league season.

Others: expansion draftee **John "Thumper" DeMerit** (1962); luckless **Craig Anderson** (1963); relievers **Danny Frisella** (1967–69) and **Bob D. Johnson** (1969); infielders **Tim Corcoran** (1986) and **Jim Lindeman** (1994); starter **Robert Person** (1995–96); utility man **Steve Bieser** (1997); and pitchers **Masato Yoshii** (1998), **Octavio Dotel** (1998–99), **Eric Cammack** (2000), and **Jorge Sosa** (2007).

Number of times issued: 28 (26 players, 1 DNP)

Longest tenured: Steve Trachsel (6 seasons, 160 games), Dave Magadan (5 seasons, 433 games), Tom Gorman (4 seasons, 98 games), Alex Treviño (4 seasons, 249 games)

Best single seasons: Viola, 1990 (20-12, 2.67, 182 strikeouts in 249.2 innings), Magadan, 1989 (.286/.367/.393 in 374 at-bats), Trachsel, 2003 (16-10, 3.78 ERA, 111 strikeouts in 204.2 innings)

Career statistical leaders: Home runs (Ken Singleton 18), RBI (Dave Magadan 131), batting average (Magadan .290), wins (Steve Trachsel 66), ERA (Frank Viola 3.29)

Decisions, Decisions

Statisticians and other astute observers understand that a pitcher's winning percentage is a poor indicator of his quality or lack of it. Especially over time, a player's winning percentage tends to resemble the overall record of his team, which is why the chart below is full of results at or near a .478 winning percentage, which happens to be the Mets' overall record through 2007 (3,496-3,817 to be precise). If you ever want to get depressed consider this: the Mets enter the 2008 season needing 18 consecutive 90-win seasons to reach .500 as a franchise. Out-winning your team overall is a feat for the lucky or exceptionally good. But it couldn't hurt to wear 16.

Following is a list of winning percentages by uniform number in Mets history through 2006. Only numbers with at least 100 wins or losses were considered.

No.	Wins	Losses	Pct.	Notes
16	162	95	.630	Thanks to Doc, no other jersey comes close. Third all time in wins.
41	203	129	.611	Almost all Seaver: his four predecessors combined to go 5-5.
35	109	111	.495	Rick Reed (59-36, .621) one of only four 35s better than .500: Kenny Greer (1-0), Mike DeJean (3-1), and Joe Smith (3-2) are the others.
39	125	134	.483	Gary Gentry (41-42) is the largest decision maker.
22	147	159	.480	Al Leiter (.586) nearly makes up for Jack Fisher (.342). Nearly.
36	229	246	.478	Winningest and losingest number in team history.
29	166	182	.477	Best percentage winner: Octavio Dotel (8-3, .727).
45	125	139	.473	Pedro Martinez (24-16) already second to Tug McGraw (47-55) in total wins.
34	110	126	.466	Winningest 34: Danny Frisella (21-16). Losingest: Bob Apodaca (16-25).
32	144	166	.465	Jon Matlack (82-81) leads the way.
40	106	126	.457	Stragglers include .333-averaging relievers Jeff Innis (10-20) and Braden Looper (6-12).
27	125	161	.437	Craig Swan (59-71) is this number's biggest winner and loser.
47	145	182	.433	Appropriately, Jesse Orosco is 47-47. Jay Hook (12-34, .261) and Wally Whitehurst (11-22, .333) bring up the rear.
38	120	184	.395	It all starts with Roger Craig (12-43, .218).

#30: NOLAN RYAN: THE ONE WHO GOT AWAY

The Mets traded **Nolan Ryan** for Jim Fregosi. Okay? Can we move on now?

It's hard to imagine how things might have been different had the Mets ever been able to resist the urge to upgrade their third basemen in the wake of 1969. It cost the Mets a fine outfielder, Amos Otis, in 1970. In 1971, it cost them an erratic but hard-throwing righthander who would become the greatest strikeout pitcher of all-time (plus three prospects!) It cost them a pitcher who could have complemented Seaver-Koosman-Matlack in the '70s, and Gooden-Darling-Fernandez in the '80s, and maybe even Gooden-Cone-Fernandez in the early '90s . . . that Ryan kid sure pitched for a while. It cost them a pitcher whose number would be retired by three other organizations.

Hey, at least we got an aging injured infielder playing out of position for a year-and-a-half out of it.

It doesn't excuse them for taking so little in return, but the Mets were losing patience with Ryan (1968–71). He suffered from recurring blisters, allowed way too many base runners via the walk or HBP, and threw too many wild pitches. He'd won a career-high 10 games in 1971 but lost 10 of his final 12 decisions. The upside was always there—he pitched seven innings in relief to win the decisive game of the 1969 NLCS and struck out batters even more prolifically than he walked them—but the Mets felt they could contend with a better offense and decided Ryan, the least-realized of the staff, was the one who had to go.

For the Angels, the Ryan trade was all the more remarkable because it replaced the Greatest Angel of All-Time with the succeeding Greatest Angel of All-Time. They would not only retire No. 30 for Ryan but also No. 11 for Fregosi. Both were deserving.

The Astros, who would retire No. 34 for Ryan, obtained the player for whom they would retire No. 33 from the Mets in **Mike Scott** (1979–82).

Scott (14-27, 4.64 as a Met) had shown little of the ability or treachery that would turn him into a force for the 1986 Astros and nearly eliminate the Mets from World Series contention. The Mets received outfielder Danny Heep in return for Scott—but the deal attracted little notice because the Mets also reacquired Tom Seaver the same day.

Dennis Ribant (1966) was the first Mets starting pitcher to fashion a winning record (11-9) and the first Met to wear number 30. He was subsequently traded to Pittsburgh.

Battle-scarred veteran **Mike Torrez** (1983–84) slogged his way toward the end of his career with the Mets. Among the lowlights: a team record for most men walked in one game (10), lasting only an inning-and-a-third in an opening-day starting assignment in 1984, and the frightening beaning of Dickie Thon.

Banished after a 1-12 record in 1962, **Bob L. Miller** (1973–74) returned to the Mets to play a small role in the 1973 stretch drive, temporarily taking the uniform number of perpetual prospect **Hank Webb** (1973, 1976). Curly haired pitcher **Jackson Todd** overcame a battle with cancer to make the Mets in 1977.

Pitching coach **Mel Stottlemyre** came around just as the Mets had pitching prospects blossoming everywhere. He coached under four managerial regimes (Johnson, Harrelson, Cubbage, and Torborg), wearing No. 30 for all but his first year with the Mets.

Defense-first catcher **Alberto "Bambi" Castillo** (1995–98) was the first non-pitcher to don the No. 30 jersey. Castillo's 14th-inning pinch single drove in the game-winning run in a 1-0 opening-day win over Philadelphia in 1998. The Mets signed lefty swingman and Queens native **Allen Watson** (1999) only to abruptly trade him just two months into his stay.

Reliever **Doug Linton** (1994) was the first post-Stottlemyre 30. Chubby first base prospect **Jorge Luis Toca** (1999–2001) saw brief duty in three seasons. Veteran hurler **Aaron Sele** (2007) made more news for being the longest holdout in the club's San Francisco head-shaving episode than for his infrequent long relief outings as a Met.

Fans applauded the bravery of **Cliff Floyd** (2003–06) when he came off the field for the last time in 2003, having put up productive numbers in spite of a painful Achilles tendon injury that required surgery. But fans eventually grew tired of waiting for Floyd to get healthy. Signed to a four-year free-agent deal, the plain-speaking, left-handed-hitting slugger had just one injury-free season as a Met, 2005, when he clubbed 34 home runs. But his lasting memory will be that of a player compromised: given a chance to be Kirk Gibson in Game 7 of the 2006 NLCS, he turned out instead to be Cliff Floyd.

Number of times issued: 15 (13 players, 1 coach)

Longest tenured: Cliff Floyd (4 seasons, 468 games), Nolan Ryan (4 seasons, 105 games), Mike Scott (4 seasons, 84 games)

Best single seasons: Floyd, 2005 (.273/.358/.505, 34 HR, 98 RBI); Ryan, 1970 (7-11, 3.42 ERA, 125 strikeouts in 131.2 innings); Dennis Ribant, 1966 (11-9, 3.20 ERA, 10 complete games)

Career statistical leaders: Home runs (Floyd 81), RBI (Floyd 273), batting average (Floyd .268), wins (Ryan 29), saves (Scott 3), ERA (Ribant 3.11)

Dirty 30 and the Unpopular Numbers

As Lotto players and roulette junkies might tell you, certain numbers just don't come up that often. In the case of Mets uniforms, the unpopular uniforms are often those boasting popular, long-time players. They also encompass the semi-retired (8, 24) and the stigma-laden (13).

Following is a list of the unretired jersey numbers, between 1 and 49, least frequently issued to players in Mets' history through 2007. For a list of the most frequently issued numbers, see Chapter 6.

No.	No. of Players	Notes
24	10	Technically still in mothballs for Willie Mays, but reissued in 2007 for coach Rickey Henderson.
8	11	Unissued since Gary Carter's Hall of Fame induction; last wearer was Desi Relaford in 2001.
47	12	Jesse Orosco kept it tied up for 9 years; Tom Glavine for 5.
30	13	Belonged longest to a coach, Mel Stottlemyre; would've been nice if Nolan Ryan had kept it warm longer.
31	13	After John Franco (9 years) and Mike Piazza (8), could be a long while before you see 31 again, unless it's hanging up on a wall permanently.
4	14	Coaches Mike Cubbage, Cookie Rojas, and Matt Galante combine for 11 years occupancy.
46	15	Not worn by a player until 1979 by Neil Allen.
13	15	Another number taken out of mothballs by Neil Allen—he was the first to wear it in 18 years in '81—it became synomomous in Queens with Fonzie and now "Enter Sandman."
9	17	Two managers wore 9 (Wes Westrum and Joe Torre).
28	19	The 1980s belonged to coach Bill Robinson.

#31: MIKE PIAZZA: THE ONE WHO CAME TO SHEA

Mike Piazza is the guy who changed everything. Even John Franco.

Piazza's arrival in a 1998 trade brought a sudden boost in attendance and a new, higher profile for the Mets overnight. His signing of a seven-year deal following the season completed a philosophical shift of direction within the organization that had begun late in the 1997 season. No longer were the Mets practicing the McIlvainian discipline of patiently building a franchise of well-scouted prospects from within. The new mission, ready or not, was this: get this team into the World Series as often as we can while this guy is still in his prime.

With Steve Phillips on the cell phone and Bobby Valentine in the dugout, they pulled it off once, in 2000. The rest of the time Piazza simply did his thing, which was to hit the ball harder than any Met ever had, stir the emotions of Mets fans like no other player, and do it all with a stoic languidness that would withstand whatever absurd fates the Mets' best player always seems destined to encounter.

Piazza remained a hard competitor and a gentleman, for instance, when fans unthinkingly booed him shortly after his arrival in 1998, when a certain knuckleheaded Yankee thug tried to assassinate him—twice—in 2000, when forced into holding a news conference to discuss his heterosexuality, when sandbagged with the revelation he was the team's new

Photo by Dan Carubia

first baseman, and so on. Even legitimate issues, such as Piazza's inability to control the opposition's running game, probably attracted more attention than they should have (and 2004's switch to first base proved to be a misguided solution).

The first base fiasco, age, and injuries made Piazza's final years in New York difficult, but unforgettable moments of longball heroism—September 21, 2001, the Trevor Hoffman game, the Billy Wagner game, the Ramiro Mendoza game, John Smoltz in Game 6, to name just a few—assure Piazza would hear the cheers of Mets fans long after his stay. He left the Mets after the 2005 season ranking first in franchise history in slugging percentage (.542), second in home runs (220) and RBI (655), and third in batting average (.296).

The trade that brought Piazza to the Mets was discussed enough beforehand that there was time to settle the looming collision between Piazza, who wore 31 with Los Angeles and Florida, and **John Franco**, then the senior Met on the squad and occupant of the 31 jersey for eight years. Franco, to his credit, volunteered to step into a new jersey (45) and welcome Piazza aboard.

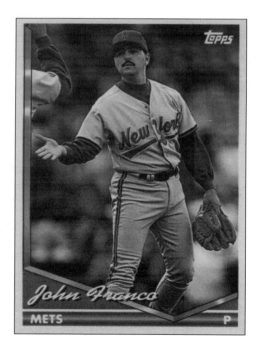

Franco to that point had appeared in 394 games, winning 35 and saving 221, numbers that made him the all-time Mets 31, and by a longshot. What he hadn't done in his career was reach the postseason, and so he gave up his number for the chance. It turned out to be a better deal than your average gold-watch-for-uni-number swap.

Franco in 1990 became the first Met ever to lead the league in saves and narrowly edged former-Met-turned-Red "Nasty Boy" Randy Myers for the Rolaids Relief Man Award. Myers won a World Series that year, making Round 1 of that challenge trade a draw. (Although when both players' careers were through, Franco had an edge of 57 saves. Both men ranked in the career top ten.)

When Franco gave up 31 he chose 45 in honor of legendary Mets fireman Tug McGraw. What he may not have known was that No. 31 previously belonged to the Mets' very first relief ace, **Larry Bearnarth**, who like Franco was a product of St. John's University.

A burly right-hander, Bearnarth (1963–66) led the team with 58 appearances as a 21-year-old rookie in 1963. Along with Al Jackson and Ron Hunt, Bearnarth was also among the few early Mets coveted by other teams.

The Mets spent their first draft pick ever on Montana schoolboy **Les Rohr** (1967–68), who made brief appearances wearing No. 31. **Jack DiLauro** as a 1969 Mets rookie threw 63.2 innings of effective relief from the left side in his only season with the club. As the most valuable member of the 1973 bullpen not named McGraw, **Harry Parker** (1973–75) picked up 8 wins and 5 saves in 1973, by far his best season with the Mets.

Freak rookie success **Mike Vail** (1975) fashioned a 23-game hitting streak in 1975 that somehow convinced the Mets it would be okay to trade Rusty Staub. Vail wrecked his ankle playing basketball that offseason and returned (wearing No. 6) as a shadow of his former self. Hard-throwing righty **Bruce Berenyi** (1985–86) had electric stuff but couldn't overcome injuries. At 29, Berenyi had been brought over from Cincinnati in June 1984 as elder statesman to New York's young yet surging rotation. He went 9-6 but was pedestrian compared to rookies Dwight Gooden, Ron Darling, and Sid Fernandez.

Iguana-eating reliever **Julio Machado** (1989) was assigned 31 before Franco arrived: he reappeared in 1990 wearing the No. 48 most recently belonging to Myers.

Others include pitchers **Ron Herbel** (1970), **Don Rose** (1971), **Roy Lee Jackson** (1977–80), and **Gene Walter** (1987). **George Bamberger** wore 31 as a Mets manager in 1982 and '83, but Bambi's heart was never really into it.

Number of times issued: 14 (13 players, 1 manager)

Longest tenured: John Franco (9 seasons, 394 games), Mike Piazza (8 seasons, 972 games)

Best single seasons: Franco, 1996 (4-3, 28 saves, 1.83 ERA); Franco, 1990 (5-3, 33 saves, 2.53 ERA); Piazza, 1999 (.303/.361/.575, 40 HR, 124 RBI); Piazza, 2000 (.324/.398/.614, 38 HR, 113 RBI)

Career statistical leaders: Home runs (Piazza 220), RBI (Piazza 655), batting average (Mike Vail .302, Piazza .296), wins (Franco 35, Harry Parker 14, Larry Bearnarth 13), saves (Franco 221, Parker 11), ERA (Franco 2.73, Bearnarth 3.43)

A True Tip of the Cap

The Mets were in Pittsburgh the morning of September 11, 2001. They had crept back to the fringes of the National League East race and were a few hours away from heading to the new PNC Park for the first time. Then the world changed. The tragedies that day at the World Trade Center, at the Pentagon in Washington, and just 64 miles south of Pittsburgh—in Shanksville—created profound sorrow and made just about every American not involved in an emergency service or the military feel utterly helpless.

Following six days of national mourning, the Mets took the field in Pittsburgh with heavy hearts. The Pirates, who were supposed to be at Shea Stadium on that date, hosted the series because Shea was still being used as a staging area for supplies to reach rescue workers. Pittsburgh, where commercials for games against the Mets a decade earlier had featured the tagline, "The Mets: Another Reason to Hate New York," now cheered the players who represented the city that had been so shaken.

The Mets wore their emotions on their sleeves, and they expressed their feelings on their heads as well. The Mets wore hats to honor the service personnel who had risked all to save others: FDNY (Fire), NYPD (Police), PAPD (Port Authority), EMS (paramedics), and OEM (Emergency Management). The Mets wore the hats before the first game in Pittsburgh on September 17 before putting on their black and blue Mets caps. Manager Bobby Valentine, who'd worked tirelessly coordinating volunteer efforts and donations, continued wearing his NYPD hat. The next night the Mets followed suit and they played in the hats honoring the services the rest of the season. Mike Piazza's black and blue catching helmet read "NYPD." An American flag was affixed to all batting helmets and uniforms for the Mets and every club (including the majors' two Canadian teams).

The Mets swept the Pirates and headed to Shea to play the city's first professional outdoor sporting event since the tragedy. Security was tight but throats were tighter as no one seemed sure they should go to something that had suddenly become, well, trivial in the grand scheme. The emergency services that had responded so quickly and given so much in a time of tragedy were at Shea in force. The Mets lined the field before the game representing them with the hats. A roll call of some players' representation that night:

Edgardo Alfonzo	FDNY
Kevin Appier	FDNY
Armando Benitez	FDNY
Bruce Chen	FDNY
John Franco	NYPD
Al Leiter	PAPD
Joe McEwing	FDNY

Jason Phillips	NYPD
Desi Relaford	FDNY
Tsuyoshi Shinjo	FDNY
Robin Ventura	PAPD
Rick White	NYPD
Todd Zeile	NYPD

There were plenty of hugs to go around. The Mets and Braves hugged before the game, fans embraced emergency personnel at every turn, and Liza Minnelli hugged Jay Payton after the first version of "New York, New York" that didn't make anyone think of the Yankees. Fittingly, it was Piazza who rose to the momentous occasion.

With the Mets down by a run in the 8th inning, Piazza launched a long two-run home run against Steve Karsay. New York had regained just a tiny bit of its swagger, even if its heart was still broken. The Mets also won the next night—their fifteenth victory in seventeen games—to pull within three and a half games of the first-place Braves. The Mets faded, but their volunteerism, compassion, and emotion remained in the minds of the faithful. The Mets played for free that Friday night, donating a day's pay, some $440,000, to Rusty Staub's Widows' and Children's Benefit Fund. Mets fan and songwriter Terry Cashman even wrote a song about what may have been Piazza's greatest moment. Every September since, as the Mets don the hats for a day in tribute to the

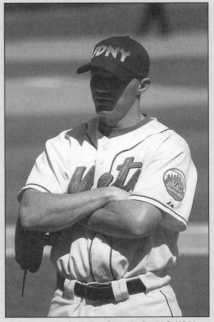

Joe McEwing. Photo by David G. Whitham

services and to the men and women who died, the chilled feeling returns from that night at Shea and that moment when, in the words of Cashman, "The ball went sailing into the night."

#32: ORNERY LEFTIES

Jon Matlack (1971–77) won in double-figures for his first five full seasons, picking up a Rookie of the Year award in 1972 and the win and co-MVP honors (with Bill Madlock) in the 1975 All-Star Game. A big left-hander with bat-shattering stuff, Matlack stepped into a rotation with Tom Seaver and Jerry Koosman and held his own.

Despite it all, he didn't have a lot of luck. Over seven seasons and 204 games, Matlack's career record was a deceptively mediocre 82-81. Poor run support—a characteristic of every Mets team to employ Matlack—was one culprit.

JON MATLACK

The Mets' first-round draft pick in 1967, Matlack was brought along slowly until debuting with 15 victories and a 2.32 ERA—fourth-best in the National League—in 1972. His sophomore season was literally more painful. Pitching to Marty Perez of the Braves that May, Matlack took a screaming line drive off his forehead and hit the ground like an empty uniform. Despite a fractured skull, Matlack was back in just eleven days and would lead the Mets into the World Series with a gutsy complete-game shutout of the favored Reds in Game 2 of the NLCS. Matlack got three starts in the World Series that year and pitched to a 2.16 ERA, but lost twice, including the decisive Game 7 on two-run homers by Bert Campaneris and Reggie Jackson.

Unhappy with the organizational strife in 1977, Matlack slumped to his worst year as a Met—7-15 with a 4.21 ERA—and would be traded to Texas in the strenuous but ultimately pointless Willie Montañez deal. He remains the gold standard for Mets 32s, particularly the lefties who followed him.

Trading for **Mike Hampton** in his walk year was a risky strategy that paid off in predictable ways: Hampton led the Mets to the World Series, and then he walked.

An ornery lefty, Hampton at his best could be a diminutive version of Matlack. He walked too many guys, but Hampton went 15-10, 3.14 in 2000 and was named MVP of the NLCS after twice beating the Cardinals, including a complete-game shutout in the decisive Game 5. But his meek opposition to Roger Clemens's World Series bat-throwing tantrum would be a dissatisfying final appearance for the Mets. His parting remarks about the quality of Colorado schools struck Mets fans as a particularly vile strain of malarkey.

Even more miscast than Hampton in Shea Stadium was once-and-future Yankee setter-upper **Mike Stanton** (2003–04), who set a team record with 83 appearances for the 2004 Mets. Stanton deserved Art Howe. Mets fans deserved neither.

Few teams in baseball embraced the player-rights movement more insincerely than did the Mets, whose tradition-bound ownership found free agency particularly abhorrent (and expensive). But to send a signal they were trying, they finally went out and bought free agent **Tom Hausman** (1978–82), an underwhelming right-handed swingman who'd amass a 12-17 record over five seasons in New York.

The Mets dealt Hausman to Atlanta to reunite him with Joe Torre for the 1982 stretch run—too late for Hausman to be on the Braves' brief postseason roster, but enough to bring back left-handed reliever **Carlos Diaz** (1982–83). Diaz had a fine season in 1983 (3-1, 2.05 ERA in 54 games), which Frank Cashen alertly parlayed into a trade for Sid Fernandez. **Paul**

Wilson (1996) was considered the surest bet of the Generation K pitchers, but injuries and ineffectiveness limited the former No. 1 overall draft pick to just 26 games for the Mets.

Remaining pitchers who wore 32: **Jack Hamilton** (1966–67), **Hal Reniff** (1967), **Dean Chance** (1970), **Dick Tidrow** (1984), **Rick Anderson** (1986), **Tom Edens** (1987), **Pete Smith** (1994), **Brent Hinchcliffe** (2001), **Bruce Chen** (2001–02), **Danny Graves** (2005), **Jeremi Gonzalez** (2006), and **Dave Williams** (2006–07). Not a keeper in the bunch.

Kevin Mitchell in his debut (1984) was the first Mets position player to wear No. 32. He was followed by outfielder **Mark Carreon** (1987–89), who, like Mitchell, would later be issued another number by the club. Also, overhyped infielder **Bill Pecota** (1992), and veteran spare-part **Eli Marrero** (one of three 2006 Mets to wear No. 32).

Number of times issued: 25 (22 players, 2 coaches 1, DNP)

Longest Tenured: Jon Matlack (7 seasons, 203 games), Tom Hausman (5 seasons, 125 games)

Best single seasons: Matlack, 1972 (15-10, 2.32 ERA, 169 strikeouts in 244 innings, Rookie of the Year); Matlack, 1974 (13-15, 2.41 ERA, 195 strikeouts in 265.1 innings); Mike Hampton, 2000 (15-10, 3.14, 151 strikeouts in 217.2 innings)

Career statistical leaders: Home runs (Mark Carreon 7), RBI (Bill Pecota 26), batting average (Carreon .318), wins (Matlack 83), saves (Mike Stanton 5), ERA (Matlack 3.03)

1967 by the Numbers

The 1967 Mets were a fascinating, if disappointing, club. Built, torn down, and rebuilt by general manager Bing Devine in his one and only full year on the job, the '67 Mets used a team-record fifty-four players (fifty-five if you count Nolan Ryan, who was on the roster in September but did not appear in a game). They were the ultimate team in transition.

The group featured twenty-seven position players and twenty-seven pitchers. Nine different players would log time at second base, eleven different men manned third base, and twenty different pitchers would make at least one start. There would also be two different managers, after skipper Wes Westrum resigned in September and was replaced on an interim basis by coach Salty Parker.

At the time, the team was the largest in National League history, breaking the record of fifty-three players set by the 1945 Brooklyn Dodgers (thanks to all the men discharged after World War II) and second only to the dreadful 1915 Philadelphia Athletics, who used fifty-six men when Connie Mack pulled a Huizenga and disbanded a pennant winner. The '67 Mets would be the largest roster in all of baseball for another twenty-nine years. (The record through 2007 is shared by the 2002 Indians and 2002 Padres, each of whom used fifty-nine men).

As the saying goes, you can't tell the players without a scorecard, but even that was difficult with the '67 Mets, considering they had fifteen sets of like-numbered teammates (including four-of-a-kind at No. 38, who, unfortunately, weren't aces):

No.	Players
2	Chuck Hiller, Phil Linz
5	Sandy Alomar, Ed Charles
6	Bart Shirley, Bob W. Johnson
18	Al Luplow, Joe Moock
19	Kevin Collins, Hawk Taylor
24	Johnny Lewis, Ken Boswell
26	Bob Shaw, Bill Graham
29	Danny Frisella, Nick Willhite
30	Dick Selma, Nolan Ryan
32	Jack Hamilton, Hal Reniff
33	Chuck Estrada, Bob Hendley
34	Jack Lamabe, Cal Koonce
35	Don Shaw, Billy Wynne
38	Ralph Terry, Dennis Bennett, Billy Wynne, Billy Connors
44	Bill Denehy, Al Schmelz

Although the crowded clubhouse (occupied by 38 different men in September, also a team record) combined to lose 101 games in the Summer of Love, the news wasn't all bad. Tom Seaver arrived with a 16-win, Rookie of the Year campaign. Behind the scenes, Devine's roster gymnastics were unearthing more good than bad. Between the time Devine was named GM in November of 1966 and the time he resigned in December of 1967 to return to the Cardinals, Devine made twenty-five trades, not including drafts or deals that didn't include major league players, gathering in Tommie Agee, Cal Koonce, Ron Taylor, Ed Charles, Al Weis, J. C. Martin, and Art Shamsky, among others. Devine also promoted third-base coach Whitey Herzog, later the manager of four different major league teams, including the mid-'80s Mets nemesis St. Louis Cardinals, to the front office for the first time. As a director of amateur scouting, Herzog led drafts during 1967 that would produce Ken Singleton, Dave Schneck, Jon Matlack, Rod Gaspar, and Gary Gentry.

Nobody might have guessed, but by the time Devine left town in '67, the vast majority of the '69 World Champion Mets were already in the organization. Only two players of significance from that team—Wayne Garrett and Donn Clendenon—would be added after Devine's departure. And his successor in the GM chair, Johnny Murphy, made no trades at all in 1968.

#33: PAIN RELIEF

In the early days of the Mets, the road to New York often went through Milwaukee.

With the Mets starving for talent and still developing a minor league system of their own, the Polo Grounds in the early 1960s became a virtual dumping ground for prospects who couldn't crack the talented Milwaukee Braves roster or suspects who did and failed.

Between 1962 and 1965 the Milwaukee-to-New York pipeline delivered Braves organization players Frank Thomas, John DeMerit, Ken MacKenzie, Rick Herrscher, Felix Mantilla, Lou Klimchock, Frank Lary, Roy McMillan, Carlton Willey, Chico Fernandez, Amado Samuel, Hawk Taylor, Dennis Ribant, and Warren Spahn, as well as hopefuls like Butterball Botz, Adrian Garrett, and Neil Chrisley, none of whom ever made the squad. Many of these players arrived via "conditional deals," whereby the Mets would pay full retail only if the acquirees met certain standards of performance that were never fully spelled out.

John McHale, the Braves' general manager at the time, would regret only one of those deals: **Ron Hunt**, a 21-year-old infielder the Mets plucked out of the Braves' Austin franchise of the Texas League following the 1962 season. Cocksure and enthusiastic, Hunt (1963–66) hustled his way into Casey Stengel's plans for 1963, and that year, still wearing the No. 33 that might be assigned to a longshot rookie, became the team's first farm-raised star.

Hunt led the Mets in runs scored, hits, doubles, batting average, and on-base percentage in his rookie year and finished second in Rookie of the Year voting to a guy named Rose. In 1964, Hunt was selected to start the

All-Star Game, held for the first and only time at Shea Stadium, and singled off starter Dean Chance. He missed half of 1965 with an injury but rebounded to a second All-Star appearance in 1966. Hunt was traded for Tommy Davis following the season.

Hunt is best remembered, though, for his willingness to absorb a fastball in the ribs. He took 41 for the team as a Met—still the franchise record—but that pales in comparison to his 50 HBPs as an Expo in 1971 and 243 career plunks. But a high tolerance for pain is a characteristic of several Met 33s.

You could ask **Eddie Murray**, but there's no guarantee he'll answer you. The gruff first baseman added to his Cooperstown résumé at Shea but happened to do it during the "Worst Team Money Could Buy" era, when tensions between writers and the Mets were at an all-time high. Murray, who rarely spoke to the press, let his bat do the talking and it had plenty to say, especially in 1993 when he drove in 100 runs. But it couldn't save that team from 103 losses.

The San Francisco Giants gave up Hall of Famer Orlando Cepeda to acquire **Ray Sadecki**, a former 20-game winner whom they shipped, four years later, to the Mets for a pair of minor leaguers: Jim Gosger and Bob Heise. It was a comparatively minor steal for the Mets, as Sadecki (1970–74, 1977) provided valuable service as a sixth man for the early '70s Mets and would eventually be traded back to the Cardinals for Joe Torre. The Mets reacquired Sadecki for a final go-round in 1977 but released him in early May.

Between Sadecki's two stints, No. 33 went to **Ken Sanders** (1975–76), a one-time relief ace of the Brewers who did some effective late-career work for the Mets. His 1975 season was interrupted by a scary injury when a return warm-up throw from catcher John Stearns struck Sanders square in the eye. Ouch.

Brooklyn-born lefty **Pete Falcone** (1979–82) battled for four difficult years but a tendency toward wildness and the gopher ball was his undoing.

One of the great revelations of 2006 was coming to realize that it was rookie **John Maine**, and not Anna Benson, or even Jorge Julio, who was the central figure in the Kris Benson trade. While several veteran teammates dropped to injury, Maine (2006–07) thrust himself into the rotation with two solid postseason starts as a rookie in 2006. Deserving of, but not selected for, an All-Star berth in '07, he quietly continued about his business and by season's end had won 15 games, which tied him with Oliver Perez for the team lead.

The rest of the 33s are backup catchers **Barry Lyons** (1986–90), **Charlie O'Brien** (1990), **Kelly Stinnett** (1994–95), **Tim Spehr** (1998), and **Mike DiFelice** (2005); lunchbucket pitchers **Chuck Estrada** (1967), **Bob Hendley** (1967), **Billy Connors** (1968), **Les Rohr** (1969), **Bill Latham** (1985), **Anthony Young** (1991), **Mike Bacsik** (2002–03), **Tyler Yates** (2004), and **Jose Santiago** (2005); and bench players **Dan Norman** (1977), **Clint Hurdle** (1983), **Andy Tomberlin** (1996–97), and **Mike Kinkade** (1998–2000). Outfielder **Bubba Trammell** (2000) had more World Series RBI (3) than any Met besides Mike Piazza against the Yankees, so of course he was immediately dispatched for worn-out reliever **Donne Wall** (2001).

Photo by Dan Carubia

Number of times issued: 28 (26 players)

Longest tenured: Ray Sadecki (6 seasons, 165 games) Ron Hunt (4 seasons, 459 games), Pete Falcone (4 seasons, 145 games)

Best single seasons: Hunt, 1964 (.303/.357/.406, 6 HR, 42 RBI, 11 HBP); Eddie Murray, 1993 (.285/.325/.467, 27 HR, 100 RBI); Sadecki, 1971 (7-7, 2.92 ERA); John Maine, 2007 (15-10, 3.91 ERA, 180 strikeouts in 191 innings); Pete Falcone, 1981 (5-3, 2.55 ERA)

Career statistical leaders: Home runs (Murray 43, Hunt 20), RBI (Murray 193, Hunt 127), batting average (Hunt .282, Murray .274), wins (Sadecki 30, Falcone 26), saves (Ken Sanders 6), ERA (Sanders 2.60, Sadecki 3.36)

Gotto's Logo Outlasts NY

In November 1961 a lot of people had no idea who or what the Mets were. Joan Payson favored Meadowlarks as the expansion club's name, but she demurred to public opinion when fans chose "Mets" in a contest. Mets seemed to fit. Newspaper writers tired of typing out "Metropolitan Baseball Club, Inc.," the company name certified by the National League eight months earlier, had already dubbed the new club "Mets." That had also been the name of an American Association club in the 1880s housed in the original Polo Grounds, just north of Central Park on 111th Street. (The "new" Mets were set to play in the fourth incarnation of the place, at 155th Street and Eighth Avenue.) But even as everyone agreed on the name, what exactly was a Met and what did one look like? Ray Gotto decided that with a flourish of his pen.

Gotto, a cartoonist who created the syndicated strip "Ozark Ike" about a hillbilly four-sport star, submitted the winning design out of five hundred entrants. Noted illustrator John Groth of *Sports Illustrated* was part of a three-man selection committee, as were representatives of two New York dailies that have long ceased to exist. Gotto was paid $1,000, while the three runners-up received season tickets. (Insert joke here.)

Gotto's iconic design featured the New York skyline, including such landmarks of the day as the Empire State Building, the Williamsburg Savings Bank, the Woolworth Building, and the United Nations. The buildings were silhouetted in Dodger blue and "Mets" was colored Giant orange—the Mets have never had a problem borrowing from their predecessors, as the team's initial roster would prove—and the bridge in the foreground was white, as was the sky behind the city. Lest anyone forget it was a baseball club, orange stitches tied together the ball motif. In case anyone wondered where it was based, "NY" was tucked in just above the "M" in "Mets," or on the side of the Williamsburg Savings Bank building.

The logo remained virtually unchanged until 1999, when "NY" was dropped and "TM" added to the right of the UN Building, lest anyone forget the logo was trademarked (a Register mark had appeared in that spot since the early 1990s). The club still had the "NY" on the logo in 1999 spring training, but "NY" was gone in the regular season. Mets exec Mark Bingham told Uni Watch at the time, "The 'NY' on the logo never matched the one on the caps. The one on the logo was more primitive looking, sort of a stick-figure 'NY.'" So the Mets got rid of it. By then, the skyline was black with "Mets" in blue and outlined in orange on the black uniforms. It remained its original color on the white and pinstriped uniforms.

If only everything stood the test of time like the Mets logo. It's essentially the same as it was forty-five years ago. Gotto's script "Mets" has appeared on countless items from ashtrays to underwear. Meanwhile, that first beer at the Polo Grounds cost 45 cents and a box seat was just $3.50. Add a zero to each and you're still not in the ballpark today. Times have changed, but so have those 120-loss Mets.

#34: IT'S A SETUP

In a uniform that's occasionally hosted players who delivered little when much was expected (see Kris Benson), **Bob Apodaca** provided a pleasant counterpoint.

Undersized and undrafted, Apodaca used an effective sinkerball to work his way into the Mets' bullpen, where he collected 16 wins and 26 saves while posting a 2.86 ERA over four-plus seasons. The Mets threw Apodaca directly into fire, asking him to close out 1974's home opener, which closer Tug McGraw missed due to illness. With two Cardinals on base, one out, and the Mets clinging to a 3-2 lead, Apodaca induced Tim McCarver to bounce into a game-ending 1-6-3 double play and saved the game for Jerry Koosman.

Apodaca, who to that point had an ERA of infinity—he'd given up a run without recording an out in his major league debut the previous September—was relieved to have finally gotten an out. He remarked to the *New York Times* that shaking Jerry Grote's hand afterward felt better than anything, "except maybe sex."

Elbow injuries ended Dack's pitching career, but he returned in 1997 to coach the Mets pitchers—itself a group of overachievers. He was removed in the warning-shot firings of 1999 and was last spotted in the 2007 World Series, directing a pitching staff in the Rockies, where, humidor or no, many thought arms would never flourish.

Apodaca was the last in a string of quietly successful setup relievers to have worn 34 for the Mets. A scrap-heap pickup from the Cubs, **Cal Koonce** (1967–70) won 6 games in relief, and saved 7, for the 1969 Mets. **Danny Frisella** (1970–72) led the Mets in appearances and saves in 1971. His right-handed forkball complemented McGraw's screwgie from the left side, as the two combined for 19 wins and a 1.82 ERA in '71. Frisella was traded to Atlanta in the Felix Millan deal. He tragically died in an offseason dune buggy accident while still an active player.

Veteran pitcher **Dave Hillman** was the first wearer of the 34 jersey in 1962, but many would follow. **Jimmy Piersall** ran the bases backwards after cracking his 100th career home run with the 1963 Mets and was summarily traded to California. Later that year, outfielder **Cleon Jones** made his earliest Mets appearances.

Dennis Musgraves (1965), **Gerry Arrigo** (1966), **Jack Lamabe** (1967), and **Phil Hennigan** (1973) all had brief employment in the Mets' bullpen, while **Nolan Ryan** (1966) made his debut in 34 (2 games, 15.00 ERA). He would switch to 30, which, along with 34, would later be retired by other teams in his honor.

Journeyman right-hander **Ray Burris** (1980) led the 1980 Mets in innings pitched and starts—not to mention losses and home runs allowed—illustrating much about the Mets pitching woes in that 95-loss season. Following Burris were **Ed Lynch** (making his Mets debut in 1981), outfield reserve **Rusty Tillman** (1982), and beloved-but-ineffectual backup catcher **Junior Ortiz** (1983–84).

The 1990s belonged to a series of brief visitors, including **Mario Diaz** (1990), **Julio Valera** (1990–91), **Chico Walker** (1992–93), **Frank Seminara** (1994), **Blas Minor** (1995–96), **Rick Trlicek** (1996), and **Chuck McElroy** (1999). Valera was a 21-year-old rookie in whom manager Bud Harrelson placed a bit too much faith in 1990. Valera started and lost a September game in Pittsburgh that helped the Pirates pull away from the Mets for good. Walker had an excellent season as a reserve in 1992, playing five positions (second base, third base, and all three outfield slots) and being the only .300 hitter on the "Worst Team Money Could Buy." He homered in his final career at-bat in 1993.

Pedro Astacio (2002–03) came to the Mets with a reputation as a talented injury risk and lived up to those expectations spectacularly. He was very good until his shredded shoulder finally gave out, at which point he was awful. **Kris Benson** (2004–05) arrived at the bloody trade deadline of 2004, but his accomplishments never lived up to the expectations placed on the former No. 1 overall draft pick. And his wife, Anna, wasn't exactly Nancy Seaver. Some believe Anna's outfit, or lack of it, during the Mets Christmas party in 2005 hastened Benson's surprise trade to Baltimore weeks later. That deal brought John Maine and **Jorge Julio** (2006), who was traded for Orlando Hernandez, so nobody much complained . . . besides Anna.

Others: knuckleballer **Dennis Springer** (2000) and relievers **Jerrod Riggan** (2000), **Tom Martin** (2001), and **Ricky Bottalico** (2004). Strapping right-hander **Mike Pelfrey** (2006–07), the Mets' top draft pick in 2005, arrived in the majors quickly but through 2007 was still learning the ropes, as his career ERA of 5.55 illustrates.

Number of times issued: 33 (30 players, 2 coaches, 1 DNP)

Longest tenured: Bob Apodaca (5 seasons, 184 games), Cal Koonce (4 seasons, 119 games), Danny Frisella (3 seasons, 122 games)

Best single seasons: Frisella, 1971 (8-5, 1.99 ERA, 12 saves); Apodaca, 1975 (3-4, 13 saves, 1.49 ERA); Chico Walker, 1992 (.308/.369/.423, 4 HR, 36 RBI, 14 stolen bases)

Career statistical leaders: Home runs (Walker 9), RBI (Walker 55), batting average (Walker .268), wins (Frisella 21, Apodaca 16, Koonce 15, Astacio 15), saves (Apodaca 26, Frisella 22), ERA (Frisella 2.70, Apodaca 2.86)

Take out That Pillbox

The 1976 bicentennial made a lot of people go a little bit loopy. Maybe it was the tall ships, maybe it was the heat, or it could have been the striped polyester pants. The summer of '76 marked the 200th anniversary of our nation as well as the 100th anniversary of the National League, so party hats were ordered for the occasion. Pillbox caps like the ones ballplayers wore back in the day were worn by the Mets, Phillies, Reds, Cardinals, and, of course, Pirates, who kept them on for a decade. (The only franchises that had existed continuously since 1876, however, were the stovepipe-free Braves and Cubs.) The National League, featuring Dave Kingman in right field, wore special white pillbox caps with red stripes and with a script "N" for the All-Star Game festivities in Philadelphia.

Pillbox fever started at Shea a few weeks shy of the Fourth of July. The Mets broke them out for the Memorial Day doubleheader against Pittsburgh. The three orange stripes that wrapped around the blue cap made some fans at home a little queasy, even watching on a black-and-white set, but when the Mets pounded out a 13-2 win in the opener, it seemed that maybe they were on to something. When the Mets predictably lost the nightcap 2-1 despite a rare yet fine start by Bob Apodaca, the sickness returned. The Mets split the July 4 twin-bill against the Cubs wearing the funny caps, and the oldtimers were forced to wear them later that month. Mostly, however, the caps were only seen gathering dust at souvenir stands.

Like the snow white caps two decades later, the next year's yearbook left no photographic evidence that the Mets ever wore such chapeaus at Shea. If only the countless other fashion sins of the '70s could have vanished so easily.

#35: IRREPLACEABLE

Rick Reed (1997–2001) was a 32-year-old journeyman, a veteran of four franchises, and a one-time strike replacement player with all of 10 major league victories when he was invited to the Mets' spring training camp in 1997.

He'd go on to win 59 games and lose 36 over the next four and a half years, becoming the kind of success the Mets had never quite had in No. 35, despite considerable efforts to find one. Among a crowd of longshots and even longer shots, Reed was a bullseye.

Relying on remarkable control and consistency, Reed at once was a revelation and a quiet guy seemingly content to slide behind higher-profile teammates even as he outperformed them. There was some ill will among the likes of John Franco about Reed's replacement player past—his mom had really needed the money—but Reed ignored the slights and performed his job outside the union and inside the strike zone. Reed went 13-9, with a 2.89 ERA in 1997, walking just 31 guys in 208.1 innings. He cut that rate slightly in 1998, when he won a team-high 16 games and made the first of two trips to the All-Star Game.

Reed pitched in five postseason games and the Mets won four of them, including their only victory in the 2000 World Series. Reed's constant strike-throwing left him vulnerable to the home run, and he was less effective as he battled injuries later in his career, but he probably should have been given a chance to finish that career as a Met. Instead he was shipped to Minnesota in 2001 for a dud outfielder, Matt Lawton, in a deal that did more to fuel tensions between Steve Phillips and Bobby Valentine than it did to help the Mets catch the Braves.

The circumstances were different, but **Joe Smith** (2007) faced Reed-like odds when he arrived at big-league camp in 2007. A hard-throwing sidewinder selected in the previous summer's college draft, and with only weeks of minor league experience, Smith rode an ability to coax ground-balls to an unexpected job in the Mets' bullpen and did not allow an earned run his first 17 appearances over 15.1 innings. Fatigue would even-tually take a toll on Smith, who pitched to an ERA of 5.28 after his torrid start and spent some time in the minors.

Chunky reliever **David Weathers** (2002–04) led the Mets in appear-ances twice and pitched to a respectable 3.22 ERA as the Mets faded from relevancy. After trading Weathers in 2004, they got **Mike DeJean** (2004–05) to take his innings. DeJean had a brief encounter with Metly suc-cess before it was revealed that he was pitching with a broken leg.

Dock Ellis once pitched a no-hitter on acid as a Pirate, but the Mets needed painkillers when he threw in 1979 (3-7, 6.04). Ellis was a Yankee before he was a Met, and the same poison may have affected the ineffec-tive lefty **Lee Guetterman** in 1992. Guetterman was all the Mets had to show for Ron Darling within a year of Darling's departure.

Billy Beane (1985) was the one-time first-round draft pick of the Mets who would become the influential general manager of the Oakland A's and tragic hero of Michael Lewis's fascinating and misunderstood book *Moneyball*. As Lewis relates, Beane was a magnificent athlete who the Mets had considered selecting ahead of Darryl Strawberry in the 1980 draft (the Mets had two first-round choices that year, including the overall top choice). Beane, however, would reject the notion of toolsy ath-leticism necessarily indicating baseball success based on his own trun-cated career with the Mets (3 hits over 18 September at-bats spanning two seasons).

M. Donald Grant's weakness for left-handed reliever **Don Shaw** inter-rupted, and nearly scuttled, the trade that brought Tommie Agee to the Mets. Shaw (1967–68), who pitched effectively before injuries intervened, would wind up being lost to the Expos in the expansion draft. Omar Minaya's weakness for veteran infielders as bench help was sated briefly by **Jose Offerman** (2005). He hit .250 in 53 games.

Southpaw **Randy Jones** (1981–82) had No. 35 retired for him—in San Diego, where he starred for the Padres. He finished second to Tom Seaver in the 1975 Cy Young voting and beat out Jerry Koosman for the trophy a year later. By the time the soft-tossing Jones got to New York, he was battling injuries that would end his career at age thirty-two. **Pat Tabler** (1990) arrived as late-season help for the 1990 stretch drive. Tabler had a freak talent for hitting with the bases loaded, batting .489 in those situations over his career. In his final game as a Met, Tabler came up with the bases loaded . . . and got hit by a pitch.

Other pitchers to don 35: **Ray "Frenchy" Daviault** (1962),**Larry Miller** (1965), **Billy Wynne** (1967), **Charlie Williams** (1971), **Randy Sterling** (1974), **Ed Lynch** (1980–81), **Joe Sambito** (1985), **Kenny Greer** (1993), and **Doug Henry** (1995).

The reserve catcher wing houses **Joe Nolan** (1972), **Luis Rosado** (1977), **John Gibbons** (1986–87), and **Orlando Mercado** (1990). Position players include prospects **Roy Staiger** (1975), **John Christensen** (1984), **Kevin Mitchell** (1986, briefly), and **Craig Shipley** (1989).

Number of times issued: 31 (29 players, 1 DNP, 1 coach)

Longest tenured: Rick Reed (5 seasons, 140 games), David Weathers (3 seasons, 180 games)

Best single seasons: Reed, 1997 (13-9, 2.89, 113 strikeouts, 31 walks in 208.1 innings); Reed, 1998 (16-11, 3.48, 153 strikeouts, 29 walks in 212.1 innings); David Weathers, 2002 (6-3, 2.91 in 71 appearances)

Career statistical leaders: Home runs (Pat Tabler 1, Jose Offerman 1), RBI (Tabler 10, Offerman 10), batting average (Tabler, .279), wins (Reed 59, Weathers 12), saves (Doug Henry 13, Weathers 7), ERA (Weathers 3.22, Reed 3.66)

Snow White and the '97 Mets

The 1997 season began strangely and kept getting stranger. The Mets opened on the West Coast, with every game seemingly held late at night. After stumbling to a 3-6 start with little sleep for the home folks, the Mets took Friday off; another bizarre move, but they didn't want to open at the same time the Yankees raised their newest championship flag. (And silly us, thinking it was because of Good Friday.) So Saturday came and fans huddled under the Grand Central Parkway overpass, grilling while it poured until officials finally saw fit to call the thing off. Then came the strangest part of all: an opening day doubleheader. On Easter.

Not only was the doubleheader crowd of 21,981 the smallest to watch a Shea opener since 1981, but the fans were blinded as well when the Mets took the field dressed in white from head to toe. Well, their spikes weren't white, but everything else was. For the first time in franchise history, the pinstripes were off the home uniform. It was called an "alternate" uniform, and many teams did this, and the Mets still wore the traditional pinstripe uniform for most games. Even the most traditional minded had to admit the snow whites didn't look bad. The hats, however, had to go.

Mets players didn't like the white hats with the blue brim one bit. The term "ice cream man" came up often, and the white hats were discreetly shelved in favor of the blue hats, which now featured an orange button on top for the first time. At least they were blue.

The '98 Mets would go *Mad* magazine—"Spy vs. Spy," white spy against black spy—as they changed uniforms willy-nilly. They wore white or black (that year's hot "alternate") almost every home game; they occasionally donned pinstripes just to throw everyone off. The Mets even pretended the whole white cap thing never happened. The 1998 yearbook used one photo of a player in a white cap: Butch Huskey on Jackie Robinson Night, with his 42 suddenly meaning more. Black or white, it was still baseball.

#36: THE KOOZ

As the story goes, **Jerry Koosman** might have been released as a minor leaguer were it not for the fact that he owed the club some money. So there was a time when Jerry Koosman was indebted to the Mets and not the other way around.

The hard-throwing lefty joined sophomore Tom Seaver in 1968 to form a one-two punch atop the Mets rotation that would last for a decade. Kooz won 19 games in '68 with 7 shutouts and a 2.08 ERA, finishing second to Johnny Bench in Rookie of the Year balloting. Koosman had 17 wins for the 1969 Mets and stepped up in the postseason, winning the crucial Game 2 and the decisive Game 5 of the World Series, allowing just 7 hits and 4 earned runs in 17.2 innings. Koosman pitched 6 postseason games between 1969 and 1973, and the Mets won them all.

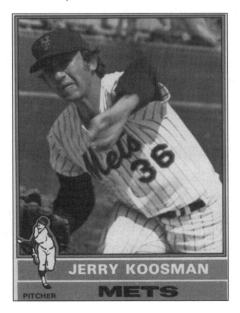

JERRY KOOSMAN
PITCHER   METS

Injuries in 1970 and 1971 robbed Koosman's career of some momentum—he never made the All-Star Game again after 1969—but he re-crafted his game to rely less on power on more on control. A 21-win season in 1976 was his best since his rookie year, but Koosman decayed along with the franchise in the years that followed, going 8-20 as the Mets dismantled in 1977 and an un-Koosmanlike 3-15, 3.75 in 1978. The best lefty starter in franchise history ended his Mets career in Joe Torre's brutal bullpen.

Koosman was traded to Minnesota that winter, then as now, ranking second in franchise history to Seaver in starts (346), complete games (108), innings pitched (2,545), and shutouts (26).

Indelicately, the Mets issued 36 the following spring to **Wayne Twitchell** (1979), a lanky veteran reliever with exceptionally poor control. The sight of Twitchell in 36 was nearly as disturbing as encountering Koosman five years down the road in Phillies jersey No. 37 (the Phils had retired 36 for Robin Roberts). Although the Mets figured Koosman was close to being finished after '78, he hung around the Twins, White Sox, and Phillies through 1985, collecting another 86 victories, including 20 in 1979 for Minnesota.

Sherman "Roadblock" Jones (1962) was the first wearer of the 36 jersey. His nickname described dominating performances as minor-league stopper in the Giants' system, but injuries blocked his opportunity to contribute to the Mets. The most notorious of these involved Jones burning his own eye in a cigarette-lighting mishap shortly before his first scheduled start.

Tracy Stallard (1963–64) was famous for having surrendered Roger Maris's 61st home run, but like most Mets pitchers of the Polo Grounds era, he was vulnerable to giving up the longball to anyone. Stallard in fact ranked tenth in the National League in home runs allowed in 1963—but fifth on his team.

The leader in that department was Stallard's hapless teammate **Roger Craig**, who famously ended his losing streak by switching from 38 to 13 in 1963 after trying and failing, on July 19, 1963, while wearing Stallard's No. 36 uniform. Neither switcheroo worked.

Cerebral right-handed junkballer **Ed Lynch** (1982–86) toiled through the early '80s for the Mets as a swingman and fifth starter before the talent of the staff he served overwhelmed him and he was traded to the Cubs during the triumphant 1986 season. Despite appearing in just one game in '86, his teammates voted him a full share of the World Series bonus. Lynch later became general manager of the Cubs.

When the Mets were in need of a starter in 1998, they sent setup man **Greg McMichael** (1997–98; 1998–99) to the Dodgers in a trade for Hideo Nomo. A month later, looking for relief, the Mets dealt with the Dodgers to get McMichael back. Between McMichael's two stints the Mets issued 36 to **Jeff Tam**. McMichael was a change-up artist whose best season was 1997 when he won 7 games and saved 7.

Grant Roberts (2000–04) was a big-time prospect who made headlines for all the wrong reasons. Embarrassing photos of him mowing down a bong surfaced in the middle of what would be his best season in 2002. He has not appeared in a major league game since the Mets released him.

Perfection in the 36 jersey is possible if the timing is right. **Manny Hernandez** (1989) pitched one inning as a Met allowing no hits, walks, or errors. Reserve catcher **Dave Liddell** (1990) had just one turn at bat in the majors, a pinch-hit single. Liddell was acquired for Lynch way back in 1986.

Others, far from perfect: pitchers **Bob G. Miller** (1962), **Jim Bethke** (1965), **Mark Bomback** (1980), **Dan Boitano** (1981), **Tony Castillo** (1991), **Mike Birkbeck** (1995), **Don Florence** (1995), **Manny Aybar** (2005), and **Henry Owens** (2006). Reliever **Willie Collazo**, who arrived late in the 2007 season, suffered the indignity of having his name spelled improperly on his home jersey (the road jersey, in which he made his debut, had it right: Two *L*'s, one *Z*, not the other way around).

Infielders **Kevin Baez** (1990, 1992) and **Tito Navarro** (1993), catcher **Kelly Stinnett** (2006), and outfielder **Chip Ambres**, whose lone hit as a 2007 Met was a game-winner, fill out the roster.

Number of times issued: 27 (25 players)

Longest tenured: Jerry Koosman (12 seasons, 376 games), Ed Lynch (5 seasons, 145 games)

Best single seasons: Koosman, 1968 (19-12, 2.08 ERA, 17 complete games, 7 shutouts, All-Star); Koosman, 1976 (21-10, 2.69 ERA, 17 complete games); Lynch, 1985 (10-8, 3.44 ERA, 6 complete games)

Career statistical leaders: Wins (Koosman 140, Lynch 33), saves (Greg McMichael 8, Koosman 5), ERA (Koosman 3.09)

Two-Timing Mets

Robert Frost wrote "Nothing Gold Can Stay" almost forty years before the Mets first took breath. If he'd lived beyond the Mets' first year of existence, Frost, a noted baseball fan, might have said, "Everything Blue and Orange Shall Return" . . . or perhaps not.

There is little literary merit concerning the second helpings of the thirty-two once-and-again Mets. To put it bluntly, few have been better the second time around, but there is something poetic about the rebirth of a player in a new form. Some have returned to Shea Stadium to add a gentle flourish to a distinguished career: Rusty Staub as a part-time player and the game's best pinch hitter in the early 1980s; Kevin McReynolds coming back as a live body in a trade for villainous Vince Coleman and calling it quits with class during the strike; and Todd Zeile, freed from the shackles of everyday playerhood, capping off an interesting career with a home run in his last at-bat, as a catcher no less (and fans gasping in horror that an out-the-door Art Howe might spoil the last line by making Zeile bat one more time).

There have also been a few career-ending clunkers: early favorite Al Jackson coming back after so much good pitching for bad clubs, being a 1969 Met and . . . stinking up the joint with a 10.64 ERA before the Reds bought him; Ray Sadecki, a versatile pitcher for Yogi Berra's believers, made the '77 club out of spring training and was released not long before manager Joe Frazier got the axe; and David Cone, who left too soon in 1992 and stayed too long in 2003, returning from retirement to allow 37 baserunners in 18 innings before getting hurt and quitting for good.

Then there's Greg McMichael, or Greg McMuffin as poet of the airwaves Steve Somers liked to call him, who was traded for prior to 1997, traded to the Dodgers in June 1998, traded for a month later, and then sent with Jason Isringhausen to Oakland in the infamous Billy Taylor debacle of '99. Original Met Bob L. Miller and backup catcher Kelly Stinnett each went twelve seasons between games for the club.

If there is any poetry in second acts at Shea, it is written by one George Thomas Seaver. And even those verses turn bitter. The Franchise was in Big Red limbo for more than five years, returning to a Mets club that wasn't much better than the one he left, but at least it was near the terminus of the club's enduring rebuilding project. Then, after a handful of pleasant reminiscences at Shea, he was gone again in a free-agent compensation snafu. Imagine Seaver on the same staff as young Dwight Gooden, giving lessons in pitching and life. As John Greenleaf Whittier wrote a century prior, "For all sad words of tongue and pen, / The saddest are these: 'It might have been!'"

Below are the once-bitten, twice-shy Mets, listed chronologically from when they became two-timers. And a one, and a two . . .

Player	1st Tour	2nd Tour	Number(s)
Frank Lary	1964	1965	17
Al Jackson	1962–65	1968–69	15/38
Jim Gosger	1969	1973–74	18/19, 5
Bob L. Miller	1962	1973–74	24/30
Ray Sadecki	1970–74	1977	33
Tim Foli	1970–71	1978–79	19
Mike Jorgensen	1968, 1970–71	1980–83	10, 16/22
Dave Kingman	1975–77	1981–83	26
Rusty Staub	1972–75	1981–85	4, 10/10
Tom Seaver	1967–77	1983	41
Bill Almon	1980	1985	25/2
Lee Mazzilli	1976–81	1986–89	12, 16/13
Clint Hurdle	1983, 1985	1987	33/13/7
Alex Treviño	1978–81	1990	29/6
Hubie Brooks	1980–84	1991	62, 39, 7/7
Jeff McKnight	1989	1992–94	15/5, 7, 17, 18
Kevin McReynolds	1987–91	1994	22
Greg McMichael	1997–98	1998–99	36
Bobby Bonilla	1992–95	1999	25
Josias Manzanillo	1993–95	1999	39
Jeff Tam	1998	1999	38, 36/36
Bill Pulsipher	1995, 1998	2000	21/25
Lenny Harris	1998	2000–01	19
Pete Walker	1995	2001–02	49/43
Roger Cedeño	1999	2002–03	19
Jeromy Burnitz	1993–94	2002–03	5/20
Tsuyoshi Shinjo	2001	2003	5
David Cone	1987–92	2003	44, 17/16
Todd Zeile	2000–01	2004	9/27
Roberto Hernandez	2005	2006	39/49, 39
Kelly Stinnett	1994–95	2006	33/36
Marlon Anderson	2005	2007	18/23

Note: The / indicates a change of number within a tour. For the Jeff McKnight story, see the last chapter.

#37: THE ONE AND ONLY CASEY

Because there was only one **Casey Stengel**, No. 37 is the only number to be issued once and only once in team history.

Managing a team to a .302 winning percentage isn't the typical route to numerical immortality, but Stengel wasn't a typical manager, and the situation he entered into in 1962 wasn't typical either. Presented with a collection of rejects as the result of a cruelly uncharitable expansion draft, Stengel embraced the role as ambassador of the Mets to help sell the team even as he led to it to new depths of futility.

Stengel had plenty of experience with poor teams, enduring managing stints with the talent-poor Brooklyn Dodgers (1934–36) and Boston Braves (1938–43) as well as a string of minor league franchises. These assignments helped Stengel develop a managing style that drew on the mentors of his playing days (Wilbert Robinson, the clown, and John McGraw, the master strategist). His break came when he was unexpectedly named manager of the Yankees in 1949 and subsequently led them to ten pennants in twelve years. His firing, along with Yankee general manager George Weiss, in the aftermath of the Pirates' surprise victory in the 1960 World Series, freed both men up to lead the new New York franchise.

The Ol' Perfesser had plenty of managerial tricks—he had a good eye for talent, and he used the bullpen and platoons effectively—but it was insufficient weaponry to fight a dearth of talent. Instead Stengel sensed an opportunity to create an attraction. His stream-of-consciousness ramblings and unique turns of phrase were enthusiastically received by writers. His calls for the "Youth of America" to join his "Amazin' Mets" helped sell the franchise to a new generation of players and fans. He even called for the club's ballparks to be decorated with "placards," to express their joy and sorrow at being part of something new. The Mets in no time were outdrawing Casey's former employers in the Bronx.

Following the game of July 24, 1965 (a 5-1 loss to the Phillies) Stengel entertained attendees for the Old Timers' Game scheduled the next day at Toots Shor's restaurant, and at some point, he fell and broke his hip. He officially retired shortly afterward, and the Mets retired jersey No. 37 on September 2 of that year.

Although Stengel is associated closely with No. 37—it was retired for him by the Mets and the Yankees—that association developed rather late in his career. Stengel never wore a number as a player—his playing career ended seven years before numbering became standard practice in 1932. His coaching and managerial career saw him dressed in 31 (Brooklyn, 1932–36), 36 (Brooklyn, 1936), 31 again (Boston Braves, 1938–39), and 32 (Boston Braves, 1940–43) before taking 37 with the Yankees in 1949.

When the Mets acquired Jimmy Piersall, a career-long wearer of No. 37, in 1963, there was some discussion of how the Mets would handle a veteran player whose favored number belonged to the manager. Among the considerations were 37A—a nod to owner Joan Payson's affininity for horse racing—and 73, before they eventually settled on 34, the *New York Times* reported. Some in the organization felt using two 37s would be acceptable, the *Times* added. "If the fans can't tell the difference between them, they don't deserve to be Met fans."

Stengel brought personality to the Mets with a capital *P*. Writers couldn't stop writing when he opened his mouth. Even after he finally put away the uniform, Stengel remained in the club's employ for the last decade of his life. He was a goodwill ambassador and his own translator of Stengel-ese, a language in which sentences rambled on forever without a point but always with a punch line.

"We got some very excellent fellows that we selected them 'cause they were college men," he said of that first Met team in spring training. "We figured if we couldn't find them that was good, we'd get them that was smart, and we checked on the college men and we selected 'em very carefully 'cause they was from Johns Hopkins, which is a very brilliant place, except we found our men was from the clinic instead of the college, and our most valuable man was the orthopedic surgeon which, thank heavens, we did not pick up in the expansion draft but got him on Park Avenue."

Casey reminded fans of the club's humble past at the 1969 World Series and celebrated in the locker room he helped break in. He continued coming to Shea for Old-Timers' Day festivities, even as his body was ravaged by cancer. He died at in 1975 at 85, just a week before Joan Payson.

Number of times issued: 1 (1 manager)
Longest tenured: Casey Stengel, 1962–65
Best single season: Stengel, 1964 (53–109)
Career statistical leader: Stengel 175-404 (.302)
Retired: September 2, 1965

Mets Uniform Controversies

When Kenny Rogers was traded to the Mets in 1999, he was presented with a problem: his favorite uniform number, 37, was retired by the club and impossible to get. Following the lead of players like Carlton Fisk, who reversed his 27 to 72 upon jumping from the Red Sox to the White Sox, Rogers suited up in 73.

Following is a list of similar cases in Mets history, when a player the Mets acquired had some equity in a number already occupied—or retired—by the club, and their resolutions.

Player	Year	# request	But it was taken by	So instead he settled for
Moises Alou	2007	18	Jose Valentin	18; Valentin switched to 22
Carlos Delgado	2006	25	Kazuo Matsui	21
Kazuo Matsui	2004	7	Jose Reyes	25; coach Don Baylor switched to 52
Braden Looper	2004	41	Retired for Tom Seaver	40; Jae Seo switched to 26
Tom Glavine	2003	47	Joe McEwing	47; McEwing switched to 11
Don Baylor (coach)	2003	25	Scott Strickland	25; Strickland switched to 28
John Valentin	2002	13	Edgardo Alfonzo	4
Jeff D'Amico	2002	13	Edgardo Alfonzo	18
Roger Cedeño	2002	19	Lenny Harris	19; Harris was traded a week later in the offseason
Jeromy Burnitz	2002	20	Mark Johnson	20; Johnson switched to 5
Mike Hampton	2000	10	Rey Ordoñez	32
Todd Zeile	2000	27	Dennis Cook	9
Kenny Rogers	1999	37	Casey Stengel	73
Mike Piazza	1998	31	John Franco	31; Franco switched to 45
Tony Fernandez	1993	1	Vince Coleman	1; Coleman switched to 11
Jeff Torborg (mgr.)	1992	10	Dave Magadan	10; Magadan switched to 29
Garry Templeton	1991	1	Vince Coleman	11
Vince Coleman	1990	29	Dave Magadan	1
John Franco	1990	31	Julio Valera	31; Valera switched to 48
Frank Viola	1989	16	Dwight Gooden	26
Lee Mazzilli	1986	16	Dwight Gooden	13

Player	Year	# request	But it was taken by	So instead he settled for
Keith Hernandez	1983	37	Retired for Casey Stengel	17
Felix Millan	1974	17	Teddy Martinez	17; Martinez switched to 23; Dave Schneck switched to 16 to accommodate Martinez
Willie Mays	1972	24	Jim Beachaump	24; Beauchamp switched to 5
Bob Aspromonte	1971	14	Gil Hodges	2; (Aspromonte, a Brooklyn native, wore 14 previously as a tribute to Hodges)
Tommy Davis	1967	12	Johnny Stephenson	12; Stephenson switched to 19
Ken Boyer	1966	14	Ron Swoboda	14; Swoboda switched to 17 (spring training), then to 4 (see Stuart, below)
Dick Stuart	1966	7	Ed Kranepool	17; Stuart was assigned No. 10 upon his arrival just prior to spring training; later that spring, he arranged to take 17 from Swoboda, who was also in uni-number limbo as the result of the newly arrived Ken Boyer
Yogi Berra	1965	8	Chris Cannizzaro	8; Cannizzaro switched to 5
Warren Spahn	1965	21	Ed Kranepool	21; Kranepool switched to 7
Jimmy Piersall	1963	37	Casey Stengel	34
Duke Snider	1963	4	Charlie Neal	11; Snider would switch to 4 following Neal's trade, July 1
Gene Woodling	1962	14	Gil Hodges	11

#38: COFFEE IS FOR CLOSERS

Number 38 in Mets history has often been a reliever's number. Many times, however, it hasn't provided nearly enough relief.

New York is especially tough on its relievers. Fans are often quick to dismiss a ho-hum 9th inning in a close win, preferring to remember the three-run home run or the starter who got them there; a 9th-inning meltdown is recalled far differently. Often forgotten is the 5th-inning error that allowed a crucial run to score or a bases-loaded strikeout by the Mets cleanup hitter—although in New York, it won't take long for these to be second-guessed—while the brunt of the blame usually falls on the man who threw the last pitch.

If you're familiar with the epic 1978 Mets highlight film (dubbed *Turning It Over*) that hit the airwaves every time Pete Flynn's crew unrolled the tarp in '79, you'll recall a poignant scene of Joe Torre removing Jerry Koosman in a 1-0 game in the 9th in favor of **Skip Lockwood** (1975–79). Lockwood then allowed a two-run home run to San Diego's Derrel Thomas, who would hit 3 homers all year. No wonder Kooz won just 3 times in '78 while Lockwood set the franchise record with 13 losses in relief.

Lockwood, a bespectacled Bostonian who started his major league career as an infielder, was actually better than dramatized. In five seasons with the Mets, he blew just 18 of 83 saves as the team's primary reliever before "closer" became the operative word. He had a 2.80 ERA in 227 career appearances for the Mets. Lockwood led the team in saves for four straight years, something no Met reliever did until John Franco came along (two of Ron Taylor's four years as leader came when saves were still an "unofficial" statistic, pre-1969).

Rick Aguilera (1985–86, 1989) began his career in the rotation but won one of the most memorable games in Mets history in relief. Aggie got the win in Game 6 of the 1986 World Series after allowing two Boston runs in the top of the inning. He switched out of 38 after the Series before jumping back in for the '89 season. By then he'd made the conversion to the pen and showed the stuff of an excellent reliever. He was a great one . . . only it was with Minnesota after he became part of the package that landed Frank Viola.

Nondescript pen men included the "not in the Hall of Fame" **Bob Gibson** (1987), **Blaine Beatty** (1989–91), **Dave Telgheder** (1993–95), **Jeff Tam** (1998), and **Jerrod Riggan** (2001).

Roger Craig (1962–63) started the first Mets game ever and was rewarded for his pioneering efforts by leading the league in losses in both his years with the Mets (24 and 22). He set a losing precedent for 38s that lasted through **Ed Bauta** (1963), **Willard Hunter** (1964), **Dave Eilers** (1965–66), **Ralph Terry** (1966–67), **Dennis Bennett** (1967), **Billy Connors** (1967), **Al Jackson** (1968–69), **Jesse Hudson** (1969), and **Rich Folkers** (1970). **Buzz Capra** (1971–73) finally managed a winning mark in 1972 (3-2). **Jerry Cram** (1974–75) never started (or won) a game as a Met, but he pitched eight scoreless innings one night in September 1974—from the 17th to the 24th against St. Louis—and the Mets promptly lost the inning after he was removed.

Jae Seo (2002) and **Pat Strange** (2002) each made their Mets/major league debut in 38. **James Baldwin** (2004) made two ineffective starts before being asked to leave.

Paul Wilson prequel **Tim Leary** debuted in 1981 as perhaps the club's most highly touted young pitcher since Tom Seaver, but Leary hurt his arm in the Chicago chill after three innings and returned as damaged goods in '83 and '84. **Dave Mlicki** (1995–98) was one of those workaday starters who marked the mid-1990s Mets. Props to Mlicki for shutting out (but not up) the Yankees in the first regular-season game between the two teams in '97.

While Mlicki has that going for him, which is nice, **Victor Zambrano** (2004–06) could never outlive the legacy of who he wasn't. In a trade certain to be debated into the ground for years, the Mets acquired Zambrano (and, don't forget, Bartolome Fortunato) from Tampa Bay for top prospect Scott Kazmir (and not-so-top prospect Jose Diaz) on July 30, 2004. Zambrano's time in New York can best be described as a lab experiment of mad scientist pitching coach Rick Peterson. Peterson deservedly kept his job; GM Jim Duquette did not. Following that fateful trade, Zambrano has won only 10 games, while Kazmir, an All-Star in 2006, has won 35 and led the American League in strikeouts in 2007.

With the 2007 bullpen reeling in a massive September swoon, the Mets hastily called up **Carlos Muniz** on September 21. But the sickness was contagious. Muniz, who spent most of the season in Class AA Binghamton, made his debut mopping up after a rotten Tom Glavine start in Washington, giving up two seemingly meaningless tack-on runs runs that loomed large when the Mets rallied for 6 in the 9th only to fall, 10-9.

Pat Howell, the only position player ever to wear No. 38 for the Mets, spent the summer of 1992 chasing flies in center field (he could go get it) and getting the occasional start at leadoff.

Number of times issued: 29 (28 players)

Longest tenured: Skip Lockwood (5 seasons, 227 games), Dave Mlicki (4 seasons, 122 games), Rick Aguilera (3 seasons, 85 games), Roger Craig (2 seasons, 71 games)

Best single seasons: Lockwood, 1976 (10-7, 2.67 ERA, 19 saves, 108 strikeouts in 94.1 innings); Aguilera, 1985 (10-7, 3.24 ERA, 74 strikeouts in 122.1 innings); Aguilera, 1986 (10-7, 3.88 ERA, 104 strikeouts in 141.2 innings)

Career statistical leaders: Wins (Aguilera 26, Lockwood 24, Mlicki 24), saves (Lockwood 65), ERA (Lockwood 2.80)

Patches, Part I: From Fair to Foul

The Mets wore a patch on their left sleeve for their first game in the major leagues. For their second game, they didn't wear any. The Mets wore the patch with the familiar Mets skyline logo only on their road uniforms from 1962 to 1966. At the Polo Grounds their sleeves were as bare as their cupboard was of talent.

The Mets moved to Shea Stadium in 1964, coinciding with the New York World's Fair. The club commemorated the event with a patch that featured the fair's icon: the "Unisphere," a twelve-story, twenty-ton, space-age globe made by U.S. Steel. The left side of the patch was blue and the right side orange with a diagonal white line splitting the image. It was the first patch worn by the Mets at home. It was worn on the road as well—on the left sleeve—with the skyline patch moving to the right sleeve on the road uniforms.

By 1966, the World's Fair was over and the Unisphere patch disappeared (the actual Unisphere remains a half-mile south of Shea), and for the first time the Mets put the skyline logo patch on the left sleeve of their home uniform. That all changed in 1969. A 100th anniversary patch with the now well-known MLB logo of a silhouetted batter (said to be modeled after Twins slugger Harmon Killebrew) was worn on the left sleeve of every team in 1969 to commemorate a century of acknowledged professional baseball. The Mets ditched the skyline logo during their signature '69 season but brought it back for the World Series. The Mets wore the skyline logo on their left sleeves and shifted the MLB logo to the right on their pinstripe uniforms.

The Mets wore no skyline logo patch at Baltimore's Memorial Stadium (they hadn't worn it on home or away uniforms against Atlanta in the first NLCS). But the skyline logo patch worked wonders at Shea. How else could anyone explain Agee's catches, Swoboda's dive, the ball glancing off J. C. Martin's wrist, the shoe polish incident, or the home runs or miracle culmination that followed?

For the next dozen years, the Mets kept the skyline patch on the left sleeve of their home and away uniforms. All National League clubs were required to wear a red, white, and blue National League patch that included a handlebar mustache and pillbox cap, plus stars and stripes on their right sleeve to honor the NL's centennial, which coincided nicely with America's bicentennial in 1976. The left sleeve was crowded with the skyline logo along with a black armband for departed Joan Payson and Casey Stengel. The skyline logo remained on the left sleeve through the Joe Torre years, even as players and fans disappeared in droves. Despite slogans to the contrary, the magic had presumably run dry by 1982. The skyline logo came off.

#39: RISK MANAGEMENT

The Mets have had some great rookies in their history, but no rookie arrived in a great season and enjoyed it quite like **Gary Gentry**. Gentry was in the middle of everything in 1969. His major league debut was the game Tommie Agee hit his one-of-a-kind blast into the upper deck at Shea; he pitched the NL East clincher against St. Louis; he started the pennant-clincher against the Braves; and was twice bailed out in Game 3 of the World Series by Agee's miraculous catches. That first year proved impossible to top.

Drafted by three different teams, Gentry spurned them all, and some felt he got what he deserved when the lowly Mets selected and signed him out of baseball factory Arizona State in 1967. He made the Mets out of spring training less than two years later. Gentry (1969–72) couldn't have picked a better place to be than Shea Stadium, making 37 starts (including two in the postseason) and winning 14 for the world champs. He remained steady, if unspectacular, through '72. Yet he still cast a large enough shadow to net Felix Millan and George Stone from Atlanta on his way out of town.

Nino Espinosa (1975–78) brought back playoff-fixture Richie Hebner just before the '79 season. Little did anyone realize how quickly Nino and his frilly fro would be missed. A 200-inning, double-digit winner on the worst team in the league was worth his weight in gold compared to a hacking, grave-digging malcontent who'd played in seven NLCS and reached one World Series.

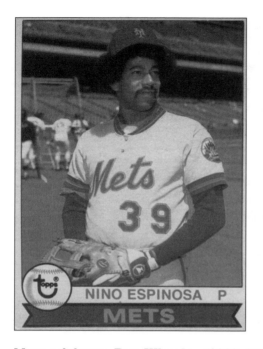

NINO ESPINOSA   P

METS

From 1982 to 1987, tuning in a Mets game and seeing 39 on the mound usually meant the Mets were in trouble or soon to be there: **Doug Sisk** was pitching. A hard-throwing sinkerballer, Sisk (known as Doug "Risk" in his day) routinely created chaos out of order. His numbers weren't bad (33 saves, 3.10 career ERA), but rarely was there a dull moment achieving them. Believe it or not, he pitched once in the 1986 NLCS *and* World Series—both losses—and allowed no runs.

Dick Selma (1966–68) paid his dues on lousy Mets teams only to wind up getting traded to the Cubs and seeing the Mets celebrate. **Dan Wheeler** (2003–04) enjoyed it the opposite way. A bargain-bin pickup, Wheeler had been one of the few pleasant surprises of 2003, but he was dealt just days before the September 2004 deadline to be on a team's postseason roster. And when the Astros finally won a postseason series after forty-two years of existence, who was on the mound to get the last out? Wheeler.

Roberto Hernandez won a bullpen role in 2005 and did well enough in New York so that Pittsburgh threw money at him in '06. No worries, though. After reliever Duaner Sanchez was injured in a cab accident—wear your seat belts, people!—the Mets swifty reacquired Hernandez. Bert, however, lost his effectiveness along the way at age forty-one. He had also lost his number to **Pedro Feliciano** (2006), but Feliciano obligingly changed digits.

The number has also served as a staging area for better times ahead for a handful of Mets hitters. **Hubie Brooks** donned 39 briefly in 1980. **Jeff Kent** wore it for a month after coming to the Mets from Toronto in the David Cone trade in 1992. And before his overpriced Kona concession ever arrived at Shea, **Benny Agbayani** was a warm body in 39 in '98.

Others: **Steve Dillon** (1963–64), **Tommy Moore** (1972–73), **John Strohmayer** (1973–74), **Phil Lombardi** (1989), **Kelvin Torve** (1990–91), **Rich Saveur** (1991), **Josias Manzanillo** (1993–95, 1999), **Juan Acevedo** (1997), **Rick Wilkins** (1998), **Jim Mann** (2000), **Dicky Gonzalez** (2001), sidearming reliever **Steve Reed** (2002), and southpaw **Vic Darensbourg** (2004).

Number of times issued: 27 (24 players)

Longest tenured: Doug Sisk (5 seasons, 263 games), Gary Gentry (4 seasons, 131 games), Dick Selma (4 seasons, 105 games)

Best single seasons: Gentry, 1969 (13-12, 3.43 ERA, 154 strikeouts in 233.2 innings); Espinosa, 1977 (10-13, 3.42 ERA, 105 strikeouts in 200 innings); Sisk, 1983 (1-3, 2.24 ERA, 11 saves, 67 games

Career statistical leaders: Home runs (Kent 3, Brooks 1), RBI (Kent 15, Brooks 10), batting average (Brooks .309, Kent .239), wins (Gentry 41, Espinosa 24), saves (Sisk 33), ERA (Sisk 3.10, Selma 3.16)

Patches, Part II: Racing the Skyline

The development of patches on Mets uniform sleeves in the 1980s was directly related to substantial changes in the uniform. A blue alternate uni plus road grays with a racing stripe led to the banishment of the skyline logo from the sleeve for eleven years

The Mets did wear a patch on their left sleeve for one year during that period: 1986. A 25th anniversary patch featured the skyline logo as the centerpiece with crossed bats set inside a diamond on a blue field. The edges of the diamond were trimmed in orange and white. The diamond had "1986" at first base and "1962" at third, and the home plate area read "25th anniversary." This was placed on top of the racing stripe. Oh, it was busy, but so were the Mets. Garment care instructions? For best results, douse repeatedly with chilled champagne.

The Mets eliminated the racing stripe and resurrected the skyline logo on the left sleeve in 1993, just in time for their worst season in twenty-eight years. The Mets wore two patches a year later. The one on the right sleeve commemorated the 125th anniversary of professional baseball. The Mets boxed the skyline logo on their left sleeve for the 25th anniversary of the "Miracle Mets." The strike wiped out two commemorative pin giveaways as well as everything else on the professional baseball landscape in year 125.

The skyline logo returned, along with the players, in 1995. Despite all the changes and additions to the uniform, the logo has remained on the left sleeve every year since then. In 1997, all major league teams honored Jackie Robinson with a right-sleeve patch. A home plate with an extended rectangle featured Robinson's signature, along with his debut year, the current year, and "50th anniversary" marked his landmark breaking of baseball's color barrier. Shea Stadium was the sight for the national ceremony fifty years to the day of his debut.

For the Mets' 2000 season opener in Tokyo, a patch was worn on the right sleeve of both the Mets and Cubs for the first two major league games ever played in Japan. The same logo was stitched on the hats for those games. A World Series logo was stitched on team hats that October.

September 11, 2001, was one of the most heartrending days in history. In the wake of the terrorist attacks, American flag patches were sewn on the back of every uniform and placed on hats and batting helmets as well. The sleeves simply read, "9-11-01." The Mets wore this remembrance with an American flag on each side of the date on the right sleeve in 2002, along with a patch commemorating the club's forty years in the National League. The gold and green patch, with "Mets" in orange and blue, featured the years 1962 and 2002 along with "40th anniversary." The '02 season ended a lot more like '62 than anyone could have imagined.

Two years later, Shea Stadium celebrated its longevity. The images of the neon pitcher and batter from the exterior of Shea were placed side by side, separated by a diagonal line reminiscent of the Unisphere patch of forty years earlier. The southpaw pitcher started his motion on the left side of the patch with a blue background, while the lefty-swinging batter took a cut on the opposite side with an orange backdrop. The years 1964–2004 as well as "40th anniversary" and "Shea Stadium" appeared in white lettering. Underneath the patch was the catchphrase "Ya Gotta Believe," signed "Tug" in honor of deceased reliever Tug McGraw. (Black armbands and special patches to honor other fallen Mets are featured in Chapter 28.) At the 2004 All-Star Game in Houston, the Shea patch was replaced on the right sleeves of Tom Glavine and Mike Piazza with a 2004 All-Star Game logo. Tug's motto remained, just as it always will in fans' hearts

The final year of Shea, 2008, will likewise feature a tribute patch. A circle shows two sides of Shea: the gray "classic" Shea complete with the colored aluminum siding on the left, and the "modern" blue version with the neon catcher on the right. Above both is a classy yet slightly different version of the familiar skyline. The patch itself reads: "Shea Stadium, 1964–2008, Mets." Go out like a lion, old friend.

#40: STONE, ZACHRY, LOOPER

Nobody likes turning 40. Naturally, that carries over to the Mets. While they've had some good seasons from players age 40, they've had relatively few by anyone wearing that number.

Like Tom Seaver, **Pat Zachry** (1977–82) was a right-handed pitcher and a former Rookie of the Year (Zachry shared the award in 1976 with the Padres' Butch Metzger). That's where the similarities ended. Even as the longest tenured of the four players returned in the Franchise-annihilating deal of 1977, the giraffish Zachry never tempted anyone to forgive M. Donald Grant or forget Tom Seaver.

Zachry's best season at Shea came in 1978, when he made the All-Star team after starting out 10-3 with a 2.90 ERA for a team that was 13 games under .500 at the midway point. But on July 24, with the shine already coming off the All-Star, Zachry allowed a single to Pete Rose in the 7th inning to push the loathed one's hitting streak to 37 straight and tie the twentieth-century NL mark set by Tommy Holmes (on the premises at Shea, because he was a Mets employee). Zachry was so incensed about the hit—and that he'd been yanked against his former team—that he kicked the dugout step, fractured his left foot, and was done for the season. Those 10 wins were the most he had in any of his six seasons as a Met.

Conversely, one of the better little trades in Mets history was the 1972 offseason swap with Atlanta that brought Felix Millan and spare-part left-hander **George Stone** to Flushing. Stone (1973–75) helped the Mets win the NL pennant by going 12-3, 2.80 in '73, though his career rapidly tanked afterward.

Former Brave **Armando Reynoso** (1997–98) seemingly came out of nowhere to lead a postseason drive in 1998, but the drive and Reynoso's Mets career petered out one game too early. His loss against Atlanta in the final game of the season cost the Mets a tie for the Wild Card and did little to redeem a strong 7-3 record. It's hard to blame the team's collapse on Reynoso, whose Musketeer-like mustache and arsenal of off-speed stuff helped compile a 13-6 career mark as a Met.

When multiple competitors all pitched worse in 2003 spring training, rookie **Jae Seo** got the last available seat on the charter to Flushing and responded with a surprisingly strong campaign (9-12, 3.82) despite the media ignoring his request to be called Jae Weong Seo. Oddly, he didn't pitch well enough to go north again in 2004. And that was after surrendering his number to newly acquired closer **Braden Looper** (2004–05). Looper did just fine for a team going nowhere. Yet fans still mastered the tricky feat of turning the "Loop" chant into old-fashioned boos during his second Shea season, when he failed to tell anyone that he was injury plagued.

Calvin Schiraldi (1984–85) did little of note while wearing a Mets uniform, but the prized prospect helped bring Bob Ojeda to Shea in trade and delivered the Mets' second world championship by suffering losses in the final two games of the '86 World Series for Boston. Mercifully, there was no

sign of 40 for the Mets outside of the celebratory pilings-on in the '86 postseason. That would have meant **Randy Niemann** was in the game. As designated mop-up man, you want to keep that guy warming up coffee—not his arm—in the pen. He remained in that vicinity as bullpen coach under several Mets regimes.

Sidearmer **Jeff Innis** (1987–93) was a beguiler in the Mets' bullpen and good clubhouse interview. He was the first Met whose last name began with *I*, and while, of course, there's no "I" in team, there was plenty of team in Innis, who gamely led the Mets in appearances during the sorry seasons of 1991–93.

Brian Bannister (2006) had the ability to fill the bases and then somehow pitch out of it, but it was running the bases that did him in, putting him on the disabled list, knocking him off the depth chart, and banishing him to Kansas City for reliever **Ambiorix Burgos**. That deal looked awful by the end of 2007. Burgos, shaky in 17 relief appearances, was lost to an elbow injury in May. In the meantime, Bannister was making a case to be the American League Rookie of the Year in Kansas City, going 12-9 with a 3.87 ERA over 27 starts in fine health.

Anyone still complaining about Rey Ordoñez's weakness at the plate ought to take a gander at the stats of shortstop **Al Moran** (1963–64), who managed a sickly .193 batting average (and 27 errors) in 119 games as a rookie for the '63 club. His sophomore season was brief.

Lefty **Dick Rusteck** (1966) fired a four-hit, complete-game shutout in his big-league debut but never won another game.

Other 40s: **Jerry Hinsley** (1967), **Bill Short** (1968), **Brent Strom** (1972), **Eric Gunderson** (1995), **Dave Telgheder** (1995), **Mike Fyhrie** (1996), one-game right fielder **Ryan McGuire** (2000), **C. J. Nitkowski** (2001), and dreadlocked pot-smoking outfielder **Tony Tarasco** (2002), the all-time offensive leader in the 40 crowd (which isn't saying much).

Number of times issued: 21

Longest tenured: Jeff Innis (6 seasons, 288 games), Pat Zachry (5 seasons, 135 games)

Best single seasons: George Stone, 1973 (12-3, 2.80 ERA in 148 innings); Zachry, 1978 (10-6, 3.33 ERA in 21 starts); Jae Seo, 2003 (9-12, 3.82 ERA in 188.1 innings)

Career statistical leaders: Home runs (Tony Tarasco 6, Al Moran 1), RBI (Moran 27, Tarasco 15), batting average (Tarasco .250, Moran .195), wins (Zachry 41), saves (Braden Looper 57), ERA (Innis 3.05, Zachry 3.62)

All Right, Pullover

By March 1978, Tom Seaver was gone, Dave Kingman was on his fifth team in nine months, Jerry Grote had been dumped, Felix Millan had been sold (to Japan), Jon Matlack and John Milner had been dealt, and Bud Harrelson was about to be shipped to Philadelphia. All of this was hard to fathom as spring training brought the threat of another season from hell. Even those so helplessly attached to the club that they vowed to just root for the uniform were in for a rude awakening. The Mets pullover had arrived.

The 1978 pullover featured blue and orange bands on each sleeve and similar piping around the neck (two blue bands surrounding an orange band). The club retained the home pinstripes and road gray, both with the skyline logo patch on the left sleeve. The two buttons around the collar of the new threads were as superfluous as the neatly stacked bats in the dugout of what would be the worst team in the National League.

The new look followed a trend that transported the audacious and multicolored outfits of the period from the stands onto the field. The National League seemed especially afflicted as the new style resulted in dizzying orange stripes in Houston, the McDonaldland look in San Diego, and road grays turned blue in Montreal, Philadelphia, St. Louis, and Chicago (the American League had six blue-road-fever victims but still had to answer for the Cleveland Indians' monochromatic maroon softball look). True, the Mets didn't have zippers on their uniforms like the Phillies; they weren't stuck in 1976—or 1876—like the Pirates with their disturbing combination of tops, bottoms, stripes, and pillbox hats; and the Mets hadn't lost all sense like the White Sox with their perpetual pajama party. But the Mets had dipped a toe in the fetid water of trendiness while others kept their shirts buttoned at home and on the road. The Mets would retain a pullover uniform, in varying styles, until 1991.

#41: TOM TERRIFIC

Tom Seaver was serious. Serious about pitching. Serious about winning. Serious when he said to lay off his family.

A signing snafu by the relocating Braves in 1966 enabled the Mets to win a three-team lottery against the Indians and Phillies for the rights to George Thomas Seaver. He was on the Mets' roster a year later and helped pitch them to a world championship two years after that. While a lot of things had to align for the heretofore horrific Mets to actually become amazin', there would have been no chance for a miracle in Flushing in 1969, or much of anything to believe in in '73, without Tom Terrific. He won the Cy Young both years and should have won in '71, too. He made up for it by winning the award in '75 to become the first right-hander with three Cy Youngs.

Seaver didn't think losing was funny and as a rookie shunned the cutesy-poo image of the stumbling expansion club, the worst team since the nineteenth-century Cleveland Spiders (at a time when your great-grandfather might have remembered seeing that team name in the bottom of the standings in the paper). For an organization that had produced zip as far as legitimate pitching prospects at the major league level, Seaver was a revelation. In his first three years he accumulated 57 wins, or more than the entire team had won in any of its first four seasons of existence. Not even Dwight Gooden's remarkable 1985—with Tom still logging innings in an ugly White Sox uniform—could surpass Seaver's '69 mark for wins (25), his '70 record for innings (291), or his '71 marks

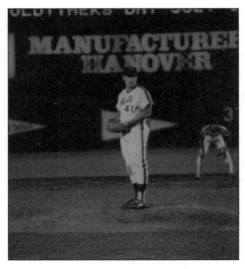

Photo by Dan Carubia

for complete games (21) and strikeouts (289). Seaver's career marks may last as long as the Mets exist. If those records ever are surpassed, including his marks for starts (395), complete games (171), shutouts (44), and innings (3,045), we hope to live long enough to see it.

A malicious 1977 *New York Daily News* column by Dick Young sparked Seaver's demand for a trade, although the deterioration of the franchise around the Franchise may have made such a deal inevitable. Young was booed at the Hall of Fame later that horrible summer when he spoke in Cooperstown. Seaver returned triumphantly in 1983 (9-14 record for a last-place team aside) and received the most thunderous applause Shea Stadium had heard since he left. One of the great moments in uniform number recognition took place at Shea that afternoon. PA announcer Jack Franchetti, after introducing the mostly forgettable starters on opening day, simply said at the end, ". . . and pitching, number 41 . . ." The fans never forgot that number.

A front-office error allowed him to go to the White Sox in '84, but let's be real: it was another team's screw-up that let Seaver become a Met in the first place. He won his 300th in the Bronx for Chicago, but his plaque in Cooperstown—affirmed by the highest percentage of any player in history—has the right "NY" on the cap.

Seaver's number hangs in left field at Shea, the only Mets player so honored. While many complain that the Mets should retire other numbers for players, no one has surpassed Seaver's legacy.

Unfortunately, 41 couldn't be retired retroactively. But at least 41 was never worn by any Mets other than pitchers. One-time Brooklyn ace **Clem Labine** (1962) was the first wearer of the 41 jersey but didn't last through April of the Mets' inaugural campaign. **Grover Powell** (1963) became an overnight sensation by throwing a four-hit shutout in his first start but just as quickly lost his way. He was struck in the face by a Donn Clendenon line drive in his next start and never won another game.

Relievers **Jim Bethke** (1965) and **Gordon Richardson** (1965–66) followed. They combined for a 4-4 lifetime record.

Number of times issued: 5

Longest tenured: Tom Seaver (11 seasons, 401 games)

Best single seasons: Seaver, 1969 (25-7, 2.21 ERA, 208 strikeouts in 273.1 innings, Cy Young Award); Seaver, 1971 (20-10, 1.76 ERA, 289 strikeouts in 286.1 innings); Seaver, 1973 (19-10, 2.08 ERA, 251 strikeouts in 290 innings, Cy Young Award); Seaver, 1975 (22-9, 2.38 ERA, 243 strikeouts in 280.1 innings, Cy Young Award)

Career statistical leaders: Home runs (Seaver, 6), RBI (Seaver, 60), batting average (Seaver, .150), wins (Seaver, 198), ERA (Seaver, 2.57), strikeouts (2,541)

Retired: July 24, 1988

Ed Lynch Called Them Earnies

Although expressing a pitcher's efforts over nine-inning increments has become a bit of quaint notion in an era of relief specialists and pitch counts, the earned-run average has withstood the scrutiny of baseball's quantitative revolution better than most stats of its age.

Anything below 3? That's very good. Over 4? Not so much. In the 1s? Extraordinary. Over 5? Send him back to Lynchburg. It may seem overly simple, but it's a fairly accurate gauge of pitching performance.

Sure, ERA+, which sets the runs allowed to league averages at a baseline of 100 and expresses the number as a percentage above or below that, is useful (Tom Seaver's 166 ERA+ in 1969 was 66 percent better than the league average) but who can figure that out? The formula for ERA (earned runs times nine divided by innings pitched) was about as complicated as a stat needs to be, which is to say, it was the only thing to inspire us to learn multiplication and long division in elementary school.

With that in mind, here's a list of earned-run average over Mets history as arranged by uniform number. Stats are current through 2007. As with strikeouts and wins, the performances of a few extraordinary performers tend to weigh most:

No.	ERA	Notes
41	2.64	Seaver, of course (2.57)
42	3.20	Relievers Roger McDowell (3.13 ERA) and Ron Taylor (3.04) set the pace.
50	3.21	With both 41 and 42 retired, 50 is the "active leader" thanks to Sid Fernandez (3.14).
16	3.24	Dwight Gooden (3.10) carrying Larry Miller (5.02), Hideo Nomo (4.82), and David Cone in 2003 (6.50).
31	3.42	John Franco (2.73) may have been the last pitching inhabitant of this number.
49	3.46	Behold your obscure leader, Dyar Miller (2.58), and his despised second-in-command, Armando Benitez (2.70).
36	3.49	Jerry Koosman (3.09) leads an otherwise shaky pack.
17	3.54	Bret Saberhagen (2.98) and David Cone (3.07) provide rare pleasantries of the early 1990s.
45	3.58	Firemen Tug McGraw (3.17) and Jeff Reardon (2.47) lead the way. John Franco's ERA while wearing 45 (3.65) is nearly a run higher than in No. 31.
32	3.59	Tough scoring off lefties Matlack (3.03) and Hampton (3.14).

#42: ROGER MCDOWELL AND MEMORIES OF JACKIE

In 1997, Major League Baseball officially retired 42 from every team in honor of groundbreaking Brooklyn Dodger Hall of Famer Jackie Robinson. Bud Selig's stunning decree occurred at Shea Stadium on April 15, the fiftieth anniversary of Robinson's legendary debut. President Bill Clinton and Rachel Robinson looked on, completely unaware that they were doing the Mets a favor in discontinuing a number that had seen its share of flops and fops at Shea.

What's a fop? A dictionary definition might lean toward a "dandy" or "trickster," and **Roger McDowell** (1985–89) managed to fill both roles during his Mets career. Memories of McDowell range from the man who made hotfoots (another dictionary definition: the affixing and subsequent lighting of a book of matches to the heel of an unsuspecting teammates' spikes) an art form to his role as the "second spitter" in his *Seinfeld* cameo, but McDowell was one of the most effective right-handed relievers the Mets have ever had. While Jesse Orosco got the deserved kudos for his yeoman's work in 1986, McDowell had more saves, became the first Met to surpass 70 appearances in a season, and won a club record 14 times in relief. He threw a somewhat forgotten five scoreless

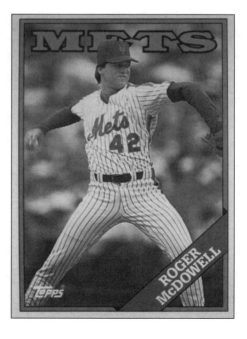

innings preceding Messy Jesse's appearance in Game 6 of the NLCS. Who got the win that clinched the world championship? It was McDowell (despite getting clubbed in his second inning of work), although Orosco's final glove fling is the enduring image of the Mets' Game 7 triumph.

Even after throwing 127-plus innings in relief in each of his first two years in the majors, McDowell remained extremely effective. His career-best 25 saves were overshadowed by the season-crushing home run he allowed to Terry Pendleton in 1987. McDowell was a setup guy who threw multiple innings and still racked up lots of saves (notching 29 more in a Mets uniform than Randy Myers, one of the guys he set up). Alas, the clownish McDowell left town not with a hot-footed bang but with a whimper. As if the 1989 Lenny Dykstra/Juan Samuel trade wasn't a big enough joke, the Mets threw Roger in, too. No one was laughing.

With a 9-4, 2.74 ERA bullpen performance in 1969, **Ron Taylor** (1967–71) played a role similar to McDowell's for the first world championship club. A member of the 1964 world champion St. Louis Cardinals, Taylor was the only man on the '69 staff with postseason experience. He came on to record the final out for the first World Series win in club history.

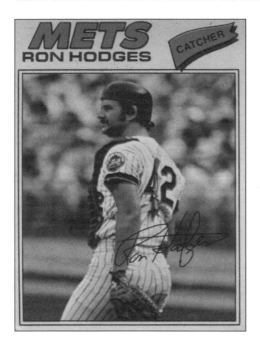

Tug McGraw, who wasn't even used in that Series, soon superseded Taylor's role as game-ending savior, but Taylor was already working toward a new career as a doctor. He eventually became team physician of the Blue Jays, a position he still holds as of the writing of this book.

Chuck Taylor (no relation) followed in 42 in '72, with **Hank Webb** debuting in the number later in the year and **Tom Hall** giving it a one-day test drive in 1975. Hall was acquired while the team was on the road, likely carrying the 42 jersey for catcher **Ron Hodges** if they needed an emergency backup. Hodges (1973–84) was in the minors at the time but had worn it before and would wear it afterward. A long time afterward.

Hodges had his greatest moment as a Met in his first few months on the job. On September 20, 1973, with the hard-charging yet still sub-.500 Mets a game and a half behind Pittsburgh, he entered a tied game in extra innings and was the recipient of the throw after "the carom" that nailed a shocked Richie Zisk at the plate in the 13th. Hodges then singled in the winning run in the bottom of the inning. He punched the clock after that, outlasting sixteen other backstops while only catching 100 games once over a dozen seasons. Lefty-hitting catchers are indeed worth their weight in gold.

Grandfathered into the 42 clause was big, freckled outfielder **Butch Huskey** (1995–98), who hinted at greatness in '97 but didn't quite get there: he switched to 42 (from 10) deliberately as a credit to Robinson. His first major league game saw the Mets get no-hit, and good luck never seemed to find him after that, although the Oklahoma kid could hit the ball a country mile . . . especially in spring training.

Although the Mets assured fans that Mo Vaughn, a former American League MVP who'd missed the entire 2001 season with an torn left bicep, would be healthy, they apparently made no promises he'd be in shape. The first baseman clubbed 26 home runs in 2002, but he could be seen from space. His 2003 campaign was an even bigger disaster, partly because Vaughn had only gotten larger, slower, and more fragile over the offseason and partly because of the fiasco of keeping him on the roster all year as an insurance dodge. Hopefully, the Mo Vaughn experience is the end of the line for a number that got off to a questionable start with 220-hitting outfielder **Larry Elliott** (1964), whose claim to fame in Mets annals is that he was traded for Ed Charles.

Number of times issued: 10 (9 players)

Longest tenured: Ron Hodges (12 seasons, 666 games)

Best single season: Roger McDowell, 1986 (14-9, 3.02 ERA, 22 saves)

Career statistical leaders: Home runs (Butch Huskey 55), RBI (Huskey 211), batting average (Huskey .268), wins (McDowell 33), saves (McDowell 84), ERA (Ron Taylor 3.04, McDowell 3.13)

Retired: April 15, 1997

Days of Remembrance

As discussed elsewhere in this book, and frequently in the ballpark, the Mets have reassuringly high standards when it comes to uniform number retirement. They've granted the honor to just three figures in team history, and to Jackie Robinson, whose number was retired throughout baseball in a surprise announcement at Shea during a 5-0 win over the Dodgers in 1997. The Mets Hall of Fame is a packed house by comparison, with twenty-one members through 2007, representing players, executives, broadcasters, and staff.

Following is a closer look at the circumstances surrounding each Mets uniform number retirement.

37:

Retired in a ceremony prior to a Thursday afternoon game against the Astros on September 2, 1965, attended by only 11,430 fans. Although the Mets rallied late, they lost to the Astros that day, 4-3. The bigger event for Casey Stengel was a press conference at the Hotel Essex three days prior, when the 75-year-old manager formally announced his retirement at the advice of doctors who recently treated Stengel's broken hip. Stengel explained he couldn't manage any longer if he couldn't walk to and from the dugout to change pitchers. Motioning with his cane he remarked, "You don't expect me to go onto the mound and take a pitcher out by putting this around his neck, do you?"

14:

The Mets were criticized for acting too quickly to name a replacement manager when Gil Hodges died suddenly prior to the 1972 season. They chose an appropriate time to memorialize him before an Old-Timers' Day crowd of 48,000 a year later. A home run from Willie Mays—himself an old-timer—provided the difference in a 4-2 win on June 9, 1973. The opponent, fittingly, was Hodges' old club, the Dodgers.

41:

Retired in a Sunday afternoon pregame ceremony on July 24, 1988, two years after Seaver's last game in baseball and twenty-two since he began his career with the Mets. Seaver asked the crowd to indulge him as he said thanks "in my own way" and proceeded to the pitcher's mound, where he turned and bowed to each section of the crowd, drawing thunderous applause from the throng of 46,000. The Mets went out and lost the game that afternoon 4-2 to the Braves, the organization that originally signed Tom Terrific but lost him on a technicality.

#43: THE LOST NATION

Number 43 may provoke the most mentions of "Who?" and "I didn't know he was a Met" of any number in the Mets numerical roster.

Appropriately, Lost Nation, Iowa-born hurler **Jim McAndrew** (1968–73) leads the collection of 43s. While McAndrew was both a '69 and '73 Met, he did not play a pivotal role on either team. That had more to do with the quality of his teammates than McAndrew's failings. He pitched some excellent ball for the early '70s Mets (11-8, 2.80 in 1972).

McAndrew was dispatched to San Diego after the '73 season for Steve Simpson, a reliever who never appeared in another major league game after the trade, but he was head and shoulders above everyone else who came and followed, save for **Terry Leach**. Leach wore the number in 1981–82, before carving out a solid Shea career in a uni number a few blocks south of this bad 43 neighborhood. Still, Leach had his best game—and one of the top performances in team history—wearing 43: a ten-inning, one-hitter against the Phillies in the final weekend of 1982 in what was just his second career start.

Former Yankee **Shane Spencer** made the Mets in 2004 and then proceeded to make an Art Howe–led club look more taken advantage of than usual. Whether it was urinating outside a pizza joint and then beating someone up about it, walking through a bar barefoot and being amazed about a foot getting cut on broken glass, or getting a DWI on a subsequent rehabilitation assignment, Spencer made you forget he was just about the best 43 with a bat the Mets have ever had. He later took his tired act on the road to Japan. Sayonara, Shane.

A promising young pitcher acquired in the Roger Craig trade, **Bill Wakefield** (1963) made a team-high 62 appearances in 1963 but never made it back to the majors again. **Dick Rusteck** (1966) fired a complete-game, four-hit shutout of the Reds in his major league debut in June of 1966 that turned out to be the only win in his career.

Then there were those youngsters whose success came only after leaving the Mets' No. 43 jersey behind. **Juan Berenguer** (1978–80) eventually found control of his wicked fastball as an American League setup man. Lefty bullpenner **Mike Remlinger** (1994–95) and slowball ace **Paul Byrd** (1995–96) were still earning a living as useful ballplayers more than a decade after leaving the Mets.

The Lost Nation: **Ted Schreiber** (1963), **Darrell Sutherland** (1965–66), **Joe Grzenda** (1967), Midnight Massacre acquiree **Paul Siebert** (1977–78), future sabermetric centerfold **Billy Beane** (1984), **John Mitchell** (1986–89), the **Kevin Brown** (1990) who was neither a jerk nor a good pitcher, **Dan Schatzeder** (1990), **Doug Simons** (1991), **Mark Dewey** (1992), **Mickey Weston** (1993), the horrendous **Toby Borland** (1997), pre-heroic **Todd Pratt** (1997), **John Hudek** (1998), **Rigo Beltran** (1998–99), **Pete Walker** (2001–02), **Jaime Cerda** (2002–03), **Bartolome Fortunato** (2004, 2006), **Royce Ring** (2006), and **Jason Vargas** (2007).

Number of times issued: 30 (28 players, 1 DNP)

Longest tenured: Jim McAndrew (6 seasons, 146 games), John Mitchell (4 seasons, 27 games)

Best single seasons: McAndrew, 1972 (11-8, 2.80 ERA, 81 strikeouts in 160.2 innings); McAndrew, 1970 (10-14, 3.56 ERA, 111 strikeouts in 184.1 innings); Bill Wakefield, 1964 (3-5, 3.61 ERA, 62 games)

Career statistical leaders: Home runs (Spencer 4, Todd Pratt 2), RBI (Spencer 26, Pratt 19), batting average (Pratt .283, Spencer .281), wins (McAndrew 36), saves (McAndrew 4, Terry Leach 3), ERA (McAndrew 3.54, Wakefield 3.61)

Styling Mets

Style is hard to define. It's especially difficult when everyone wears the same outfit. Still, any longtime follower of the Mets must admit that there have been a few players whose dress has made them stand out above the crowd, even as the team has endured more costume changes than a high school production of Gilbert and Sullivan's *Mikado*. What follows are a few prime examples in terms of individual dress. Check local listings or search uniwatchblog.com for more.

Player	Digression	Style analysis
Lee Mazzilli	Uniform tighter than the rest	It was the '70s; Maz was the "Italian Stallion"; a screaming female teenager might buy a hot dog, a pretzel, and an RC Cola.
John Pacella	Hat several sizes too small	It flew off after almost every pitch, and he had a handlebar mustache; both more memorable than his pitching in 1980.
Roy McMillan	Nerd specs	Wait, that wasn't an ironic display of cool but actual nerdiness.
Ron Swoboda	Love beads	Leader of the 1960s Mets counterculture reportedly had his snatched away by conservative veteran teammate Don Cardwell on a team flight, nearly leading to fisticuffs before peace triumphed, man.
Bruce Bochy	Gargantuan helmet	After arriving in New York in 1982, his extra-large cranium would not fit in any Mets helmet and he had to wait until his was rushed up from Tidewater before he could play.
Rusty Staub	High socks	Many have tried this, but the '80s Rusty flew in the face of the trend of low stirrups on the way to no stirrups.
Jose Cardenal	Afro hairstyle	Mid-'70s Mets like Nino Espinosa and Billy Baldwin wore afros when they carried more heft as a signal of racial pride, but they couldn't match Cardenal for volume.

Player	Digression	Style analysis
Keith Hernandez	Racing stripes perfectly aligned	A few '80s Mets may have been guilty of this level of fastidiousness, but he's admitted a mild obsession about it; he's also Keith Hernandez.
John Olerud	Batting helmet in the field	A brain aneurysm in college didn't alter his sweet swing, but he thereafter wore a flapless helmet in the field for protection—and as a message to his mom.
Turk Wendell	Necklace of animal teeth on mound	He was getting national press for quirkiness while still in the minors, what did you expect? Turk forever rules the rosin slam!
Tsuyoshi Shinjo	Triple-wide orange sweatbands	The Jim Palmer of Japan, Shinjo is a noted underwear model in his home country. He took to wearing argyle-patterened sweatbands during his final baseball season there.
Derek Bell	Mr. Baggy Pants	Was he too big for his britches, or was it the other way around? Either way, that's just style, man.
Lastings Milledge	Enormous crucifix necklace	Useful in the event he breaks a bat.
Jason Phillips	Helmet facing forward under mask	Really, this is just an excuse to mention those Bono glasses again.
Tom Wilson & Jose Parra	Wearing wrong Met uniform at Yankee Stadium in 2004	Donned the black "Mets" jersey instead of the "New York" road jersey worn by the rest of the team; we know there are too many jerseys, but couldn't they have made this faux pas in Montreal?

#44: POWER OUTAGE

Forty-four is a slugger's number. The Yankees had Reggie Jackson, the Giants had Willie McCovey, while the Braves—and even the Brewers—laid claim to Hank Aaron. The Mets had . . . **Jay Payton**?

That Mets fans had to wait a long time for the oft-injured Payton (1999–2002) to arrive was even more aggravating, but he finally showed up, injury-free at last, as the only groomed member of Bobby Valentine's rag-tag outfield. Payton won the starting center field job in 2000 and made a case for Rookie of the Year. His career stalled amid yet more injuries in 2001. Finally getting it together in 2002, he was shipped off to Denver as part of the final Steve Phillips trading deadline fiasco.

Mike Cameron (2004–05) was more along the lines of the type of 44 Mets fans had in mind. He arrived from Seattle with a reputation for great play in center field and prolific strikeout numbers. Cameron saw his position taken away by Carlos Beltran as 2005 dawned. In fairness, Cammy managed 30 home runs and solid play once he recovered from an early-season injury in '04. Although he was unhappy about moving to right field the following year, he showed great natural ability at the position until he ran smack-dab into Beltran in what may have been the scariest collision in club history. Cameron was fortunate to recover fully from the facial injuries sustained in the collision and wind up patrolling center field in sunny San Diego, where the gruesome scene played out.

For five games in May of 1991, **Howard Johnson** tried to channel Hank, Reggie, and Willie in 44 as he battled a slump. He switched back to 20 after admitting he felt "uncomfortable" in his new number, and that his wife disapproved. It was a wise choice, as HoJo wound up having his best season. (While it's not our place to suggest numbers, it would have been intriguing if HoJo had gone orange-roof crazy with 28—made famous as the number of the ice cream flavors available at his namesake restaurant and hotel chain—but that might have made him feel like an advertising tool, or worse, hungry.)

A Mets outfielder wearing 44 once made the cover of *Sports Illustrated*. Unfortunately, it was diminutive **John Cangelosi** (1994) about to be punched by ex-Met Charlie O'Brien after an ill-advised mound charge. The Cangey-man, with 135 homer-free trips to the plate

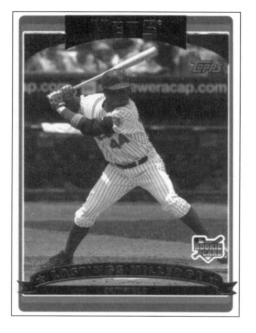

as a Met, was released shortly after creating his own version of the "*SI* Cover Jinx."

Lastings Milledge (2006–07) has more than enough magnetism and style to fill the No. 44 jersey, but questions over whether he had the substance may have sparked his trade to Washington. He could be the one who got away, or another in a long line of underachieving outfielders with Met bloodlines.

Devoid of true sluggers in the 44 slot, the Mets did have an honest-to-goodness power pitcher in that jersey. **David Cone** (1987–91) was at his Mets best in 44: as a brief rookie sensation in '87 before getting hurt, going a sterling 20-3 the next year, and then winning his first NL strikeout crown before heading for the teens during the 1991 season.

Coney was clearly the best of a group of arms that also included **Al Schmelz** (1967), **Bob Rauch** (1972), **Mac Scarce** (1975), **Bob Myrick** (1976-78), **Andy Hassler** (1979), **Ray Searage** (1981), **Bill Latham** (1985), **Tim Burke** (1991–92), **Tom Filer** (1992), and **Kevin Lomon** (1995).

Other Mets wore the number for a time and had a lot on the ball: **Jeff Reardon** (1981)—traded for a man with a tremendous right arm, Ellis Valentine, who had become, sadly, a pitch-shy outfielder who had started hitting like a pitcher—and a young **Ron Darling** (1983–84). Darling led the charge of Mets hurlers to lower numbers when he switched to 12; he was stylish and gifted enough to pull it off with aplomb.

Another talented young Met pitcher was **Jason Isring-hausen** (1995–97, 1999). Izzy was issued No. 29 when he joined the team in 1995, but he switched to 44 prior to his first

DAVID CONE

start as a reminder of the lowly round in which the Mets drafted him: no Met draftee, in fact, had ever made the major league roster from such a low pick. While he didn't get the win in his debut against his homestate Cubs, Izzy did go 9-2 with a 2.81 ERA that year, allowing even hardened Met fans to believe Generation K was more than a PR myth. Alas, it was a pipe dream that even Eugene O'Neill would have thought too cruel for production.

After sticking with Isringhausen through seemingly endless injuries and confounding behavior, Steve Phillips traded the 26-year-old reliever to Oakland just in time for him to blossom as a short reliever. A two-time All-Star, his 47 saves for the Cardinals led the National League in 2004.

Human power failures **Harry Chiti** (1962), **Leroy Stanton** (1972), **Tom Paciorek** (1985), **Ryan Thompson** (1992–93), and an end-of-the-line **Jay Bell** (2003) also wore 44. Chiti, a veteran reserve catcher, was acquired from Cleveland in April of 1962 for a player to be named later. Chiti hit just .195 in 15 games for the Mets, who farmed him to Jacksonville on June 15 before quietly returning him to Cleveland to complete the trade. The Mets, as often pointed out, got fleeced in the Chiti-for-Chiti deal. No Met dared put on the jersey again until **Bill Denehy** (1967), a 21-year-old with a 1-7 record and a drinking problem, who was sent to Washington—along with $100,000—for manager Gil Hodges.

Number of times issued: 26 (25 players, 1 DNP)

Longest tenured: Jay Payton (4 seasons, 353 games), David Cone (4 seasons, 127 games), Jason Isringhausen (4 seasons, 60 games), Bob Myrick (3 seasons, 82 games)

Best single seasons: Cone, 1988 (20-3, 2.22 ERA, 213 strikeouts in 231.1 innings); Cone, 1990 (14-10, 3.23 ERA, 233 strikeouts in 211.2 innings); Isringhausen, 1995 (9-2, 2.81 ERA, 55 strikeouts in 93 innings); Mike Cameron, 2004 (.231/.319/.479, 30 HR, 76 RBI, 22 SB); Payton, 2000 (.291/.331/.447, 17 HR, 62 RBI)

Career statistical leaders: Home runs (Cameron 42, Payton 33), RBI (Payton 128, Cameron 115), batting average (Payton .277, Lastings Milledge .257), wins (Cone 56, Isringhausen 18), saves (Andy Hassler 4), ERA (Cone 3.09, Myrick 3.48)

What's in a Name?

When the Mets came into the National League in 1962, it had been thirty years since the requirement that every major leaguer be numbered. As time passed, a public watching baseball games at football stadiums craved additional information that the National Football League had already acquiesced to: names on the back of the uniforms.

Bill Veeck, not surprisingly, was the first to do so with the White Sox, but the Mets had kept the same uniform with the number and no name through 1977. After a horrific season in which nothing went right on the field, the Mets started tinkering with the tailoring. The pullover with piping on the sleeves and neck arrived in '78; a year later came the names. If the names had been "Schmidt" or "Bench" or heaven help us, "Seaver," Mets fans certainly would have volunteered to do the stitching.

Instead, the Mets had "Youngblood." That was the first name with double-digit letters on the back of the uniform. Longer names, like harder times, were bound to come. There have been many names over ten letters since then—as well as several that predated nameplates—but next time you spy a curved surname in skinny letters numbering ten or more on a player's back, keep in mind that only one such Met has been an All-Star or played in a World Series at Shea: Darryl Strawberry.

The style with which the Mets displayed those names has changed over the years. Letters initially were affixed onto a swath of fabric that was then stitched to the back of a jersey. That style—still used by chintzy organizations like the Braves—was dropped by the Mets in 1988. (Incidentally, when the Mets presented Tom Seaver with a retired jersey that year it was unplated—a style of jersey Seaver had never worn in his playing days with the club.)

The font also slimmed from thick, boxy letters used in 1981 to a leaner style in 1982, although some players holding over were never refitted with the new style, leading to non-uniform uniforms. They would also get more sophisticated as time went on. Although Willie Montañez qualified, Alex Treviño in 1980 was the first Met to sport a tilde on his nameplate.

Following are the lengthiest statements ever made on the back on a Mets uniform:

Length	Name (Met Debut)	Debut Uni Number
12 letters	Isringhausen, Jason (1995)	44
11 letters	Christensen, John (1984)	35
	Allensworth, Jermaine (1998)	23
	Hinchcliffe, Brett (2001)	32
	Christensen, McKay (2002)	23
	Middlebrook, Jason (2002)	27
	Darensbourg, Vic (2003)	39
	Mientkiewicz, Doug (2005)	16
	Schoeneweis, Scott (2007)	60
10 letters	Youngblood, Joel (1979)*	18
	Washington, Claudell (1980)	15
	Gardenhire, Ron (1981)	19
	Strawberry, Darryl (1983)	18
	Winningham, Herm (1984)	21
	McReynolds, Kevin (1987)	22
	Candelaria, John (1987)	45
	Whitehurst, Wally (1989)	47
	Schatzeder, Dan (1990)	43
	Saberhagen, Bret (1992)	17
	Guetterman, Lee (1992)	35
	Manzanillo, Josias (1993)	39
	Strickland, Scott (2002)	25
Managers	None	
Coaches	Monbouquette, Bill (1982)	56
	Stottlemyre, Mel (1984)	48
	Stephenson, John (1992)	51
Pre-1979	Cannizzaro, Chris (1962)	8
	Throneberry, Marv (1962)	2
	Christopher, Joe (1962)	23
	Stephenson, John (1964)	49
	Sturvidant, Tom (1964)	47
	Richardson, Gordon (1965)	41
	Aspromonte, Bob (1971)	2
	Strohmayer, John (1973)	39
Coach	McCullough, Clyde (1962)	54

*Youngblood debuted with the Mets in 1977, two years before the team used nameplates.

#45: TUG MCFRANCO AND SIR PEDRO

If the Mets were a deck of cards, the first three aces in the pack would be easy to pick: Tom Seaver, Jerry Koosman, and Dwight Gooden. A quick scan of the Mets' record book confirms these findings. But who would that fourth ace be? You could try the ace that got away: Nolan Ryan. The great lefties who came to Shea after long careers as Braves: one, Warren Spahn, didn't work out; another, Tom Glavine, was a crafty old cat likely to run back to Atlanta if you left the door open. Jon Matlack? Ron Darling? Sid Fernandez? David Cone? Bobby Jones? Al Leiter? All fine choices. But if you need to win a hand, you can't go wrong drawing the ace of hearts.

Pedro Martinez (2005–07) wasn't even in the original pack. Underappreciated in Montreal and loved too much in Boston (although not enough to outbid the Mets), Pedro brought the swagger back to Shea. Fans squealed when Pedro took the mound in 2005. He danced when the sprinkler went off mid-game. He threw the most complete games by a Met in seven years. He shrugged off Braden Looper's blown saves. He made fans think no-hitter when he took the mound, although even Pedro could only do so much.

Pedro made one of Omar Minaya's biggest gambles pay off, if only for a year. Injuries quieted him after that, but what he did in 2005 for the franchise—and to opponents—cannot be downplayed. Pedro came as close as anyone of living up to the tradition set forth by the first man to wear the uniform number. **Ron Locke**? No, not him. (Locke won once in 25 games as a '64 Met.) Make that the man who owned that number the longest.

Tug McGraw (1965–67, 1969–74) was one of the true characters (and best pitchers) in the history of the Mets. He was a starter for Casey

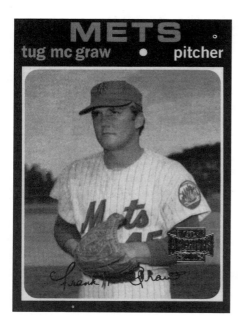

tug mc graw • pitcher

METS

Stengel, a trusted reliever for Gil Hodges, and he brought the Mets from the dead to the pennant in '73. His rallying cry of "Ya Gotta Believe!" lives on whenever teams are counted out but there are still games on the schedule and pages on the calendar.

The club's first true stopper, Tug collected 85 saves with the Mets and averaged two innings per outing over a five-season span. He was a perfect 12-for-12 in save tries for the '69 club. He was 11-4 in 1971. The next year he was the winning pitcher in the All-Star Game, saved 27, and finished with a 1.70 ERA for the second straight year. He pitched a career-high 118.2 innings in '73, plus 18.2 more in the postseason. The Mets dealt their king of hearts to the rival Phillies after the 1974 season in a head-scratcher of a deal that netted John Stearns, and the Flushing faithful were forced to watch his thigh-slapping and screwgie through many a close contest and October with that annoying *P* on his hat.

The downgrading of the save by the sheer increase in its volume makes for invariable and complicated comparisons between McGraw and **John Franco** (1998–2001, 2003–04). Let's just say these different era closers both showed plenty of spunk. The Franco that gave up the No. 31 he'd worn at Shea since 1990 for Mike Piazza's 1998 arrival had only about a year left as a compiler of saves. Yet the 45 Franco may have actually been more valuable—and more like Tug—than the one that set the standard for career saves by a southpaw. He still was in big trouble if teams ignored his sinking stuff, but he began compiling big outs in earlier innings like Tug, whose uniform number he took as a tribute. Franco opted for Tommy John surgery at age forty-one, stayed around a little too long, and was booed a little too harshly in his Shea return as an Astro, but he looked like a one-eyed jack beating a flush when he threw his high-school-speed fastball past Barry Bonds with all the cards on the table in the 2000 Division Series.

A wild card is the only non-pitcher in the group: pinch-hitting stalwart **Mark Carreon** "Luggage" (1990–91), who wore the number in tribute to his father, Cam Carreon. Mark was the club's all-time pinch-hitting power specialist. His 8 pinch-hit homers are the all-time club record, and his 4 bench blasts for the 1989 Mets (wearing 32) tied Danny Heep's 1983 mark.

Rick Baldwin (1975–78) was dealt a tough hand as follower of Tug in 45, but Baldwin left behind good numbers: 3.60 ERA, 105 games, 182.2 innings, and 7 saves. **John Candelaria** was a Met for 3 starts in the closing weeks of the 1987 season and won twice. He was ineligible for the postseason, but his teammates made sure that wasn't a problem. The Candy Man went to the sugar daddy in the Bronx after the season, but he was never able to regain the form that made him a 20-game winner and All-Star for the 1977 Pirates. He stuck around to gain 177 wins in the bigs; 2 as a Met.

Two Gibsons wore 45: **Paul Gibson** (1992–93) and **Bob Gibson** (1981). The latter Gibson should not to be confused with the Bob Gibson who spent his last week in the majors as a 1987 Met (wearing 38). One of the most intense competitors of his era, Bob Gibson the Cardinal (in fearsome 45) started nine times in the World Series, completed eight, and won seven, not to mention garnering two Cy Young Awards and carrying a 1.12 ERA in 1968 that would have made Christy Mathewson blush. Gibson wore 45 when he joined old pal Joe Torre's staff in 1981 as a co-pitching coach with Rube Walker. While Gibson was inducted into the Hall of Fame upstate in Cooperstown that summer, the downstate New York experience (complete with cataclysmic strike) went so well that the whole staff was fired after the season. Torre, Gibson, and Walker, plus Joe Pignatano, reemerged with a division title in Atlanta in 1982.

Discounting the first two years from hard-throwing **Jeff Reardon** (1979–80), the rest of the 45 deck has been stacked with face cards and forgettable pitchers: **Darrell Sutherland** (1966), **Billy Connors** (1968), **Butch Metzger** (1978), **Brent Gaff** (1982–84), **Edwin Nuñez** (1988), **Mauro Gozzo** (1993–94), and **Jerry Dipoto** (1995–96).

Number of times issued: 20 (16 players, 2 coaches)

Longest tenured: Tug McGraw (9 seasons, 361 games), John Franco (6 seasons, 302 games), Rick Baldwin (4 seasons, 105 games)

Best single seasons: Tug McGraw, 1973 (5-6, 3.87 ERA, 25 saves, 81 strikeouts in 118.2 innings); McGraw, 1972 (8-6, 1.70 ERA, 27 saves, 92 strikeouts in 106 innings); McGraw, 1969 (9-3, 2.24 ERA, 12 saves, 92 strikeouts in 100.1 innings); Pedro Martinez, 2005 (15-8, 2.82 ERA, 208 strikeouts in 217 innings); John Franco, 2000 (5-4, 3.40 ERA, 56 strikeouts in 55.2 innings)

Career statistical leaders: Home runs (Mark Carreon 14), RBI (Carreon 47), batting average (Carreon .256), wins (McGraw 47, Martinez 24), ERA (Jeff Reardon 2.47, McGraw 3.17), saves (McGraw 85, Franco 56)

Somebody Save Me

Nolan Ryan recorded the first official save in Mets history on April 9, 1969. At the behest of Chicago newspaper writer Jerome Holtzman—later named MLB grand poobah of history and such—baseball adopted the save as an "official" statistic that year. Baseball historians have generally taken the rules of the save (getting the last out with a three-run lead or less, pitching the last three innings regardless of score, or coming in with the tying run on deck) and applied them retroactively.

If you go by that logic, the real first save in Mets history belongs to Roger Craig, who came out of the bullpen to nail down the first Mets extra-inning win (for otherwise luckless Craig Anderson) on May 6, 1962. Imagine the modern-day Mets waiting until May for their first save of the year—or the twentieth game, for that matter—and bringing in a starter to get the last outs? Lucky for the Mets there was no WFAN to rail about their 4-16 start. Comedy Central might've helped, though.

Because we can, we are mixing old and new, the official and the unofficial, to provide the uniform numbers in Mets history with the most saves through 2007. You may want to avert your eyes upon seeing names like Armando Benitez and Braden Looper . . . and you may also be surprised to see how many times these names came through.

Number	Saves	Notes
31	235	Love him or hate him, John Franco racked up the saves: 221 wearing this number and 56 more down the road at 45.
49	164	Maligned Armando pushes 49 to the second spot with his 160 saves.
45	162	Tug McGraw (86) was emphatic and Franco (56) could be erratic, but the Mets would've done more celebrating if these two had shared the same pen.
47	116	Messy Jesse all the way at 107.
42	114	The number's been retired, but so was the side with the likes of Roger McDowell (84) and Ron Taylor (28).
13	113	Billy Wagner has raced to 74 saves in two years.
38	81	They say bad teams don't need good closers . . . well, nuts to that! Thanks, Skip Lockwood, for those 65 saves.
48	73	Before he was a "Nasty Boy," Randy Myers (56) was wicked at Shea.
40	64	Remember when the cry was "Loop!" not "Boo!" for Looper (57)?
34	60	Underrated Bob Apodaca (26) and tragic Danny Frisella (22) showed guile and guts for the '70s Mets.

#46: RICKEY, DON'T USE THAT NUMBER

Number 13 is generally considered unlucky, but **Neil Allen** figured it had to be better luck than 46. The first wearer of 46, Allen got his big break in the big leagues when he got hurt in May of 1979. The Mets then had to put the rookie on the disabled list instead of sending him to Tidewater, as his 7.06 ERA and 0-5 record demanded. When Allen came back, he was one of the very few pleasant developments in an otherwise horrific '79 season. He went 6-5 with a 2.45 ERA after the injury. Allen was fourth in the NL with 22 saves in 1980—a remarkable achievement given the team he was pitching for—before rolling the dice with 13.

Oliver Perez came to New York and donned 46 because someone else got hurt. Duaner Sanchez, the club's top setup man in 2006, was lost for the year (and beyond) after being injured in a cab ride from hell in Miami during the early hours of the July 31 trading deadline. The resulting trade was a knee-jerk grab into the team's recent past to rescue Roberto Hernandez from the Pirates. But Omar Minaya also pulled Perez, a fireballing left-handed prospect

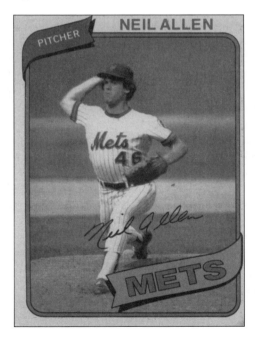

turned bust at age twenty-four, out of that deal. To do so, Minaya surrendered likeable, hard-hitting right fielder Xavier Nady, the best player (and only one) in club history with a first name that started with an *X*.

Hernandez wasn't close to as good as he'd been in 2005, and Perez came up to the big club only after spending a few weeks in Norfolk. Perez showed flashes of promise, averaging more than a strikeout per inning with the Mets, but his combined major league totals for the year were 3-13, 6.55 ERA. Injuries to yet other pitchers put him on the NLCS roster, where fate intervened. With the Mets down to the Cardinals in the series, he won Game 4 in St. Louis. Four nights later he was called on to start the deciding game, making Perez the pitcher with the worst record of any Game 7 starter in major league history. He then joined Al Leiter (Game 5, 2000 World Series) among the great wasted efforts in franchise postseason history. When the hurt wore off, it became clear that Perez thrived under the most difficult circumstances. He won 15 games and whiffed 174 in 2007, all while leaping over foul lines in a single bound and excelling against enemies like Atlanta and the Yankees.

Dallas Green wore 46 for parts of four seasons as manager of the Mets, surviving the 103-loss season in '93, the strike in '94, plus a brutal start in '95 before Generation K collapsed right over his head. Dallas could have used big **Brian Bohanon** (1997–98), but then Bohanon was a Bobby Valentine/Apodaca reclamation project who hit hard (.255 batting average) and threw soft (3.57 ERA). **Tim Hamulack** (2005) stands out in the crowd because his Mets ERA of 23.14 was more than half that of his high uniform number. Don't try this at home, kids.

Others: future coach material **Randy Neimann** (1985); highly touted trade bait **David West** (1988–89); **Chris Jelic** (1990), whose lone major league hit was a homer; towering bust **Terry Bross** (1991); washed-up fireman **Barry Jones** (1992); brief visitor **Willie Blair** (1998); Norfolk shuttler **Jermaine Allensworth** (1999); and **Rich Rodriguez** (2000), who pitched poorly for eight teams but was at his absolute worst for a top-notch Mets club (props to his old roommate Steve Phillips for the free-agent contract).

Tyler Walker tempted fate in 2002 and got claimed by the Tigers on waivers. Rookie spot-starter **Jeremy Griffiths** (2003) fit right in with this motley group. Days after Griffiths was traded in '04, his uni number was replaced by **Jose Parra**, who continued the bad luck streak by suffering a freak injury—a line drive breaking a finger—during a rehab appearance for a minor injury. He hasn't appeared in a major league game since. Don't say we didn't warn him.

Number of times issued: 15 (all to players)

Longest tenured: Neil Allen (2 seasons, 109 games), Brian Bohanon (2 seasons, 44 games)

Best single seasons: Allen, 1980 (7-10, 3.70 ERA, 22 saves, 79 strikeouts in 97.1 innings); Oliver Perez, 2007 (15-10, 3.56 ERA, 174 strikeouts in 177 innings); Bohanon, 1997 (6-4, 3.82 ERA, 66 strikeouts in 94.1 innings)

Career statistical leaders: Home runs (Jermaine Allensworth 3), RBI (Allensworth 9), batting average (Bohanon .255, Allensworth .219), wins (Perez 16), saves (Allen 30), ERA (Bohanon 3.57, Allen 3.61)

Managing to Get By

The Mets have often been a team defined by their managers: that two of the three numbers ever retired by the club were for managers should say as much.

There were the clownish-but-endearing early 1960s Mets and their clownish-but-endearing manager, Casey Stengel. As a Mets manager, Stengel was probably well beyond his prime as a strategist but at the peak of his abilities to create an attraction. The Mets stopped being a laughingstock and started to gain respect when manager Gil Hodges possessed the same qualities.

The Mets at other times in their history were young and made mistakes (Joe Torre), were brash and offensive-minded (Davey Johnson), strategic and conniving (Bobby Valentine), or passionless and distracted (Art Howe).

Two Mets managers have worn No. 9 (Wes Westrum and Joe Torre), and two have worn No. 55 (Joe Frazier and Frank Howard). Nine were former Mets players, with Hodges (14), Berra (8), Torre (9), Bud Harrelson (3), and Willie Randolph (12) wearing the same numbers they wore as players to the manager's office. Following is a chronological list:

No.	Manager	Years	Notes
37	Casey Stengel	1962–65	Zany but endearing
9	Wes Westrum	1965–67	Stengel-like results without the charisma
54	Salty Parker	1967	Strictly interim
14	Gil Hodges	1968–71	Made the Mets respectable, then more than respectable
8	Yogi Berra	1972–75	Ya gotta believe . . . or underachieve
51	Roy McMillan	1975	Interim, and not really even cut out for that
55	Joe Frazier	1976–77	No match for Seaver or Grant
9	Joe Torre	1977–81	Players loved him, but . . . Hall of Fame managing careers have to start somewhere

No.	Manager	Years	Notes
31	George Bamberger	1982–83	Heart wasn't in it
55	Frank Howard	1983	Enormously interim
5	Davey Johnson	1984–90	Created a monster
3	Bud Harrelson	1989–91	Not cut out for it
4	Mike Cubbage	1991	Strictly interim
10	Jeff Torborg	1992–93	Worst manager money could buy
46	Dallas Green	1993–96	Too much tough, not enough love
2	Bobby Valentine	1996–2002	Charisma, excitement, ego to spare
18	Art Howe	2003–04	Caretaker of organization in chaos
12	Willie Randolph	2005–07	Efficient, businesslike; went down with the ship in '07, and he'll need to get this crew into shape for the entire voyage

#47: JESSE

Even after starting off their inaugural season 0-9, it was inevitable (on paper, at least) that the original Mets would win a game. That it fell to **Jay Hook** (1962–64), an engineer from Northwestern with a strong right arm, was proof that in baseball every team will beat every other team, even if one team has a 9½-game lead on the other on April 23. The great Leonard Koppett said of Hook, "He could throw as hard as anyone, and he was intelligent and eager, and he could even show with diagrams and equations why a ball curved." He beat the Pirates that night, and of Mets pitchers with 10 or more decisions, his .296 winning percentage topped the '62 club. At 8-19, he was responsible for 20 percent of the club's wins and only 16 percent of its losses. The Mets won 15 of his 56 career starts for the club. They should have retired 47 right then and there.

If they had, however, maybe the Mets would not have become the first expansion team to win multiple world championships. Reliever **Jesse Orosco** (1979, 1981–87) made it happen, getting the final outs for the pennant and World Series while most Mets fans were contorted into whatever "lucky" position had worked to that point. Orosco was acquired for Jerry Koosman in what became a trade of the pitcher on the mound for the final out of both the Mets' World

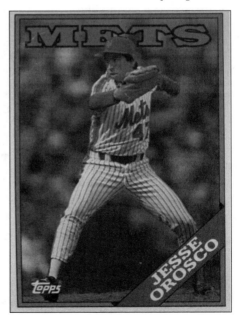

Series clinchers. Messy Jesse saved 107 games as a Met, and had a career ERA of 2.74, second only to Tom Seaver. His best season, though, turned out to be the team's fifth last-place finish in seven years. In 62 games for the '83 Mets, Orosco tossed 110 innings and had a ridiculous 1.47 ERA with 17 saves and 13 wins for a team that couldn't even get Seaver into double digits in the victory column.

Orosco was reacquired in the 1999 offseason, only to be traded again before the season began. That was probably for the best since Orosco's career record of 47-47 confirmed his place as the Met most deserving of the number. All in favor, fling your gloves skyward.

The second Orosco deal actually netted the best 47 with the bat: **Joe McEwing** (2000–02). Super Joe was nothing special as a hitter—he's also the only 47 to date who wasn't a pitcher—but versatility, humility, and random bursts of offense kept him employed.

McEwing knew his place on the club, and he willingly surrendered 47 when veteran enemy lefty **Tom Glavine** (2003–07) signed on board. A sure Hall of Famer, Glavine deserved better than to walk into an Art Howe rebuilding project (although no one twisted his arm). The team's terrible bullpen seemed to pick Glavine starts for every blown save. He went 9-14 his first year with the club twenty years after another Hall of Fame–bound Tom struggled through the same record for an equally inept club. Working diligently at his craft, Glavine persevered and earned two berths as a Mets All-Star and increased his win total by two each of his first four years with the club. And in 2007, he finally notched win 300.

But no sooner had fans finally warmed up to Glavine—some were referring to him as Tom, by George—than the relationship soured again. Glavine was last seen getting booed off the mound before the first inning was complete in what would be the final Mets game of 2007.

And the rest: knuckleballer **Tom Sturdivant** (1964), **Darrell Sutherland** (1964), **Mardie Cornejo** (1978), **Wally Whitehurst** (1989–92), Rule 5 pick **Mike Draper** (1993), **Jason Jacome** (1994–95), **Reid Cornelius** (1995), and **Derek Wallace** (1996), whose career was cut short by a blood clot, but he still became the first Met with four strikeouts in an inning (while earning a save against the Braves).

Number of times issued: 12 (all to players)

Longest tenured: Jesse Orosco (8 seasons, 370 games), Tom Glavine (5 seasons, 164 games), Wally Whitehurst (4 seasons, 127 games), Joe McEwing (3 seasons, 308 games), Jay Hook (3 seasons, 81 games)

Best single seasons: Orosco, 1983 (13-7, 1.47 ERA, 17 saves, 84 strikeouts in 110 innings); Glavine, 2006 (15-7, 3.82 ERA, 131 strikeouts in 198 innings); McEwing, 2001 (.283/.342/.449, 8 HR, 30 RBI)

Career statistical leaders: Home runs (McEwing 13), RBI (McEwing 75), batting average (McEwing .242), wins (Glavine 61, Orosco 47), saves (Orosco 107), ERA (Orosco 2.74, Whitehurst 3.83)

Eight Miles High

On April 4, 2002, at Shea Stadium, the Mets ran out a starting lineup whose combined uniform number totaled 274—which by our count is the highest total in team history.

Fan expectations on this day were about as high. It was only the third game of the 2002 season, the club's fortieth. The Mets had made several changes to a 2001 team that fell too far behind in the first half to make a strong second half meaningful. So out were Robin Ventura and Todd Zeile and Benny Agbayani. In were Roberto Alomar, Mo Vaughan, and Jeromy Burnitz. It was a swap of one set of veterans for another, but this one, as Casey Stengel would say, "hadn't failed here yet" (well, Burnitz had). The pitching staff also included Shawn Estes, making his Mets debut against the Pirates.

Joe McEwing, getting a start against Pirates left-hander Jimmy Anderson, homered to lead off the home first that afternoon. Alomar walked and Vaughn was hit by a pitch, but big-inning momentum subsided when Piazza hit into a double play and Alfonzo grounded out.

And that was all that was heard from the Mets until Burnitz parked a solo home run in the 7th. The Pirates in the meantime scratched three runs off Estes in seven innings, two on a homer by Kevin Young, and the Pirates won 3-2, taking the season's opening homestand.

And that's the way the year went for the 2002 Mets, destined to finish last in the NL East and 26½ games out of first place. The 274 lineup would be together only this once. Estes would be so insignificant, they'd trade him away and still make deals designed to improve the club for the stretch run. One of those trades would cost Jay Payton. Alomar, Vaughn, and Burnitz would all struggle. McEwing would make it through the year but bat .199. Scandal and a twelve-game losing steak in August would cost manager Bobby Valentine his job.

The lineup: 47 McEwing, 12 Alomar, 42 Vaughn, 31 Piazza, 13 Alfonzo, 20 Burnitz, 44 Payton, 10 Ordoñez, 55 Estes

#48: HOT DOG

Number 48 was first issued to a Mets player (Joe Nolan) who didn't play in a game. Then **Nino Espinosa** (1974) pitched twice and abandoned it. **Juan Berenguer** (1978) wore it for a few weeks without winning.

Randy Tate (1975) was the first to wear 48 and win a game, but it didn't happen often for him. His 5-13, 4.45 season—including going 0 for 41 at the plate—was his only year in the major leagues and included a heartbreaking loss to the Expos on August 4. The 22-year-old rookie had a no-hitter, a 3-0 lead, and 12 strikeouts through 7.1 innings when Jim Lyttle slapped a single to left to break up the no-hitter.

A cruel progression of future Mets followed: Pepe Mangual walked. Jim Dwyer struck out. Gary Carter singled. And Mike Jorgensen whacked a three-run homer to left. Mets and Randy Tate lose, 4-3.

In a special pregame ceremony on May 25, 1980, the Mets presented reliever **Ed Glynn** with a hot-dog steamer bearing his No. 48.

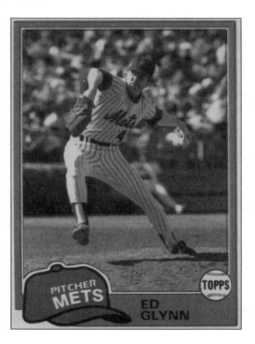

The gift recalled the Flushing-born Glynn's first career—as a vendor at Shea.

Glynn (1979–80), a lefty known as the "Flushing Flash" could cut the mustard out of the bullpen, too, as his 7 saves in 1980 attest. He lasted with the Mets for two seasons, or about as long as the average hot dog remains in the bottom of a steamer box.

Randy Myers (1985–89) might have been called a hot dog, but no one wanted to incite someone whose off-field interests were headlined by camouflage and gun magazines. Randall K. Myers, as Tim McCarver always called him (the K stood for Kirk, if you're dying to know), saved 56 games in his too-brief Shea career, averaging well over a strikeout per inning. His best year was 1988, when he saved 26 and compiled a 1.72 ERA. Mets fans still shake their heads that the southpaw wasn't brought in to face Mike Scioscia in Game 4 of that year's NLCS, when a 3-1 series lead seemed just a K away.

Many hours of therapy got fans over that, but watching Myers cavort on the mound for the world champion Reds two years later as leader of the "Nasty Boys" caused a few relapses. The Mets had sent him to Cincy in a straight-up challenge blockbuster for John Franco after the '89 season. Myers moved around but continued to get the job done as the Mets went to seed. When he set the then-NL record with 53 saves for the 1993 Cubs, the Mets won 59 times all season.

In 1999, the Mets pulled off a considerably more minor challenge trade, sending brief visitor **Dan Murray** to Kansas City for **Glendon Rusch** (2000–01). Rusch proudly wore 48 into a starting job in 2000 and turned out to be one of the biggest surprises in baseball. That season, at least. The Mets held onto the man that *Baseball Weekly* proclaimed as "the best number five starter in baseball." Then he proceeded to pitch like several previous number 48s. Rusch went to Milwaukee in the Jeromy Burnitz deal and really started the roller coaster. He won 10 games in his first year as a Brewer, but he hasn't reached double digits since. In 2003, he was 1-12 in 19 starts. Makes his 8-12 mark for the 2001 Mets seem like Cy Young stuff.

Aaron Heilman (2003–07) has also experienced the up-and-down ride of the major leagues since he became a first-round pick out of Notre Dame in 2001. Heilman looked like a bust when he lost 10 of his first 13 career decisions as a starter. The Mets gave him another chance in 2005, and he tossed a one-hit shutout, opening a lot of eyes and seemingly fixing it in his mind that he *should* be a starter despite his bullpen success and the organization telling him no (repeatedly).

While he had a 5.93 ERA and 22 home runs in 133.2 career innings as a starter, Heilman had a 0.68 ERA out of the pen after the 2005 All-Star break, the best of anyone in baseball. He pitched 74 times in '06 and was generally successful, until Yadier Molina took out his banjo in Game 7 of the NLCS and made the faces at Shea look as sour as Heilman's. Although still vulnerable to the occasional gut-punch home run, by the end of 2007 Heilman was the team's only reliable reliever.

Among the lower 48: **Julio "Iguana-Man" Machado** (1990), babyfaced lefty **Pete Schourek** (1991–93), veteran setter-upper **Roger Mason** (1994), the other **Pedro Martinez** (1996), highly unsuccessful reliever **Ricardo Jordan** (1997), and hard-throwing **Kane Davis**, who made the squad in 2002 and subsequently blew out his arm.

Number of times issued: 18 (14 players, 1 DNP, 3 coaches)

Longest tenured: Aaron Heilman (5 seasons, 227 games), Randy Myers (5 seasons, 185 games), Pete Schourek (3 seasons, 98 games), Glendon Rusch (3 seasons, 65 games)

Best single seasons: Myers, 1988 (7-3, 1.72 ERA, 26 saves, 69 strikeouts in 68 innings); Rusch, 2000 (11-11, 4.01 ERA, 157 strikeouts in 190.2 innings); Heilman, 2005 (5-3, 3.17 ERA, 106 strikeouts in 108 innings)

Career statistical leaders: Wins (Rusch 19, Heilman 19, Myers 17), saves (Myers 56, Heilman 6), ERA (Myers 2.74, Ed Glynn 3.53)

Ghosts in the Machine

Somewhere beyond right-center field at Shea Stadium, perhaps in an auto salvage yard over by the Roosevelt Avenue Bridge, is the place where Phantom Mets gather. It's where Mac Suzuki approaches Randy Bobb and, fighting backs tears, asks, "Wanna have a catch?"

Vagaries of the waiver rules, poor planning, bad luck, injuries, trades, or other roster-changing events have resulted in sixteen such men. This group is a bit different than "paper Mets" who may have been acquired over an offseason and traded immediately, like Jim Kern, or guys who were traded for but never made it out of the minors. Phantom Mets differ in that they occupied space on the active roster during a season, meaning they were eligible to play and thereby occupied a number. They count, and yet they don't.

Following is a list of Met uniforms worn by players who never made it into an official game while wearing that uniform in that year. (They are the mysterious players listed as DNP in various chapters.) Some of the players accrued considerable time in other Mets uniforms, while others haunt the Iron Triangle.

No.	Player	Year	Notes
3	Jason Phillips	2001	Phillips would gather in three additional numbers in subsequent call-ups. He couldn't get No. 3 back because it belonged at the time to Vance Wilson, his rival for the role of Mike Piazza's backup.
5	Jerry Moses	1975	One of three catchers to start the year with the Mets (Jerry Grote and rookie John Stearns were the others), the veteran Moses was sold to San Diego when they had a sudden catching crisis.
9	Randy Bobb	1970	Duffy Dyer won the backup catcher job in 1970, although Bobb rode the bench in September.
16	Mike Jorgensen	1969	Gil Hodges liked small groups. Jorgensen didn't even get a post-clinching inning, although he played in this number subsequently.
21	Ron Gardenhire	1986	Cut shortly after the season began, Gardenhire kept his sense of humor. Fearing he might wind up driving a tractor in Kansas he quipped, "I could go from Dear John to John Deere." Fear not, Ron, a managerial career awaited.
21	Terrel Hansen	1992	Minor league slugger recalled briefly when Kevin Baez and Vince Coleman were injured; he was sent back down before appearing. Never got a turn at-bat or an inning in the field but hit nearly 200 home runs over thirteen minor league seasons.
22	Billy Cotton	1972	Another minor league catcher who couldn't take innings from Duffy Dyer.
23	Bob G. Miller	1962	Acquired in a trade, then reassigned to the minors before appearing in a game. When Miller returned, Joe Christopher was in 23, so Miller switched to 36.
29	Jason Isringhausen	1995	Asked for—and received—No. 44 before his mound debut.
32	Tyler Yates	2002	When Satoru Komiyama injured his finger in his electric garage door, Yates had three days in the bullpen, but that door never opened. He returned two years and one arm surgery later, wearing No. 33.

No.	Player	Year	Notes
34	Mac Suzuki	1999	In what wouldn't be considered Steve Phillips's brightest procedural moment, Suzuki was acquired in a trade for Allen Watson but claimed by Kansas City on waivers when the Mets tried to sneak him down to AAA days later.
35	Jon Matlack	1970	Just getting a September taste; would be up to stay a year later in No. 32.
43	John Gibbons	1985	With the Mets in a pennant race, it was more difficult than usual getting playing time from Gary Carter.
44	Jim Bibby	1970, 1971	Right-hander Bibby had a 12-year career ahead of him, including a no-hitter, but none of it was with the Mets (natch), who in consecutive years promoted Bibby to the club in September only to leave him seated in the bullpen. Traded after the '71 season to St. Louis in an eight-player deal.
48	Joe Nolan	1973	Catcher was rushed from Tidewater when Jerry Grote suffered a broken arm, Nolan became superfluous when the Mets traded for Jerry May.
56	Anderson Garcia	2006	Last of the Armando Benitez trade booty, Garcia came and went to fill a space between the entertaining yet ineffective Jose Lima and Alay Soler.

#49: ARMANDO

When they write the book about the Mets— and the guess here is this qualifies— **Armando Benitez** (1999–2003) will go down as one of the top relievers in Mets history. Granted, the Mets have a lineage of great relievers, and Benitez famously (or rather, infamously) coughed up the lead in many a crucial spot, but by sheer volume of saves, the chest-thumping, leadoff-batter-walking, longball-allowing Armando makes the list. He could throw a ball through a wall, but unfortunately batted balls seemed to go off said walls or fly over them at the most inopportune times.

Armando had the first 40-save seasons in club history (2000, 2001), and his 160 saves for the Mets ranks ahead of any reliever not named Franco. Considering he didn't take over the closer's role until midway through 1999 and was finally run out of town in July 2003, he averaged close to 40 saves per season. Total blown saves in that time: 25. Seven of those ruined chances came during his one truly awful year as a Met in 2003; ironically, that was the same year he earned his lone All-Star berth as a Met (and never made it back to Shea from the festivities).

Steve Phillips stole Benitez from the Orioles for a player the Mets only owned on paper for a few hours (Charles Johnson), and a well-timed finger injury to John Franco enabled the Mets to insert the hard-throwing righty for the soft-tossing southpaw in the 9th inning. Getting a save often seemed automatic for Armando. It was when he didn't get the save that the image of Brian Jordan or J. T. Snow or Paul O'Neill repeated in your head again and again as night gave way to dawn.

The relievers that have followed Benitez in 49 have predictably had tough times. **Orber Moreno** (2003–04) got hurt, **Felix Heredia** (2005) got hurt and then suspended for steroids, and **Roberto Hernandez** wore the number for only a few days in 2006 before going back to 39. Still, the mojo must have rubbed off and Bert wasn't nearly the same pitcher he'd been in '05. Here's hoping that **Philip Humber**—a starter—changes 49's fortunes for the good (or picks a different number), although 2003's top Mets draft pick has been slow to make an impact.

Walt Terrell (1982–84) was the first 49 of note in Mets history. Like Benitez, he was pilfered from an AL team (Texas, with Ron Darling in tow). Terrell was 19-23 as a Met with a downright upright 3.53 ERA. His most memorable day came when he homered twice and drove in all four runs in his win at Wrigley in a rare Mets NBC *Game of the Week* appearance in 1983. He left town in a similarly brilliant move; the prize returned from Detroit was Howard Johnson.

Bearded lefty **Kevin Kobel** (1978–80) had experience in losing. He came from a Milwaukee team that finished fifth, fifth, and sixth his first three years in the majors. That proved to be a perfect apprenticeship for a Mets club that would finish sixth, sixth, and fifth in his three years in Flushing. Kobel was not altogether horrible in a swingman role in 1978, fashioning 5 wins and a 2.91 ERA. He started 27 games with a 3.51 ERA in 1979.

If the Mets' failure to chase down a division title in 1989 can be traced to a single game and a single goat, it might be the August 20 affair at Shea when veteran **Don Aase** (1989) coughed up four 9th-inning runs and a lead to the Dodgers, highlighted by a home run from the guy currently in the dugout, Willie Randolph.

Ed Hearn (1986) shined as only someone playing Gary Carter's understudy when the lights were brightest could shine. That is to say, not quite as incandescently, but bright enough, especially for a reserve backstop whose high number illustrated what a longshot he was. Fondly remembered as a piece of the '86 puzzle, and afterward outbound freight in the David Cone heist.

Others wore 49 while passing through: **John Stephenson** (1964), **Dyar Miller** (1980–81), **Don Schulze** (1987), **Mike Birkbeck** (1992), **Joe Vitko** (1992), **Pete Walker** (1995), and **Bob MacDonald** (1996). No. 49 was also the first number for Todd Hundley (1990–1991).

Joe Crawford was effective (4-3, 3.30) and yo-yoed back to Norfolk during his lone year as a Met in 1997, but he went for the cash and security in Japan. He later became pitching coach for the independent Bridgeport Bluefish and was the kind of guy who left messages on ultimatemets.com. Go, Joe! **Brad Clontz** (1998) did nada in his two-game Mets tenure in 1998, but the next year he threw the most important regular-season wild pitch for a New York team since Jack Chesbro's 95 years earlier. Pitching for Pittsburgh in the bottom of the 9th in a tie game on the last day on the schedule, Clontz's first pitch to Mike Piazza with the bases loaded skipped away and brought in Melvin Mora with the run that sent the Mets to a one-game playoff in Cincinnati. What a Clontz!

Number of times issued: 19 (all to players)

Longest tenured: Armando Benitez (5 seasons, 333 games), Kevin Kobel (3 seasons, 76 games), Walt Terrell (3 seasons, 57 games)

Best single seasons: Benitez, 1999 (4-3, 1.85 ERA, 22 saves, 128 strikeouts in 78 innings); Benitez, 2000 (4-4, 2.61 ERA, 41 saves, 106 strikeouts in 76 innings); Terrell, 1984 (11-12, 3.52 ERA, 114 strikeouts in 215 innings); Kobel, 1979 (6-8, 3.51 ERA, 67 strikeouts in 161.2 innings)

Career statistical leaders: Home runs (Ed Hearn 4), RBI (Hearn 10), batting average (Hearn .265), wins (Terrell 19, Benitez 18), saves (Benitez 160), ERA (Benitez 2.70, Terrell 3.53)

Keeping up Appearances

While the Mets have had some excellent pitching talent in their history, they've also had a lot of mound melancholy. And how does one deal with poor pitching? By bringing in more pitchers, of course. As the game has evolved and well-pitched games often require three and four hurlers—if not more—to complete, the Shea grounds crew has been on its toes to make sure Mets managers and pitching coaches don't wear out a path between the dugout and the mound. (At least they don't have to worry about skid marks from the bullpen car anymore.)

Below are the numbers that have been called in to the game the most often in Mets history, with cumulative games for the top ten. It includes starters, closers, and many classifications of manly men: middle men, setup men, mop-up men, and firemen. Watch out for the odd LOOGY (Left-handed One Out Guy) floating around. It can get a little messy.

No.	Games	Notes
45	1,239	When a Mets manager has wanted an arm, he's signaled for 45 more than anyone else. And why not? Tug McGraw (361 games) and John Franco (301) make up more than half of those calls.
36	992	Although Jerry Koosman (376) was one of a kind, he had a lot of followers; none of whom, including Ed Lynch (145) and Greg McMichael (144), were in the same ballpark.
39	935	Get out the straightjackets, folks! Doug Sisk (263) is your leader.
38	895	Skip Lockwood entered 227 games as a Met; Dave Mlicki appeared 122 times, but only one game against the Yankees seemed memorable.
47	865	It's pretty much a lot of starters, stiffs, and Jesse Orosco (371).
40	852	Jeff Innis (288) proved that you don't have to be great; you just have to be there.
27	808	What Craig Swan (229) would have given to have been on one of the Mets clubs Dennis Cook (255) pitched so unpredictably for.
34	807	Cal Koonce (119), Danny Frisella (122), and Bob Apodaca (184) provided solid relief in this uniform from the Summer of Love to the Summer of Sam.
48	804	Aaron Heilman (227 appearances) has been on call more often than any Met 48.
35	781	David Weathers (180) *always* wanted the ball; Rick Reed (140) and Doug Henry (109) follow.

#50: HAWAII 5-0

In an era when educators complain that students are lacking general knowledge in many subjects—geography among them—the Mets have taught plenty of people about our fiftieth state. Hawaii was home for a popular pitcher of the 1980s and a thumping folk hero who rode in on a wave of home runs in 1999 and hit the latest game-ending postseason home run in franchise history (if you ignore the first two words in Robin Ventura's grand-slam single).

Portly portsider **Sid Fernandez** (1984–93) was one of the best pitchers the Mets have ever had. No Met since Tom Seaver has gone out there with no-hit stuff more frequently. El Sid was lucky to have pitched in the era before pitch counts or he would have been yanked for exceeding 100 pitches often enough to have dwindled his win total to nothing. Maybe his career would have lasted longer if that powerful left arm had been babied, but it's hard to imagine him lasting longer than the ten seasons he spent at Shea, three of which saw El Sid post the best ratio of hits per nine innings in the National League.

The Mets stole him from the Dodgers and put him in the rotation in July 1984. He only pitched in relief once in his first three seasons, but it was his masterful bullpen work in Game 7 of the 1986 World Series that put the Mets in position to rally to win the world championship.

Fernandez certainly would have reached 100 wins as a Met if his last club hadn't been the brutal '93 edition that he wasted a 2.93 ERA on before getting hurt (5-6 mark in 120 innings). Of his list of impressive numbers, something that can't be overlooked is how he made a uniform number in the 50s fair game for players (thirty-four coaches and managers—and only a handful of call-ups—had worn numbers 50 or higher pre-Sid). Fernandez was proud of his Hawaiian roots and claimed *Hawaii 5-0* to be his favorite program, so 50 it was. No Mets player had worn the number before, and none has lived up to El Sid's legacy. But one guy sure tried hard.

Benny Agbayani (1999–2001) burst onto the scene and became an instant hero and cult figure. Shane Spencer had come up the previous year for the Yankees and crushed homers at an impressive rate. Big whoop. The Yankees were ahead by a hundred games and Shane merely kept the yawning down among the arrogant. The following May, the Mets were in need of an outfielder and brought up the stocky, hardworking, Honolulu product with the funny name. Whereas Agbayani wore 39 for his unimpressive first tour in '98, this time he snagged 50. He hit 10 homers in his first 19 starts and helped the Mets reach the postseason for the first time in eleven years.

The next year there was no spot for Benny, but the roster flexibility afforded for the season-opening series with the Cubs in Japan got him a seat on the long plane trip to Tokyo. After losing the opener to a poor Cubs club, the second game went into the 11th inning tied, two outs, bases loaded, pitcher's spot up. Why not Benny? Why not indeed. Agbayani's grand slam won the game, and he stayed with the team all year, settling in as a thumper in the eighth spot until Melvin Mora was traded and Benny moved up in the order. He had another solid season and saved his heroics for when they were most needed. Game 3 Division Series, tie game, tie series, 14th inning, wind howling in from left field. Whap! Gone. Shea goes nuts. Everyone loves Benny just a little bit more.

He should have kept his mouth shut when asked for his World Series prediction, but unlike his teammates, he at least brought his bat to the first real Subway Series in forty-four years, driving in the tiebreaking run in the only win for the Mets. But that was it. The spell ended, and those big hits no longer came. Fans started liking the exotic new flavor of Tsuyoshi Shinjo. Agbayani was traded and eventually had a reunion with Bobby Valentine and Matt Franco in Japan; this time toasting the championship with no Yankee rabble to ruin things.

As thrilling as the dual Hawaiian 5-0s were, others suffered by comparison.

Victor Diaz hit an Agbayani-esque home run in the 9th at Shea to start the 2004 Cubs on the road to ruin not unlike the '07 Mets (or '69 Cubs). After he switched to 20, Diaz seemed to find a way of hitting the off switch on his brain at the wrong time. He was quietly dealt during the 2006 season for minor league catcher Mike Nickeas.

Duaner Sanchez went unscored upon in his first 22 innings as a Met in 2006, including seven multiple-inning appearances, as the Mets roared to a big lead in the standings. Even when the National League caught up to him a little, the goggled one was still as good as any reliever the Mets—or the league—had to offer. Then he took a taxi. Not Harry Chapin's taxi either. If you could go back in time—and you'd already ended poverty, hunger, war, and talked Harry Frazee into keeping Babe Ruth—would you run onto the field before Aaron Heilman's fateful pitch to Yadier Molina or fasten Duaner Sanchez's seat belt? If you chose the latter, there'd have been no Oliver Perez to start that game so magnificently. But if Duaner wasn't hurt, would the Mets have even needed a Game 7? Call it the Duaner Quandary.

Not so thought provoking were the 50 portions of the careers of **Juan Castillo** (1994), **Rick Trlicek** (1997), the miserable **John Thomson** (2002), and **Matt Watson** (2003).

Number of times issued: 10 (8 players, 2 coaches)

Longest tenured: Sid Fernandez (10 seasons, 255 games), Benny Agbayani (3 seasons, 311 games)

Best single seasons: Fernandez, 1986 (16-6, 3.52 ERA, 200 strikeouts in 204.1 innings); Fernandez, 1989 (14-5, 2.83 ERA, 198 strikeouts in 219.1 innings); Agbayani, 2000 (.289/ .391/.480, 15 HR, 60 RBI); Duaner Sanchez, 2006 (5-1, 2.60 ERA, 44 strikeouts in 55.1 innings)

Career statistical leaders: Home runs (Agbayani 35), RBI (Agbayani 129), batting average (Agbayani .282), wins (Fernandez 98), saves (Fernandez 1), ERA (Fernandez 3.14)

"C" You Real Soon

In the early days of professional baseball, a captain also performed the duties of today's manager. The captain played, made out the lineup, and settled player disputes while the manager operated more like a general manager or business manager of today. Eventually the captain and manager monikers merged, and there didn't seem much purpose for a captain.

And after winning two world championships in their first twenty-five years of existence, the captain-free Mets seemed to do just fine (forgetting, of course, that period from 1962 to 1968 and that eternity between 1977 and 1983). On May 6, 1987, the Mets named their first captain: Keith Hernandez. It seemed an inspired choice. The first baseman was the leader on the field and in the locker room, handing out bon mots as needed to the press that swarmed around his smoky locker.

As if this didn't distinguish him enough, a *C* was stitched on his uniform. They also sewed one on the upper right corner of Gary Carter's jersey. The Mets doubled—or halved—the honor and made the catcher a captain for '88.

Why co-captains? George Vescey of the *New York Times* forwarded a theory: "The group-think is that appointing the fiery Hernandez was [Davey] Johnson's natural instinct, and that appointing the sunny Carter six months later was Johnson's way of appeasing Frank Cashen." But two captains couldn't outflank Major Orel Hershiser in battle in the NLCS.

The captains went out together, limping into the sunset—or Cleveland and San Francisco—after their injury-marred 1989. The Kid and Mex were two different personalities, but both were essential to the glory the Mets achieved as a unit in 1986.

The naming of the next captain came a season following another World Series appearance, albeit not a successful one. John Franco, a forty-year-old relief pitcher, was named captain on May 4, 2001. This germinated from the mind of none other than Turk Wendell. Wild-eyed Turk got the idea from hockey, where a captain actually has necessary on-ice duties. About the only official function a captain has in baseball is to take the lineup card to home plate (sometimes). Franco did this on his first night wearing the *C* and explained a Shea Stadium ground rule incorrectly. (He said that a ball hitting off the black backdrop in the picnic area was a live ball. It's not. But with meticulous Bobby Valentine in the dugout, players didn't sweat rule idiosyncrasies.) Franco did get the save that night, though.

The captaincy left with Franco following the 2004 season. Willie Randolph, a former Yankee co-captain with Ron Guidry (1986–89), named no Mets captain. "I feel like right now I'm the leader, so to speak," he told Mark Hale of the *New York Post* in 2007 spring training. "I think sometimes you've got to be careful with that because what happens is if you look for one guy to be the leader, then everyone else ceases to lead."

#51–99: THE HIGH NUMBERS

PROGRESSION:

Player	Years
Cookie Lavagetto (coach)	1962–1963
Wes Westrum (coach/manager)	1964–1965
Roy McMillan (coach/manager)	1973–1976
Denny Sommers (coach)	1977–1978
Dick Sisler (coach)	1979–1980
Deron Johnson (coach)	1981
Jim Frey (coach)	1982–1983
Vern Hoscheit (coach)	1984–1987
Tom Spencer (coach)	1991
John Stephenson (coach)	1992
Mike Maddux	1993–1994
Lance Johnson	1996
Mookie Wilson (coach)	1997
Mel Rojas	1997–1998
Rick White	2000–2001
Dave Engle (coach)	2002 (to June 12)
Chris Chambliss (coach)	2002 (from June 12)
Rick Peterson (coach)	2004–2007

Numbers over 50 are sort of the netherworld of Metdom. If not for Kenny Rogers (73) and Turk Wendell (99), teammates on a memorable Mets club with a 55 (Orel Hershiser), even us hardcores would have a hard time remembering anyone wearing a number beyond the Fernandez-Agbayani Equator. While these rough waters are on the map, the stats grow sparse as the beguiling trek commences. Few will last more than a year.

Number 51
Can we turn back now?

In this land of the frightening relievers, **Mike Maddux** is the first stop. He went 3-8 with a 3.80 ERA in a thankless role for the 1993 Mets. As the team improved, Maddux imploded. He was brutal in '94 and only the strike could wipe away any recall of the "Bad Maddux," who actually turned into a good pitching coach. (Having Greg Maddux as your little brother can't hurt in an interview.)

Rick White (2000–01) was kind of scary looking, but he did all right on the mound. He was part of that Steve Phillips Friday trading spree in July 2000 that resulted in Bubba Trammell and Mike Bordick both homering in their first Mets at-bats. White, just in from Tampa Bay, picked up a win in his first Mets appearance. He got an even more important win in Game 3 of that year's Division Series. He did some solid work for the Mets in 2001 as well.

There's just no explaining **Mel Rojas** (1997–98). One day he's a superb closer for the Expos. Next, the Cubs sign him to a huge contract and he becomes a batting-practice pitcher. Steve Phillips strolls by with his new allowance and pays full price for Rojas, who clearly belongs in the 99-cent bin. After trying to hide Rojas and his 6.05 ERA from the Shea boo-birds

247

in '98, the Mets shipped him to Los Angeles for none other than Bobby Bonilla.

Lance Johnson, part of that original deal for Rojas, obligingly changed to 51 for a game in 1996 to let Mookie Wilson have his own day and his own number when he was inducted into the Mets Hall of Fame. "We had to do what we could to make this day perfect," Johnson explained.

While fourteen coaches have worn 51, including **Rick Peterson** (who couldn't fix Victor Zambrano but patched several other holes and generally sounded smart until the chassis fell off the jalopy in September '07), two coaches have ridden the number to the manager's chair. **Wes Westrum** finished out the 1965 season in 51 as the hand-picked successor of the incapacitated Casey Stengel, but the following spring he snagged number 9 from Jim Hickman, who took on 6. A press corps hooked on Stengel-ese wished Westrum could have grabbed a fistful of personality while he was at it. Some of those same reporters still on the beat must have had a similar wish when **Roy McMillan** succeeded the colorful, quotable Yogi Berra as manager to finish out the 1975 season. McMillan returned to the quiet coaching lines the following spring.

Number of times issued: 18 (4 players, 14 coaches)

Best single season: Rick White, 2001 (4-5, 3.88 ERA, 2 saves, 51 strikeouts in 69.2 innings)

PROGRESSION:

Player	Years
Solly Hemus (coach)	1962–1963
Don Heffner (coach)	1964–1965
Harvey Haddix (coach)	1966–1967
Joe Pignatano (coach)	1968–1981
Greg Pavlick (coach)	1985–1986, 1988–1991, 1994–1996
Dave Wallace (coach)	1999–2000
Dave Engle (coach)	2001
Randy Niemann (coach)	2002–2003
Rick Waits (coach)	2003
Tony Clark	2003 (from June 5)
Don Baylor (coach)	2004
Guy Conti (coach)	2005
Howard Johnson (coach)	2007

Number 52

The next time you're fed up with the Mets or Willie Randolph, think back to 2003 and the Art Howe–led Mets. **Tony Clark** was the team's chief power source once Cliff Floyd left to polite applause due to a leg injury in late August. To Clark's credit, he remade himself at Shea a season after hitting just .207 with 3 homers as a regular for the Red Sox. Clark reached 30 homers for the first time in six years as a 2005 D-Back.

Number of times issued: 13 (1 player, 12 coaches)
Best single season: Tony Clark, 2003 (.232/.300/.472, 16 HR, 43 RBI)

PROGRESSION:

Player	Years
Rogers Hornsby (coach)	1962
Ernie White (coach)	1963
Mel Harder (coach)	1964
Sheriff Robinson (coach)	1966–1967
Eddie Yost (coach)	1968–1976
Tom Burgess (coach)	1977
Dal Maxville (coach)	1978
Chuck Cottier (coach)	1979–1981
Bud Harrelson (coach)	1982
Bobby Valentine (coach)	1983
Eric Hillman	1992–1994
Rafael Landestoy (coach)	1996
Tom Robson (coach)	1997–1999, 2000–2001
Mickey Brantley (coach)	1999
Dave Engle (coach)	2001
Mark Guthrie	2002
Verne Ruhle (coach)	2003
Jerry Manuel (coach)	2005
Chad Bradford	2006

Number 53

Mark Guthrie had a 27-inning scoreless streak for the 2002 Mets that stretched over 34 appearances. Did we mention he's left-handed? The streak ended and he got his first loss as a Met when he allowed a three-run blast to Luis Gonzalez that flushed the season down the toilet in early August, culminating with the sorry ending of the Bobby Valentine era. Guthrie, who'd come from the Art Howe Show in Oakland, did not stick around for the East Coast revival.

Chad Bradford, of *Moneyball* fame, was excellent in his one year as a Met, 2006. He took 53, Marty Noble reported on mlb.com, because he had a thing for 8 and liked to add: 5 + 3. His knuckle-dragging, sidearm slowball drove hitters nuts. It made Peter Angelos a little crazy as well because he threw $10.5 million at Bradford to bring him to Baltimore for three years. It was sad to see Bradford go, replaced (for a time) with the sidewinder in the hole, Joe Smith.

Eric Hillman (1992–94) was extremely tall (6-foot-10) and had a Mets career that was all or nothing (mostly the latter). Hillman got a chance to start regularly for the putrid 1993 club, throwing two masterful complete-game victories and losing his other nine decisions.

The Mets didn't score much between 1968 and 1976, so it was crucial that the man in charge of sending runners home be daring yet efficient. **Eddie Yost** was both. He was also loyal. He came to the Mets from Washington with Gil Hodges and fellow coaches Rube Walker and Joe Pignatano. Yost watched in disbelief as his trusted friend died in front of him after a round of golf in 1972, and he stayed through Yogi Berra's tenure and lasted a year into Joe Frazier's brief and unhappy reign before hightailing it to Boston. They called him "The Walking Man" because of the staggering 1,614 walks he drew with the old Senators (still in the top ten all-time), but Mets fans knew that keen eye also could see when to try to squeeze a little more offense from a slow-footed Mets runner rounding third on a one-hop single.

Until Willie Mays, the best player in history to serve as a Mets coach was **Rogers Hornsby** for the 1962 club. "Rajah" was a career .358 hitter who won seven batting titles—six in a row—including an unfathomable .424 average for the 1924 Cardinals. He was a prime example of a great hitter who failed to comprehend how someone couldn't hit an outside fastball one-hop off the wall. Every time. Having arguably the greatest-hitting second baseman of all-time coach hitters for arguably the worst team in modern history wasn't a great match. He scared the kids, disturbed the veterans, and at sixty-seven probably could have hit better than any second sacker the '62 Mets could muster. He died that winter, as did coach Red Kress. Makes one wonder how anyone survived that club.

Number of times issued: 19 (3 players, 16 coaches)

Best single seasons: Mark Guthrie, 2002 (5-5, 2.44, 44 strikeouts in 48 innings), Chad Bradford, 2006 (4-2, 2.90 ERA, 2 saves, 45 strikeouts in 62 innings)

Number 54

GM Joe McIlvaine snagged **Mark Clark** from Cleveland just before the 1996 season started, figuring he needed a veteran to offset Generation K. Good idea. Clark led the Mets in wins, ERA, strikeouts, and innings, while Jason Isringhausen and Paul Wilson combined for 11 wins and a 5.05 ERA (Bill Pulsipher missed the entire year). Clark was solid but not as good in '97, so new GM Steve Phillips sent him home to Illinois in a six-player deal with the Cubs. It's the kind of multiplayer deal that seems rare today because all the players involved were major leaguers. This was the deal that brought fellow high numberers Brian McRae (56), Mel Rojas (51), and Turk Wendell (99) to Shea.

PROGRESSION:

Player	Years
Red Ruffing (coach)	1962
Clyde McCullough (coach)	1963
Whitey Herzog (coach)	1966
Salty Parker (coach/manager)	1967
Rube Walker (coach)	1968–1981
Rob Dromerhauser (coach)	1988–1991
Mark Clark	1996–1997
Al Jackson (coach)	1999–2000
Charlie Hough (coach)	2001–2002
Rick Waits (coach)	2004 (see also 52)
Rick Down (coach)	2005–2007 (to July 13)
Brian Lawrence	2007 (from Aug. 2)

The 2007 Mets tried Mike Pelfrey, Jason Vargas, Dave Williams, and Chan Ho Park for a combined thirteen No. 5 starter appearances before reclamation project **Brian Lawrence** became the first pitcher to win a game (and in his first try). The aforementioned quartet was 0-10 with an 8.28 ERA. After winning in his debut, Lawrence was 0-2 in his five subsequent starts for the Amazin's.

Salty Parker is the least known of any Mets manager. And given that he spent one year as a Mets coach and went 4-7 in his brief tilt at the skipper's wheel in 1967, it should stay that way.

If any coach is ever considered for the Mets Hall of Fame, it should be **Rube Walker**. Taking into account that the process for induction into the exclusive circle located in the waiting area outside the Diamond Club has become as hard to interpret as the puffs of smoke from the College of Cardinals (in Rome not St. Louis), don't hold your breath that Rube will ever get the nod. But consider that Walker served as pitching coach from 1968 to 1981, nurtured the greatest array of pitching talent in club history, started the practice of the five-man rotation to protect those arms, and served faithfully under Gil Hodges, Yogi Berra, Roy McMillan, Joe Frazier, and Joe Torre without losing his mind (or job). The old Brooklyn catcher should receive a posthumous medal. There wasn't much about baseball that **Whitey Herzog** didn't know, except when it came to kissing up to those who paid the bills. Herzog coached the 1966 team, moved up to director of player development, helped put together the budding farm system, and probably could have moved into the general manager's seat when Johnny Murphy died in 1969 or the manager's office when Gil Hodges passed in 1972. Obviously neither job came his way. Herzog couldn't keep from continuously telling board chairman and stockbroker M. Donald Grant to stop interfering with personnel matters. How we all wish we could have said that to the Simon Legree of Shea. Maybe that would have made those three 1980s pennants Herzog won for the Cardinals at the Mets' expense a little easier to swallow.

Number of times issued: 12 (2 players, 10 coaches)
Best single season: Mark Clark, 1996 (14-11, 3.43, 142 strikeouts in 212.1 innings)

Number 55

Odd-looking former Mets nemesis **Orel Hershiser** (1999) showed Shea fans, at long last, why his teammates had called him "Bulldog" throughout his career. With nearly nothing left in the tank, Orel worked awfully hard to win a miraculous 13 games—including the 200th of his career—as a Met in '99. Who could forget Hershiser casually flinging the ball to second base in an improvised hidden ball trick as he was about to be lifted from a key game with the Braves? Or starting that final game of the season that the Mets *had* to win against powerful Pirates rookie Kris Benson, who hadn't yet been worn down by his wife, Anna. Or Hershiser's gritty 3.1 innings out of the pen in epic Game 5 of the NLCS. It was nice for the Mets to have the Bulldog on their side this time.

Shawn Estes (2002) will be remembered forever as the guy who missed Roger Clemens's butt but who humiliated him with a home run when Clemens finally showed his cowardly face at Shea. Disappointing and disowned, Estes went to Cincinnati in August for a few players, including **Pedro Feliciano** (2002–03). This Pedro wasn't any better than the other slop-throwers that clogged the Mets at the time, but Feliciano honed his craft as a Norfolk Tide, Fukuoka Daiei Hawk, and Shea mop-up guy upon his return stateside (wearing 39 and then 25) to become that lefty that every team desperately craves for their bullpen.

Joe Frazier had the name of a fighter. **Frank Howard** looked like one. Frazier was GM Joe McDonald's idea of a good manager when he came up from Tidewater to take over the 1976 Mets. With Tom Seaver coming off his third Cy Young, Jerry Koosman winning 20 and making a push for his own Cy Young, and Jon Matlack winning a career high 17 with 6 shutouts—not to mention Dave Kingman launching balls to Astoria (until he got hurt)—the Mets won 86 times while never even remotely contending in the NL East. His French Army–like collapse the following spring set the stage for the Joe Torre era (not the one they talked about on *Letterman*). Howard, a 6-foot-7 sweetheart, took over when George Bamberger could no longer hack managing in 1983. Hondo played the kids and let the Mets get the last bit of seven seasons of losing out of their system. He then returned to coach for Davey Johnson as if nothing had happened.

Number of times issued: 8 (3 players, 5 coaches)

Best single season: Orel Hershiser, 1999 (13-12, 4.58 ERA, 89 strikeouts in 179 innings)

PROGRESSION:	
Player	Years
Dyar Miller	1980
Bill Monbouquette (coach)	1982
Gene Dusan (coach)	1983
Jeff Kaiser	1993
Bob Apodaca (coach)	1996
Brian McRae	1997–1999
Darren Bragg	2001
Edwin Almonte	2003
Dave Racanelli (coach)	2004
Guy Conti (coach)	2006–2007

Number 56

A man came right from the office to Shea Stadium one Friday night in August 1997, unaware of Steve Phillips's first trade. The Shea patron stared blankly at the lineup posted on the scoreboard and mumbled in a baffled tone, "Who is number 56, and why is he batting first?" That's how **Brian McRae** came to Shea. B-Mac (1997–99) was the son of Hal McRae, the best designated hitter until Paul Molitor put away his glove. B-Mac possessed power from both sides of the plate, plus speed and fielding skills his father couldn't dream of, yet the numbers he put together in his one full season as a Met didn't resonate like dear old Dad's. Fans got on him, B-Mac got on them back—although not in the same league as Hal's famous Kansas City ashtray-tossing tirade—and the McRae era at Shea lasted just 300 games. It would be the longest and most productive stint of any Met to wear 56. Read on.

Darren Bragg, of Waterbury, Connecticut, chose 56 for Lawrence Taylor, a Giant in a different field. Bragg accrued 57 at-bats somewhat quickly in 2001 and then was set adrift just as fast to ply his hand at evil as a Yankee. Don't like to Bragg, but Darren lasted longer and fared better in Queens than the Bronx.

Dyar Miller was the first Met to break out 56. He did it in his breakout season of 1980. Yes, Mets had occasional breakout seasons in this time period; just nobody knew about them. A 1.93 ERA and 1 home run allowed stabilized a rocky bullpen—even with his penchant for allowing hits on other pitchers' accounts—and Joe Torre should have used him more on a team in perpetual need of relief. Miller slipped into 49 the next year and his breakout broke.

Jeff Kaiser (1993) and **Edwin Almonte** (2003) had forgettable months with really bad teams a decade apart.

Mostly, though, 56 belongs to coaches. It's been worn by **Bill Monbouquette** in a thankless role as George Bamberger's pitching coach,

Bob Apodaca before he got his 34 back, and **Guy Conti**, the affable bullpen coach for Willie Randolph.

Number of times issued: 9 (5 players, 4 coaches)

Best single seasons: Brian McRae, 1998 (.264/.360/.462, 21 HR, 79 RBI, 20 stolen bases); Dyar Miller, 1980 (1-2, 1.93 ERA, 1 save, 28 strikeouts in 42 innings)

Number 57

PROGRESSION:	
Player	Years
Tom Robson (coach)	2002 (see also 53)
Jason Roach	2003 (June 14–18, July 7–10, and from July 29)
Bobby Floyd (coach)	2004 (see also 55)
Eric Valent	2004 (from April 6)–2005 (April 4–May 28)

Eric Valent holds the distinction of wearing the highest number in club history while hitting for the cycle; he was also the last major leaguer—and only non-Expo—to do so at Stade Olympique. On the afternoon of July 29, 2004, Valent, batting seventh—ahead of David Wright!—hit a speaker with his high fly for a ground-rule home run. His 7th-inning triple got him the cycle, one of two three-baggers he had all year. That was enough to tie for the team lead. (Lest ye forget, *second baseman* Jose Reyes was hurt most of 2004.) The next year Valent couldn't get on track, and 57 was 86ed. He has not appeared in a major league game since.

Jason Roach was brought up three times during the 2003 season and was pummeled twice.

Number of times issued: 4 (2 players, 2 coaches)

Best single season: Eric Valent, 2004 (.267/.337/.481, 13 HR, 34 RBI)

Number 58

PROGRESSION:	
Player	Years
Luis Rosado	1980
Anderson Garcia	2006 (did not play)

Quick stop at 58. **Luis Rosado** is the only Met to appear in a game wearing that number, and he didn't get a hit.

Number of times issued: 2 (1 player, 1 DNP)

Number 59

This number brings out the GM, the defector, and the cheater.

Guillermo Mota would have been easier to forgive if he'd struck out Scott Spiezio in Game 2 of the 2006 NLCS, or if Shawn Green had come down with Spiezio's deep drive. That series-changing moment was one of the few failures on Mota's Mets résumé . . . at least until his drug test results were made public a few weeks later. Pre-Mets he was pitching batting practice in '06, with a 6.21 ERA in 34 games for Cleveland; Mota was 4-0 with a 2.39 earned run average in 25 games after the one-sided deal, including seven postseason appearances. He took it like a man, but he still got pinched and sat out 50 games in 2007.

How quickly things change when a man puts on your uniform. Mota was vilified after Mike Piazza went after him in spring training and both were suspended for brawling in 2003 while Mota was a Dodger. When Mota returned after his '07 suspension, he received heartfelt applause at Shea. This applause quickly died down—and eventually turned into a Shea-engulfing boo before he finished his jog in from the bullpen—when Mota showed himself to be a far less effective reliever than he had been pre-ban. That Willie Randolph continued to rely on him made the booing even louder.

Alay Soler (2006) started his major league career by walking the first three Phillies he faced, allowing a hit to the next batter, and then being victimized by an error that scored two runs. He persevered and wound up having a marvelous debut. Soler didn't get the win, but the Mets did. He won twice on the ensuing road trip from heaven, including a rare complete game in the Rick Peterson world. Then Soler, who'd risked all to defect from Cuba, couldn't get outs and found himself back in the minors. Despite a million Mets mound questions in spring training 2007, he was one of the first guys cut.

Brooklyn-born **Ed Lynch** wound up a general manager with the Cubs, but his first major league win came against Chicago on Senior Citizens' Day before a Saturday throng of 7,259 in 1980. He even picked up his first major league hit that day. Acquired a year earlier as the prospect portion of the Willie Montañez deal with Texas (Mike Jorgensen was the player part), Lynch would slip off 59 for lower numbers and stick around to see other prospects prosper around him.

> **Number of time issued:** 3 (3 players)
> **Best single season:** Guillermo Mota, 2006 (3-0, 1.00 ERA, 19 strikeouts in 18 innings)

PROGRESSION:

Player	Years
Al Odmundsen (coach)	1979–1980
Rob Dromerhauser (coach)	1987
Juan Lopez (coach)	2002–2003, 2006
Scott Schoeneweis	2007

Number 60

When Chad Bradford escaped New York to Baltimore and the market for veteran brand-name relievers went kerflooey along with him, the Mets abruptly reached into their pockets to be sure they didn't miss **Scott Schoeneweis** (2007). That was their second mistake. The lefty with the three-year deal proved remarkably unreliable, although he did wind up with a few late-season saves when Billy Wagner collapsed. The dam still burst. Then, while other teams, teams that had been in fourth place while the Mets had been in first, made preparations for a one-game playoff the Monday after the season ended, Schoeneweis was outed for receiving shipments of steroids when he was with the White Sox in 2003–04.

> **Number of times issued:** 4 (1 player, 3 coaches)

PROGRESSION:

Player	Years
Jesse Orosco	1979
Mario Ramirez	1980
Jeff Duncan	2003
Chan Ho Park	2007

Number 61

Jesse Orosco wore 61 for only a day, but he did the undoable. He got the last out in a game for the 1979 Mets. This didn't happen often. On April 5 that year, with two outs in the bottom of the 9th, and Dwight Bernard knocked out of a mop-up situation at packed Wrigley Field on opening day, Orosco induced his lone batter, Bill Buckner, to fly out. It was the first of his record 1,252 appearances in the majors and his only one not wearing 47. The number and the pitcher—he'd been in rookie ball the previous year with the Twins—needed to age a bit. He returned more experienced and transformed into one of the greatest relievers the franchise has seen.

While the Mets suffered through Mike Piazza's groin injury in May 2003, the already depleted club reached all the way to Class AA and made **Jeff**

Duncan's life. The 24-year-old outfielder had two hits in his first start, and the team was bad enough and banged-up enough that he played in 56 games despite the fact that he couldn't hit. When Mets continued getting hurt the next year, the smooth-fielding Duncan was back at Shea, but his .067 average assured there would be no third invitation.

Chan Ho Park was a subplot throughout 2007 spring training, but he dropped out of New York's plans like a stone after getting rocked the second time through the order in his only start. While **Mario Ramirez** (1980) spent almost as little time in 61 as Park, he did come back to see further action at No. 3.

Number of times issued: 4 (4 players)
Best single season: Jeff Duncan, 2004 (.197/.291/.245, 1 HR, 10 RBI)

Number 62

PROGRESSION:	
Player	Years
Hubie Brooks	1980

Fresh off the farm, **Hubie Brooks** came to the majors wearing 62. Fittingly, the Mets had been searching for a quality third baseman since '62. Hubie would do quite nicely. Brooks wore this number, the highest in Mets history until Turk Wendell hopped over the chalk, for a few games after his September summons. "It was the only uniform they had when I came up, so I had to take it," Brooks told the *New York Times.* "I'm kind of superstitious, so I told [equipment manager Herb Norman] I'd take any number under 62." They gave him 39. He received a respectful 7 the next spring.

Hubie's arrival signaled a shift from the jokes about the multitude of mediocre Mets at the position to a succession of third baseman who could hit, field, and lead, each seemingly better than the last.

Number of times issued: 1

Number 73

PROGRESSION:	
Player	Years
Kenny Rogers	1999

Kenny Rogers, "The Gambler," came a-riding in from the west to save the day for the '99 Mets. Save the day? Yes. Take a look at his 12 starts with the Mets that year.

Rogers led the Mets in complete games and won his first five decisions as the team went 10-2 in his starts. A sixth win was denied him when he was injured a few outs shy of qualifying for the win. With everyone assuming the Mets were finished the last weekend of the season, Rogers struck out 10—more than in his three previous starts combined—and the Mets won in extra innings and somehow ended up in the 11th inning of the NLCS with a chance to force a seventh game.

Maybe this is where we should mention he had some control issues and was not at his best pitching for New York teams in the postseason. The Gambler, whose uniform said 73 because the number he wore in every city except New York was retired for Casey Stengel (37), was back in the American League in his accustomed digits the following spring.

Rogers has continued to pitch through television cameraman tirades, Detroit dousings of fans, and World Series gems tossed with suspiciously smudgy fingers uncovered on national TV. That cameraman should watch out; you never know what Kenny Rogers might do.

> **Number of times issued:** 1 (1 player)
> **Best single season:** Kenny Rogers, 1999 (5-1, 4.03 ERA, 2 complete games, 58 strikeouts in 76 innings)

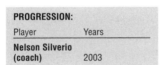

Number 84

Nelson Silverio was Art Howe's bullpen catcher in 2003. Why the son of 1970s California Angel Tom Silverio felt compelled to wear 84 is unknown, but at 5-11, 245, he could be a tight end . . . on a team bound for the basement.

PROGRESSION:	
Player	Years
Nelson Silverio (coach)	2003

> **Number of times issued:** 1 (1 coach)

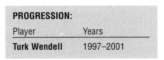

Number 99

Turk Wendell (1997–99) said he chose 99 because 13 was already gone. A lot of big numbers were doled out the day he got to Shea. The August 8, 1997, trade between the Mets and Cubs sent away advanced-digit wearer Mark Clark (54), one-day 51 Lance Johnson, plus the unadventurous—except when it came to hiding his steroids stash—Manny Alexander (6); in return came Mel Rojas (51), Brian McRae (56), and

PROGRESSION:	
Player	Years
Turk Wendell	1997–2001

Wendell in the high-numbers deal of the century for the Mets. Wendell, somewhat dismissed at the time of the trade, turned out to be the most significant player who changed places that day.

Wendell was a man of the people, befriending everyone he came in contact with at Shea and everywhere else. He pumped his fist, slammed the rosin bag, leapt over baselines, and brushed his teeth between innings. He got lost hunting mountain lions and wore a necklace of turkey teeth that could have severed his jugular. Behind all that flakiness, though, he worked hard and was willing to do anything within the rules to win, just as it was desire and not sideshows that marked the careers of Tug McGraw and Roger McDowell, the Mets relievers Wendell so vividly brings to mind.

Wendell set a Mets record by appearing in 80 games in 1999 (the year prior he set a club record by pitching in 9 successive games). His career ERA as a Met was a terrific 3.34 over an astonishing 285 games in four-plus seasons. His rubber arm fell off from a million sliders too many after he was traded to Philadelphia, but he was one Phillie it was hard to root against.

Number of times issued: 1 (1 player)

Best single season: Turk Wendell, 1999 (5-4, 3 saves, 3.05 ERA, 77 strikeouts in 80 games/85.2 innings)

Collage of Coaches

Coaches. Without them there'd be no one to hold on to baserunners' shin guards and batting gloves, no one to yell at when someone gets thrown out at home, and no one to fire when the team doesn't hit. It may sound like a thankless job, but it keeps a lot of old ballplayers close to the game while aiding the development of younger players. Some coaches are more helpful in developing skills like scratching, spitting, and cursing.

Coaching allowed Willie Mays to wear a Mets uniform for an extra five seasons. It gave the great Rogers Hornsby a foot in the door in 1962, which Rajah used to kick the backside of any rookie who looked in his direction. It put Hall of Fame pitchers Bob Gibson, Red Ruffing, and Warren Spahn in Mets uniforms way too late to be of much help. And it brought a lot of smart baseball minds into the Shea dugout where they either were in sync with the manager (Rube Walker and Mel Stottlemyre as prime examples) or banged their heads against the wall in frustration (too many to mention).

Mets coaches are listed by the uniform number each wore first as part of the coaching staff (followed by subsequent numbers in the order they were worn). Johnny Murphy spent the last week and a half of the 1967 season as a coach before taking over as general manager, but the number he wore—if any—is unknown. The rest are numbered below.

Number	Coach	Tenure
2	Gary Pettis	2003–2004
2	Sandy Alomar[1]	2005–2007
4	Mike Cubbage[1,2,3,5]	1990–1996
4, 8	Cookie Rojas	1997–2000
7	Bobby Wine	1993–1996
8	Yogi Berra[1,2,3,4]	1965–1971
8, 4	Matt Galante	2002–2004
10	Rusty Staub[1,4]	1982
12	John Stearns[1]	2000–2001
13, 8	Steve Swisher	1993–1996
15	Darrell Johnson	1993
15	Denny Walling	2003–2004
20	Bruce Benedict	1997–1999
21	Warren Spahn[1,4]	1965
22	Chuck Hiller[1]	1990
24	Willie Mays[1]	1974–1979
24	Rickey Henderson[1]	2007
25, 52	Don Baylor	2003–2004
26, 28	Bill Robinson	1984–1989
26	Barry Foote	1992–1993
27, 10	Tom McCraw	1992–1996
28	Dave LaRoche	1992–1993
32	Doc Edwards	1990–1991
34	Sam Perlozzo	1987–1989
44, 50	Phil Cavaretta	1975–1978
45	Bob Gibson	1981
45, 48, 52	Randy Niemann[1]	1997–1999, 2001–2002
48	Red Kress	1962
48, 30	Mel Stottlemyre	1984–1993
50, 3	Manny Acta	2005–06
51	Cookie Lavagetto	1962–1963

Number	Coach	Tenure
51	Wes Westrum[2,3]	1964–1965
51	Roy McMillan[1,2,3,5]	1973–1976
51	Denny Sommers	1977–1978
51	Dick Sisler	1979–1980
51	Deron Johnson	1981
51	Jim Frey	1982–1983
51	Vern Hoscheit	1984–1987
51	Tom Spencer	1991
51, 32	John Stephenson[1]	1992–1993
51, 1	Mookie Wilson[1]	1997–2002
51	Chris Chambliss	2002
51	Dave Engle	2001–2002
51	Rick Peterson	2004–2007
52	Solly Hemus	1962–1963
52	Don Heffner	1964–1965
52	Harvey Haddix	1966–1967
52	Joe Pignatano[1]	1968–1981
52	Greg Pavlick	1985–1986, 1988–1991, 1994–1996
52	Dave Wallace	1999–2000
52, 56	Guy Conti	2005–2007
52, 54	Rick Waits	2003–2004
52	Howard Johnson	2007
53	Rogers Hornsby	1962
53	Ernie White	1963
53	Mel Harder	1964
53, 55	Sheriff Robinson	1966–1967, 1972
53	Eddie Yost	1968–1976
53	Tom Burgess	1977
53	Dal Maxvill	1978
53	Chuck Cottier	1979–1981
53, 23, 3	Bud Harrelson[1,2,3]	1982, 1985–1990
53, 22, 28	Bobby Valentine[1,2]	1983–1985
53	Rafael Landestoy	1996
53, 57	Tom Robson	1997–1999, 2000–2002
53	Mickey Brantley	1999

Number	Coach	Tenure
53, 51	Dave Engle	2001–2002
53	Verne Ruhle	2003
53, 35	Jerry Manuel	2005–2007
54	Red Ruffing	1962
54	Clyde McCullough	1963
54	Whitey Herzog	1966
54	Salty Parker[2,3]	1967
54	Rube Walker	1968–1981
54	Rob Dromerhauser	1987–1991
54	Al Jackson[1]	1999-2000
54	Charlie Hough	2001–2002
54	Rick Down	2005–2007
55	Joe Fitzgerald	1973–1975
55	Frank Howard[2,3,5]	1982–1984, 1994–1996
55	Tom Nieto	2005–2007
56	Bill Monbouquette	1982
56	Gene Dusan	1983
56, 34	Bob Apodaca[1]	1996–1999
56	Dave Racanelli	2004
57, 55	Bobby Floyd	2001, 2004
60	Al Odmundsen	1979–1980
60	Juan Lopez	2002–2003, 2006–2007
84	Nelson Silverio	2003

[1]one-time Mets players who later coached the team
[2]coaches who later became Mets managers
[3]coaches who directly replaced a Mets manager
[4]player-coaches
[5]those who returned to the Mets as coaches after managing the team

#0–00: LESS THAN ZERO

Number 0

Some would say the career of **Rey Ordoñez** was a big, fat zero. That isn't true. Only the first two years of it were.

Ordoñez debuted as 0 on April Fool's Day, 1996, in an opening day downpour at Shea Stadium. He gunned down a runner at the plate from his knees in left field as the Mets staged a comeback from 6-0 down against the Cardinals. Ordoñez wowed the crowd with his remarkable range, popup slides, and bullet throws. His bat work, however, left a lot to be desired. Ordoñez hit .257—high for him—but he swung at everything, walking just 22 times with a mere 10 unintentional bases on balls in 151 games. He finished fifth in the Rookie of the Year balloting, but a *Newsday* scribe said anyone who voted for Ordoñez "just isn't paying attention."

Rey-Rey's attention drifted even more in 1997. He lost playing time to Manny Alexander after breaking a bone on his glove hand diving for a ball. After Alexander was traded, Luis Lopez saw plenty of time at short. Ordoñez homered on September 2—his only one of the year—and proceeded to go on an 0-for-37 skid, breaking the 35-year-old franchise mark for position players set by original Met Don Zimmer and tied by Tommie Agee in 1968 (0 for 34). Ordoñez fell just shy of pitcher Randy Tate's 0 for 41 set in his immortal hitless season of '75. The shortstop finished the year at .216, reaching base a quarter of the time while posting an unfathomable .256 slugging percentage. He did increase his unintentional walk total to 15 and stole 10 more bases than in his rookie year, though.

With Ozzie Smith retired, Ordoñez was the best-fielding shortstop in the league, and he won the first of three consecutive Gold Gloves in 1997. If he'd played in most other eras, when shortstops were expected to field everything and keep the game moving with unproductive at-bats, there'd have been few complaints. But now there was Jeter—a rookie the same year as Ordoñez—an offensive catalyst across town; A-Rod, already a batting champ in Seattle; and this kid in Boston named Nomar, who seemed like quite the hitter. Ordoñez still used a translator, but he had to know that the expectations at the position were getting higher.

So Ordoñez changed. Numbers. He took 10 in spring training in 1998, stating, "I want to be more than nothing." Oh, he's that. And more.

Outfielder **Terry McDaniel** was the first 0 in franchise history. He debuted on August 30, 1991, and disappeared into nothing just a month later.

Number of times issued: 2
Best single season: Rey Ordoñez, 1996 (.257/.289/.303, 1 HR, 30 RBI)

Number 00

PROGRESSION:	
Player	Years
Tony Clark	2003 (to June 5)

According to numerologists, zero is the number of nothingness and potentiality. **Tony Clark** asked for a double dose.

Clark arrived in 2003 having worn 17 and 44 as Tony the Tiger before switching to 22 for what became a down year with the Red Sox in 2002. Clark was one of several free agents in camp, but unlike Tom Glavine and Mike Stanton, Clark had to earn his spot. General manager Steve Phillips invited anyone who could walk to spring training, hoping to catch lightning in a bottle. With such a big group in camp, Clark was offered the choice of 00 or 88. He said, "I didn't want to hear any wide-receiver jokes." Instead, he heard a lot of Mr. Met jokes.

When too many school kids asked why he had Mr. Met's number, Clark switched to 52 on June 5 and homered his first time up in the new number. Ten of Clark's 16 homers came following the switch, but none came after Cliff Floyd left the lineup in mid-August. The powerless, punchless Mets stunk up the joint.

Number of times issued: 1
Single season: Tony Clark, 2003 (.196/.271/.443, 7 HR, 19 RBI)

Tony Clark vs. Mr. Met

Tony Clark, meet Mr. Met. For the chilly opening day festivities on March 31, 2003, the Mets had two 00s: Clark, the backup first baseman, and the team's longtime mascot, Mr. Met. How awkward.

At 6-foot-10, Mr. Met stood just three inches taller than Clark, but he towered over his adversary in so many ways. Mr. Met had first appeared on the cover of the 1963 yearbook in cartoon form, and a year later a man dressed as the mascot, a baseball first, roamed the stands at new Shea Stadium. It was a much more primitive—and smaller—head that Dan Reilly cavorted around in than today's noggin, but the kids loved Mr. Met right off the bat.

And since he was popular and beloved, it only made sense that M. Donald Grant put the kibosh on it. Mr. Met was rarely seen through the dwindling days of the deRoulet regime—why bother when there's Mettle the Mule!— and not at all when Doubleday and Wilpon took over.

Mr. Met emerged from hiding . . . to make a buck. A venture with Nickelodeon turned Shea

into an amusement park beyond right field in 1994. Mr. Met returned for good with a state-of-the art head and sporting 00 on his pinstripe uniform. It may have been cheesy, but at least someone was having fun as the screeches of kids could be heard above the agony on the field. Kids left the amusement park after the game to run the bases at Shea on certain Sundays.

The strike brought a premature end to Nick and the Mets' plans, but Mr. Met stuck around. He got new wardrobes as the Mets broke out new uni after new uni. When it rained he wore a yellow slicker and matching cap not unlike the Gorton's Fisherman of the Islanders' brief logo disaster.

Mr. Met got higher profile, popping up in commercials and TV guest spots, showing his head at civic functions and schools, and appearing at the odd birthday party. Mrs. Met sometimes appeared, but it mostly seemed like a marriage of convenience. "Hot dogs for dinner? Again!"

Then Tony Clark came along taking his number. Mr. Met didn't say anything, but Clark knew when he was licked. The night after a long rain delay perhaps gave him time to think, Clark switched to 52. "Mr. Met had 00 long before I got here, and he'll be here long after I leave," Clark told John Rowe of the *Record*. "It's his to keep."

#5, 7, 15, 17, 18: THE JEFF MCKNIGHTMARE

No player in Mets history has worn as many uniform numbers as Jeff McKnight. Over a sporadic four-year stint with the Mets, the bespectacled utility man suited up in an amazin' five different uniform numbers. His story, naturally, is one of persistence and versatility.

Jefferson Alan McKnight had a long journey into Mets history. Born on February 18, 1963, in Conway, Arkansas, McKnight, the switch-hitting son of former Cubs utility man Jim McKnight, was selected by the Mets in the second round of the January 1983 free-agent draft. He spent the next six and a half years in the Mets' farm system, developing into the kind of player who does many things adequately and none particularly well. McKnight could—and did—play all nine positions as a minor leaguer, yet he lacked the power, speed, and fielding skill to project as a big league starter at any of them. Never even invited to major league camp, by 1987 McKnight had settled into a reserve role for AAA Tidewater, and it appeared his chances for success in the big leagues were slim.

Then came 1989. The Mets' bid to repeat as Eastern Division champions would run off the tracks early, when All-Star starters Gary Carter and Keith Hernandez hit the disabled list within a week of one another in May. And when starting second baseman Tim Teufel sprained an ankle while jogging outside Wrigley Field on June 5, McKnight, who had logged 1,795 minor league at-bats to that point, finally got the call. The following day, pinch hitting from the left side for Roger McDowell, in the stadium his father played in, McKnight drove a 2-1 delivery from Calvin Schiraldi into left field for a single.

McKnight was wearing No. 15 then. He would see action in another 5 games, including 2 starts, before being optioned to Tidewater on June 18 when Teufel returned to active duty. McKnight spent the rest of the season there.

The story might have ended then, as the Mets released McKnight following the '89 season. However, he caught on with Baltimore and spent the next two years as a part-time Orioles backup and DH, becoming one of thirty-one second basemen to play alongside Cal Ripken during the Iron Man's consecutive-games streak. Non-tendered by Baltimore following the 1991 season, McKnight again caught on with the Mets, who offered him a non-roster invitation to spring training in 1992.

This time, he made the team, wearing No. 5 (Kevin Elster had 15 at that time and 13—McKnight's uni number with the O's—belonged then to Rodney McCray). McKnight spent all of April and most of August and September with the Mets that year. In 1993, McKnight again had to fight for an opening-day job—and won it—despite seeing his No. 5 issued to hotshot rookie Jeromy Burnitz, who'd debut later that season. McKnight instead opened 1993 in No. 7 but changed jerseys on May 22 when manager Jeff Torborg and his staff were fired. Dallas Green's new coach, Bobby Wine, wanted No. 7 and got it. McKnight switched to 17; but for the first time as a Met, he spent an entire year without a visit to Norfolk. (During all McKnight's number switching and moving, his former summer home had transformed from Tidewater to Norfolk without changing its address.)

Once again in 1994, McKnight found himself—and his number—pushed aside for a higher profile teammate. This time it was pitcher Bret Saberhagen, who was unhappy with the No. 18 issued him in 1993 and began '94 in McKnight's 17. Accepting the lot of the twenty-fifth man, McKnight acquiesced and took No. 18. Jeff would learn soon enough what Sabes disliked about 18: struggling with a .143 average in June, McKnight went onto the disabled list with a strained rib cage. The *Record* gave him a midseason grade of F, noting that his "only value to the Mets [is that] he's a Bob Dylan fan."

Newspapers speculated that summer that the Mets had "disabled" McKnight merely to create roster space artificially ("You can believe what you want to believe," Jeff told writers). But they hadn't stopped jerking him around. Sent to a Norfolk rehab assignment in July, McKnight was recalled to the majors on August 11 so that the team could send its promising young players—Burnitz and Fernando Viña—to AAA so they'd continue to play in the event of a strike. That night in Philadelphia, in the top of the 12th inning of a 1-1 game, McKnight entered as a pinch hitter for Eric Gunderson and singled off Tom Edens, only to be thrown out at second trying to stretch it into a double. The Phillies won the game in the bottom of the 12th, the players struck as threatened at midnight, and Jeff McKnight would never play another major league game. His New York legacy was 4 home runs, 28 RBI, a .250 average, and a record that might never be broken: five different Mets uniform numbers.

* * * * *

If Jeff McKnight leads the lineup of multiple-number wearing Mets, Ed Lynch is its starting pitcher.

Fans best remember Lynch for wearing No. 36—his digits for 145 of his 167 career games with the Mets. But his 22 other appearances were divided among three numbers on his back during 1980 and 1981.

Lynch owes much of his number collection, indirectly, to Craig Swan, the veteran Mets pitcher whose frequent breakdowns over the tail end of his career provided Lynch with his first three opportunities—and first three uni numbers. Shoulder trouble suffered by Swan in late August of 1980 required the Mets to summon Lynch while on a West Coast trip. Like several Mets call-ups in 1980, Lynch was initially issued a high number (59) for his debut appearance in San Francisco. But Lynch was wearing No. 35 shortly after the Mets returned home to Shea.

In April of 1981, Lynch reappeared in No. 35 after Swan was taken out of action by his own teammate: attempting to catch Tim Raines stealing second in the first inning, catcher Ron Hodges' throw drilled Swan in the back, breaking one of Swan's ribs (needless to say, Raines was safe; he eventually scored to hand Swan an especially hard-luck loss). Lynch was sent back to Tidewater shortly after Swan was reactivated, mere days before a two-month strike interrupted the season. Baseball resumed anew in August, but Swan's shoulder was only older and rustier, and Lynch was back; only this time, he was wearing No. 34. That's because Randy Jones, the former All-Star whose 35 jersey would one day be retired by the Padres, apparently decided during the strike to take back his familiar number (Jones was in 25 previously).

Lynch finally won a roster spot on his own ability in 1982 and remained a good Met soldier until 1986, in his familiar No. 36.

Utility infielder Kevin Collins also wore four different numbers—one for each truncated visit with the Mets over four seasons. He debuted in 1965 as No. 10, returned for a September call-up in 1967 as 19, spent four months wearing No. 16 in 1968, and finally inherited Jerry Buchek's former No. 1 in 1969 before becoming outbound freight in the famous Donn Clendenon trade with Montreal.

From the Office of McKnight, Lynch, & Collins

Ron Darling switched numbers when he felt like it. Roger Craig changed jerseys to change his luck. But the majority of Mets triple threats were bit players who took what they were given and/or assembled their jersey collection on the way to establishing an identity.

Typical of the below list is Jason Phillips, the backup catcher who suited up in Nos. 7, 26, and 23—and technically, at least, in No. 3. Phillips was called up to Mets from AA Binghamton in May of 2001 due to a player shortage occurring when reliever Tom Martin went down with a sudden injury and outfielder Darryl Hamilton was a day short of returning from the disabled list. Phillips then was issued a jersey, No. 3, but did not appear in a game before being sent back down when Hamilton returned the next day. Later that year, Phillips made his "official" Mets debut in No. 26—his No. 3 had in the meantime been issued to reserve backstop Vance Wilson. No. 26 was issued to Marco Scutaro prior to Phillips's September call-up of 2002, so Phillips instead wore No. 7. But in the spring of 2003, the Mets reserved No. 7 for superstar-in-waiting Jose Reyes and told Phillips to take No. 23 instead. That would be his number for the remainder of his Mets career.

Following is a list of membership in the Mets' exclusive three-number club, through 2007:

Name	Numbers Worn
Jeff McKnight	5, 7, 15, 17, 18
Kevin Collins	1, 10, 16, 19
Ed Lynch	34, 35, 36, 59
Darrell Sutherland	43, 45, 47
Cleon Jones	34, 12, 21
John Stephenson	12, 19, 49
Jim Hickman	6, 9, 27
Mike Jorgensen	10, 16, 22
Hank Webb	22, 29, 30
Hubie Brooks	62, 39, 7
Clint Hurdle	7, 13, 33
Chuck Carr	1, 7, 21
Kevin Elster	2, 15, 21
Charlie O'Brien	5, 22, 33
Ron Darling	12, 15, 44
Jason Phillips	7, 23, 26
David Cone	16, 17, 44
Jae Seo	40, 38, 26
Roger Craig	13, 36, 38
Lee Mazzilli	12, 16, 13
Pedro Feliciano	55, 39, 25
Mike DiFelice	6, 33, 9

COMPLETE NUMERICAL ROSTER

Following is an alphabetical list of all Mets players and their uniform numbers. An asterisk (*) indicates that the player was assigned that number but did not appear in a game while wearing it.

A

Don Aase (1989)	15, 49
Kurt Abbott (2000)	20
Juan Acevedo (1997)	39
Jon Adkins (2007)	39
Benny Agbayani (1998–2001)	39, 50
Tommie Agee (1968–72)	20
Rick Aguilera (1985–89)	38, 15
Jack Aker (1974)	22
Manny Alexander (1997)	6
Edgardo Alfonzo (1995–2002)	13
Neil Allen (1979–83)	46, 16
Jermaine Allensworth (1998–99)	46, 23
Bill Almon (1980, 1987)	25, 2
Edwin Almonte (2003)	57
Roberto Alomar (2002–03)	12
Sandy Alomar Jr. (2007)	19, 28
Sandy Alomar (1967)	5
Jesus Alou (1975)	23
Moises Alou (2007)	18
George Altman (1964)	2
Luis Alvarado (1977)	19
Chip Ambres (2007)	36

Craig Anderson (1962–64)	20, 29
Jason Anderson (2003)	17
Marlon Anderson (2005, 2007)	18, 23
Rick Anderson (1986)	32
Bob Apodaca (1973–77)	34
Kevin Appier (2001)	17
Jerry Arrigo (1966)	34
Richie Ashburn (1962)	1
Tucker Ashford (1983)	11
Bob Aspromonte (1971)	2
Pedro Astacio (2002–03)	34
Benny Ayala (1974, 1976)	18
Manny Aybar (2005)	36

B

Wally Backman (1980–88)	28, 6
Mike Bacsik (2002–03)	33
Carlos Baerga (1996–98)	6, 8
Kevin Baez (1990, 1992–93)	36, 1
Bob Bailor (1981–83)	4
Billy Baldwin (1976)	21
James Baldwin (2004)	38
Rick Baldwin (1975–77)	45
Brian Bannister (2006)	40
Lute Barnes (1972–73)	1
Jeff Barry (1995)	18
Kevin Bass (1992)	21
Ed Bauta (1963–64)	38
Billy Beane (1984, 1985)	43, 35
Larry Bearnarth (1963–66)	31

Blaine Beatty (1989, 1991)	38
Jim Beauchamp (1972–73)	24, 5
Rich Becker (1998)	6
Derek Bell (2000)	16
Gus Bell (1962)	3
Heath Bell (2004–06)	19
Jay Bell (2003)	44
Carlos Beltran (2005–07)	15
Rigo Beltran (1998–99)	43
Armando Benitez (1999–2003)	49
Dennis Bennett (1967)	38
Gary Bennett (2001)	7
Kris Benson (2004–05)	34
Butch Benton (1978, 1980)	15, 19
Juan Berenguer (1978–80)	43
Bruce Berenyi (1984–86)	27, 31
Dwight Bernard (1978–79)	28
Yogi Berra (1965)	8
Jim Bethke (1965)	41, 28, 36
Steve Bieser (1997)	29
Mike Birkbeck (1992, 1995)	48, 36
Mike Bishop (1983)	11
Willie Blair (1998)	46
Terry Blocker (1985)	21
Bruce Bochy (1982)	9
Tim Bogar (1993–96)	23, 11
Brian Bohanon (1997–98)	46
Bruce Boisclair (1974, 1976–79)	26, 4
Danny Boitano (1981)	36
Mark Bomback (1980)	36
Bobby Bonilla (1992–95, 1999)	25

Mike Bordick (2000)	17
Toby Borland (1997)	43
Don Bosch (1967–68)	17
Daryl Boston (1990–92)	7, 6
Ken Boswell (1967–1974)	24, 12
Ricky Bottalico (2004)	34, 20
Ed Bouchee (1962)	11, 3
Larry Bowa (1985)	2
Ken Boyer (1966–67)	14
Chad Bradford (2006)	53
Mark Bradley (1983)	9
Darren Bragg (2001)	56
Craig Brazell (2004)	9
Ed Bressoud (1966)	1
Rico Brogna (1994–96)	26
Hubie Brooks (1980–84, 1991)	62, 39, 7
Terry Bross (1991)	46
Kevin Brown (1990)	43
Leon Brown (1976)	23
Mike Bruhert (1978)	26
Brian Buchanan (2004)	10
Jerry Buchek (1967–68)	1
Damon Buford (1995)	2
Ambiorix Burgos (2007)	40
Tim Burke (1991–1992)	4
Jeromy Burnitz (1993–94, 2002–03)	5, 20
Larry Burright (1963–64)	6
Ray Burris (1979–80)	26, 34
Brett Butler (1995)	22
Paul Byrd (1995–96)	43

C

Miguel Cairo (2005)	3
Mike Cameron (2004–05)	44
Eric Cammack (2000)	29
John Candelaria (1987)	45
John Cangelosi (1994)	44
Chris Cannizzaro (1962–65)	8, 5
Buzz Capra (1971–73)	38
José Cardenal (1979–80)	6
Don Cardwell (1967–70)	27
Duke Carmel (1963)	1
Chuck Carr (1990–91)	7, 1, 27
Mark Carreon (1987–91)	32, 45
Gary Carter (1985–89)	8
Alberto Castillo (1995–98)	30
Juan Castillo (1994)	50
Luis Castillo (2007)	1
Tony Castillo (1991)	36
Ramon Castro (2005–07)	11
Roger Cedeño (1999, 2002–03)	19
Jaime Cerda (2002–03)	43
Rick Cerone (1991)	13
Elio Chacon (1962)	7
Dean Chance (1970)	27
Kelvin Chapman (1979, 1984–85)	10, 11
Ed Charles (1967–69)	24, 5
Endy Chavez (2006–07)	10
Bruce Chen (2001–02)	32
Rich Chiles (1973)	29
Harry Chiti (1962)	44

John Christensen (1984–85)	35, 7
McKay Christensen (2002)	23
Joe Christopher (1962–65)	23
Galen Cisco (1962–65)	26
Brady Clark (2002)	15
Mark Clark (1996–97)	54
Tony Clark (2003)	00, 52
Donn Clendenon (1969–71)	22
Gene Clines (1975)	1
Brad Clontz (1998)	49
Choo Choo Coleman (1962–63, 1966)	17, 20
Vince Coleman (1991–93)	1, 11
Willie Collazo (2007)	36
Kevin Collins (1965, 1967–69)	10, 19, 16, 1
David Cone (1987–1992, 2003)	44, 17, 16
Jeff Conine (2007)	28, 19
Bill Connors (1967–68)	38, 33, 45
Cliff Cook (1962–63)	6, 1
Dennis Cook (1998–2001)	27
Tim Corcoran (1986)	29
Mark Corey (2001–02)	27
Mardie Cornejo (1978)	47
Reid Cornelius (1995)	47
Billy Cowan (1965)	3
Roger Craig (1962–63)	38, 36, 13
Jerry Cram (1974–75)	38
Joe Crawford (1997)	49
Mike Cubbage (1981)	3

D

Jeff D'Amico (2002)	13
Vic Darensbourg (2004)	39
Ron Darling (1983–91)	44, 12, 15
Brian Daubach (2005)	13
Ray Daviault (1962)	35
Kane Davis (2002)	48
Tommy Davis (1967)	12
Mike DeJean (2004–05)	35
Carlos Delgado (2006–07)	21
Wilson Delgado (2004)	17
John DeMerit (1962)	29
Bill Denehy (1967)	44
Joe DePastino (2003)	10
Mark Dewey (1992)	43
Carlos Diaz (1982–83)	32
Mario Diaz (1990)	34
Victor Diaz (2004–06)	50, 20
Mike DiFelice (2005–07)	33, 6, 9
Jack DiLauro (1969)	31
Steve Dillon (1963–64)	39
Jerry Dipoto (1995–96)	45
Chris Donnels (1991–92)	23
Octavio Dotel (1999)	29
D. J. Dozier (1992)	7
Sammy Drake (1962)	12
Mike Draper (1993)	47
Jeff Duncan (2003–04)	61, 10
Shawon Dunston (1999)	12
Jim Dwyer (1976)	25
Duffy Dyer (1968–74)	18, 10
Lenny Dykstra (1985–89)	4

E

Damion Easley (2007)	3
Tom Edens (1987)	32
Dave Eilers (1965–66)	38
Larry Elliot (1964, 1966)	42, 17
Dock Ellis (1979)	35
Kevin Elster (1986–92)	2, 21, 15
Scott Erickson (2004)	19
Alex Escobar (2001)	25
Nino Espinosa (1974–78)	48, 39
Alvaro Espinoza (1996)	12
Shawn Estes (2002)	55
Chuck Estrada (1967)	33
Francisco Estrada (1971)	5
Carl Everett (1995–97)	3

F

Jorge Fabregas (1998)	12
Pete Falcone (1979–82)	33
Pedro Feliciano (2002–04, 2006–07)	55, 39, 25
Chico Fernandez (1963)	7
Sid Fernandez (1984–93)	50
Tony Fernandez (1993)	1
Sergio Ferrer (1978–79)	3, 1
Tom Filer (1992)	44
Jack Fisher (1964–67)	22
Mike Fitzgerald (1983–84)	20
Shaun Fitzmaurice (1966)	5
Don Florence (1995)	36
Gil Flores (1978–79)	17

Cliff Floyd (2003–06)	30
Doug Flynn (1977–1981)	23
Tim Foli (1970–71, 1978–79)	19
Rich Folkers (1970)	38
Brook Fordyce (1995)	5
Bartolome Fortunato (2004, 2006)	43
Larry Foss (1962)	27
George Foster (1982–86)	15
Leo Foster (1976–77)	1, 19
Joe Foy (1970)	5
John Franco (1990–01, 2003–04)	31, 45
Julio Franco (2006–07)	23
Matt Franco (1996–2000)	15
Jim Fregosi (1972–73)	11
Bob Friend (1966)	20
Danny Frisella (1967–1972)	29, 34
Mike Fyhrie (1996)	40

G

Brent Gaff (1982–84)	45
Bob Gallagher (1975)	22
Dave Gallagher (1992–93)	8
Danny Garcia (2003–04)	12
Karim Garcia (2004)	20
Ron Gardenhire (1981–85)	19, 21*
Jeff Gardner (1991)	19
Rob Gardner (1965–66)	29
Wes Gardner (1984–85)	27
Wayne Garrett (1969–76)	11
Rod Gaspar (1969–70)	17

Gary Gentry (1969–72)	39
John Gibbons (1984, 1986)	8, 35, 43*
Bob Gibson (1987)	38
Paul Gibson (1992–93)	45
Shawn Gilbert (1997–98)	12
Brian Giles (1981–83)	23, 15
Bernard Gilkey (1996–98)	23
Joe Ginsberg (1962)	12
Matt Ginter (2004)	13
Mike Glavine (2003)	27
Tom Glavine (2003–07)	47
Ed Glynn (1979–1980)	48
Carlos Gomez (2007)	27
Jesse Gonder (1963–65)	16, 12
Dicky Gonzalez (2001)	39
Jeremi Gonzalez (2006)	32
Raul Gonzalez (2002–03)	21
Dwight Gooden (1984–94)	16
Greg Goossen (1965–68)	20, 10
Tom Gorman (1982–85)	29
Jim Gosger (1969, 1973–74)	18, 19, 5
Ruben Gotay (2007)	6
Mauro Gozzo (1993–94)	45
Bill Graham (1967)	26
Wayne Graham (1964)	4
Danny Graves (2005)	32
Dallas Green (1966)	27
Pumpsie Green (1963)	18
Shawn Green (2006–07)	20
Charlie Greene (1996)	7
Kenny Greer (1993)	35

Tom Grieve (1978)	2
Jeremy Griffiths (2003)	46
Jerry Grote (1966–1977)	15
Joe Grzenda (1967)	43
Lee Guetterman (1992)	35
Eric Gunderson (1994–95)	40
Mark Guthrie (2002)	53
Ricky Gutierrez (2004)	6

H

Don Hahn (1971–74)	25
Tom Hall (1975–76)	42, 19
Shane Halter (1999)	11
Darryl Hamilton (1999–2001)	18
Jack Hamilton (1966–67)	32
Ike Hampton (1974)	20
Mike Hampton (2000)	32
Tim Hamulack (2005)	46
Todd Haney (1998)	18
Jason Hardtke (1996–97)	19
Shawn Hare (1994)	19
Tim Harkness (1963–64)	3
Pete Harnisch (1995–97)	27
Bud Harrelson (1965–1977)	3
Greg Harris (1981)	20
Lenny Harris (1998, 2000–01)	19
Greg Harts (1973)	6
Andy Hassler (1979)	44
Tom Hausman (1978–1982)	32
Ed Hearn (1986)	49

Richie Hebner (1979)	3
Danny Heep (1983–86)	25
Jack Heidemann (1975–76)	12
Aaron Heilman (2003–07)	48
Bob Heise (1967–69)	23, 28
Ken Henderson (1978)	10
Rickey Henderson (1999–2000)	24
Steve Henderson (1977–1980)	5
Bob Hendley (1967)	33
Phil Hennigan (1973)	34
Doug Henry (1995–96)	35
Bill Hepler (1966)	28
Ron Herbel (1970)	31
Felix Heredia (2005)	49
Anderson Hernandez (2005–07)	1, 4
Keith Hernandez (1983–89)	17
Manny Hernandez (1989)	36
Orlando Hernandez (2006–07)	26
Roberto Hernandez (2005–06)	39, 49
Tom Herr (1990–91)	28
Rick Herrscher (1962)	6
Orel Hershiser (1999)	55
Jim Hickman (1962–66)	9, 27, 6
Joe Hicks (1963)	22
Richard Hidalgo (2004)	15
Joe Hietpas (2004)	10
Chuck Hiller (1965–67)	2
Dave Hillman (1962)	34
Eric Hillman (1992–94)	53
Brett Hinchliffe (2001)	32
Jerry Hinsley (1964, 1967)	24, 40

Gil Hodges (1962–63)	14
Ron Hodges (1973–1984)	42
Scott Holman (1980, 1982–83)	26, 28
Jay Hook (1962–64)	47
Wayne Housie (1993)	2
Mike Howard (1981–83)	5
Pat Howell (1992)	38
John Hudek (1998)	43
Jessie Hudson (1969)	38
Keith Hughes (1990)	12
Philip Humber (2006–07)	49
Todd Hundley (1990–98)	49, 9
Ron Hunt (1963–66)	33
Willard Hunter (1962, 1964)	29, 38
Clint Hurdle (1983, 1985, 1987)	33, 13, 7
Jonathan Hurst (1994)	13
Butch Huskey (1993, 1995–98)	10, 42

I

Jeff Innis (1987–93)	40
Kaz Ishii (2005)	23
Jason Isringhausen (1995–97, 1999)	29,* 44

J

Al Jackson (1962–65, 1968–69)	15, 38
Darrin Jackson (1993)	3
Roy Lee Jackson (1977–1980)	31
Mike Jacobs (2005)	27
Jason Jacome (1994–95)	47

Gregg Jefferies (1987–1991)	9
Stan Jefferson (1986)	27
Chris Jelic (1990)	46
Ben Johnson (2007)	4
Bob D. Johnson (1969)	29
Bob W. Johnson (1967)	25, 6
Howard Johnson (1985–1993)	20, 44
Lance Johnson (1996–97)	1, 51
Mark Johnson (2000–02)	5, 20
Barry Jones (1992)	46
Bobby J. Jones (1993–2000)	28
Bobby M. Jones (2000, 2002)	21
Chris Jones (1995–96)	5
Cleon Jones (1963, 1965–1975)	34, 12, 21
Randy Jones (1981–82)	25, 35
Ross Jones (1984)	21
Sherman Jones (1962)	36, 28
Ricardo Jordan (1997)	48
Mike Jorgensen (1968, 1970–71, 1980–83)	10, 16, 22
Jorge Julio (2006)	34

K

Jeff Kaiser (1993)	56
Rod Kanehl (1962–64)	10
Takashi Kashiwada (1997)	18
Jeff Kent (1992–96)	39, 12
Jeff Keppinger (2004)	6
Dave Kingman (1975–77, 1981–83)	26
Mike Kinkade (1998–2000)	33
Wayne Kirby (1998)	11

Bobby Klaus (1964–65)	6
Jay Kleven (1976)	22
Lou Klimchock (1966)	6
Ray Knight (1984–86)	22
Kevin Kobel (1978–1980)	49
Gary Kolb (1965)	18
Satoru Komiyama (2002)	7
Dae-Sung Koo (2005)	17
Cal Koonce (1967–1970)	34
Jerry Koosman (1967–1978)	36
Ed Kranepool (1962–1979)	21, 7
Gary Kroll (1964–65)	25

L

Clem Labine (1962)	41
Jack Lamabe (1967)	34
David Lamb (2000)	26
Hobie Landrith (1962)	5
Ced Landrum (1993)	26
Frank Lary (1964–65)	17
Bill Latham (1985)	44, 33
Brian Lawrence (2007)	54
Matt Lawton (2001)	23
Terry Leach (1981–82, 1985–89)	43, 26
Tim Leary (1981, 1983–84)	38
Ricky Ledee (2006–07)	9
Aaron Ledesma (1995)	11
Al Leiter (1998–2004)	22
Johnny Lewis (1965–67)	24
Dave Liddell (1990)	36

Cory Lidle (1997)	11
Jose Lima (2006)	17
Jim Lindeman (1994)	29
Doug Linton (1994)	30
Phil Linz (1967–68)	2
Mark Little (2002)	21
Graeme Lloyd (2003)	17
Paul Lo Duca (2006–07)	16
Ron Locke (1964)	45
Skip Lockwood (1975–79)	38
Mickey Lolich (1976)	29
Phil Lombardi (1989)	39
Kevin Lomon (1995)	44
Terrence Long (1999)	26
Braden Looper (2004–05)	40
Luis Lopez (1997–99)	17
Al Luplow (1966–67)	18
Ed Lynch (1980–86)	59, 35, 34, 36
Barry Lyons (1986–1990)	33

M

Rob MacDonald (1996)	49
Julio Machado (1989–1990)	31, 48
Ken MacKenzie (1962–63)	19
Elliott Maddox (1978–1980)	21
Mike Maddux (1993–94)	51
Dave Magadan (1986–1992)	29, 10
Pat Mahomes (1999–2000)	23
John Maine (2006–07)	33
Pepe Mangual (1976–77)	11, 21

Phil Mankowski (1980, 1982)	2, 8
Jim Mann (2000)	39
Felix Mantilla (1962)	18
Barry Manuel (1997)	26
Josias Manzanillo (1993–95, 1999)	39
Eli Marrero (2006)	32
Dave Marshall (1970–72)	18
Jim Marshall (1962)	6
Mike G. Marshall (1981)	28
Mike A. Marshall (1990)	6
J. C. Martin (1968–69)	9
Jerry Martin (1984)	9
Tom Martin (2001)	34
Pedro A. Martinez (1996)	48
Pedro Martinez (2005–06)	45
Ted Martinez (1970–74)	17, 23
Roger Mason (1994)	48
Jon Matlack (1971–77)	35,* 32
Kaz Matsui (2004–06)	25
Gary Matthews (2002)	25
Mike Matthews (2005)	27
Jerry May (1973)	20
Brent Mayne (1996)	17
Willie Mays (1972–73)	24
Lee Mazzilli (1976–81, 1986–89)	12, 16, 13
Jim McAndrew (1968–1973)	43
Bob McClure (1988)	27
Terry McDaniel (1991)	0
Roger McDowell (1985–89)	42
Chuck McElroy (1999)	34
Joe McEwing (2000–04)	47, 11

Tug McGraw (1965–67, 1969–1974)	45
Ryan McGuire (2000)	40
Jeff McKnight (1989, 1992–94)	15, 5, 7, 18, 17
Greg McMichael (1997–99)	36
Roy McMillan (1964–66)	11
Brian McRae (1997–99)	56
Kevin McReynolds (1987–1991, 1994)	22
Doc Medich (1977)	22
Carlos Mendoza (1997)	6
Orlando Mercado (1990)	35
Butch Metzger (1978)	45
Jason Middlebrook (2002–03)	27
Doug Mientkiewicz (2005)	16
Felix Millan (1973–77)	16, 17
Lastings Milledge (2006–07)	44
Bob G. Miller (1962)	23,* 36
Bob L. Miller (1962, 1973–74)	24, 30
Dyar Miller (1980–81)	56, 49
Keith Miller (1987–91)	25
Larry Miller (1965–66)	35
Ralph Milliard (1998)	26
Randy Milligan (1987)	27
John Milner (1971–77)	28
Blas Minor (1995–96)	34
John Mitchell (1986–89)	43
Kevin Mitchell (1984, 1986)	32, 35, 7
Vinegar Bend Mizell (1962)	26
Dave Mlicki (1995–98)	38
Herb Moford (1962)	26
Willie Montañez (1978–79)	25
Joe Moock (1967)	18

Tommy Moore (1972–73)	19, 39
Bob Moorhead (1962, 1965)	22, 21
Melvin Mora (1999–2000)	6
Jerry Morales (1980)	25
Al Moran (1963–64)	40
Jose Moreno (1980)	4
Orber Moreno (2003–04)	49
Kevin Morgan (1997)	10
Guillermo Mota (2006–07)	59
Carlos Muniz (2007)	38
Billy Murphy (1966)	23
Dale Murray (1978–79)	22
Dan Murray (1999)	48
Eddie Murray (1992–93)	33
Dennis Musgraves (1965)	34
Jeff Musselman (1989–1990)	13
Randy Myers (1985–89)	48
Bob Myrick (1976–78)	44

N

Xavier Nady (2006)	22
Danny Napoleon (1965–66)	16
Tito Navarro (1993)	36
Charlie Neal (1962–63)	4
David Newhan (2007)	17
Randy Niemann (1985–86)	46, 40
C. J. Nitkowski (2001)	40
Junior Noboa (1992)	3
Joe Nolan (1972)	35
Hideo Nomo (1998)	16

Dan Norman (1977–80)	33, 8
Edwin Nunez (1988)	45
Jon Nunnally (2000)	26

O

Charlie O'Brien (1990–93)	22, 33
Tom O'Malley (1989–90)	27
Alex Ochoa (1995–97)	22
Jose Offerman (2005)	35
Bob Ojeda (1986–1990)	19
John Olerud (1997–99)	5
Darren Oliver (2006)	26
Jose Oquendo (1983–84)	2
Rey Ordoñez (1996–2002)	0, 10
Jesse Orosco (1979, 1981–87)	61, 47
Joe Orsulak (1993–95)	6
Junior Ortiz (1983–84)	34
Brian Ostrosser (1973)	19
Ricky Otero (1995)	1
Amos Otis (1967, 1969)	28, 25
Henry Owens (2006)	36
Rick Ownbey (1982–83)	20

P

John Pacella (1977, 1979–1980)	20
Tom Paciorek (1985)	44
Juan Padilla (2005)	28
Craig Paquette (1998)	18
Chan Ho Park (2007)	61

Harry Parker (1973–75)	31
Rick Parker (1994)	11
Jose Parra (2004)	46
Tom Parsons (1964–65)	27
Jay Payton (1998–2002)	25, 44
Bill Pecota (1992)	32
Al Pedrique (1987)	25
Mike Pelfrey (2006–07)	34
Brock Pemberton (1974–75)	2
Alejandro Pena (1990–91)	26
Oliver Perez (2006–07)	46
Timo Perez (2000–03)	6
Yorkis Perez (1997)	25
Robert Person (1995–96)	29
Roberto Petagine (1996–97)	20, 10
Bobby Pfeil (1969)	1
Jason Phillips (2001–04)	3*, 26, 7, 23
Mike Phillips (1975–77)	5
Tony Phillips (1998)	6
Mike Piazza (1998–2005)	31
Jimmy Piersall (1963)	34, 2
Joe Pignatano (1962)	5
Grover Powell (1963)	41
Todd Pratt (1997–2001)	43, 7
Rich Puig (1974)	6
Charlie Puleo (1981–82)	25
Bill Pulsipher (1995, 1998, 2000)	21, 25

R

Gary Rajsich (1982–83)	21

Mario Ramirez (1980)	61, 3
Lenny Randle (1977–78)	11
Willie Randolph (1992)	12
Bob Rauch (1972)	44
Jeff Reardon (1979–81)	45, 44
Prentice Redman (2003)	20
Darren Reed (1990)	28, 6
Rick Reed (1997–2001)	35
Steve Reed (2002)	39
Desi Relaford (2001)	8
Mike Remlinger (1994–95)	43
Hal Reniff (1967)	32
Jose Reyes (2003–07)	7
Ronn Reynolds (1982–83, 1985)	8, 9
Tommie Reynolds (1967)	16
Armando Reynoso (1997–98)	40
Dennis Ribant (1964–66)	17, 18, 30
Gordie Richardson (1965–66)	41
Jerrod Riggan (2000–01)	34, 38
Royce Ring (2005–06)	22, 43
Luis Rivera (1994)	3
Jason Roach (2003)	57
Kevin Roberson (1996)	18
Dave Roberts (1981)	15
Grant Roberts (2000–04)	36
Rich Rodriguez (2000)	46
Kenny Rogers (1999)	73
Les Rohr (1967–69)	31, 33
Mel Rojas (1997–98)	51
Luis Rosado (1977, 1980)	58, 35
Brian Rose (2001)	23

Don Rose (1971)	31
Don Rowe (1963)	29
Glendon Rusch (1999–2001)	48
Dick Rusteck (1966)	43, 40
Nolan Ryan (1966, 1968–71)	34, 30

S

Bret Saberhagen (1992–95)	18, 17
Ray Sadecki (1970–74, 1977)	33
Joe Sambito (1985)	35
Amado Samuel (1964)	7
Juan Samuel (1989)	7
Duaner Sanchez (2006)	50
Rey Sanchez (2003)	10
Ken Sanders (1975–76)	33
Rafael Santana (1984–87)	3
Jose Santiago (2005)	33
Mackey Sasser (1988–92)	2
Doug Saunders (1993)	2
Rich Sauveur (1991)	39
Mac Scarce (1975)	44
Jimmie Schaffer (1965)	17
Dan Schatzeder (1990)	43
Calvin Schiraldi (1984–85)	40
Al Schmelz (1967)	44
Dave Schneck (1972–74)	23, 16
Scott Schoeneweis (2007)	60
Dick Schofield (1992)	11
Pete Schourek (1991–93)	48
Ted Schreiber (1963)	43

Don Schulze (1987)	49
Mike Scott (1979–82)	30
Marco Scutaro (2002–03)	26
Ray Searage (1981)	44
Tom Seaver (1967–1977, 1983)	41
David Segui (1994–95)	10, 21
Aaron Sele (2007)	30
Dick Selma (1965–68)	39
Frank Seminara (1994)	34
Jae Seo (2002–05)	38, 40, 26
Art Shamsky (1968–1971)	24
Bob Shaw (1966–67)	26
Don Shaw (1967–68)	35
Norm Sherry (1963)	5
Tsuyoshi Shinjo (2001, 2003)	5
Craig Shipley (1989)	35
Bart Shirley (1967)	6
Bill Short (1968)	40
Paul Siebert (1977–78)	43, 48
Doug Simons (1991)	43
Ken Singleton (1970–71)	29
Doug Sisk (1982–87)	39
Bobby Gene Smith (1962)	16
Charley Smith (1964–65)	1
Dick Smith (1963–64)	16
Joe Smith (2007)	35
Pete Smith (1994)	32
Esix Snead (2002, 2004)	23, 1
Duke Snider (1963)	11, 4
Alay Soler (2006)	59
Jorge Sosa (2007)	29

Warren Spahn (1965)	21
Tim Spehr (1998)	33
Shane Spencer (2004)	43
Bill Spiers (1995)	19
Dennis Springer (2000)	34
Steve Springer (1992)	13
Larry Stahl (1967–68)	25
Roy Staiger (1975–77)	35, 2
Tracy Stallard (1963–64)	36
Leroy Stanton (1970–71)	23, 44
Mike Stanton (2003–04)	32
Rusty Staub (1972–75, 1981–85)	4, 10
John Stearns (1975–84)	16, 12
John Stephenson (1964–66)	49, 19, 12
Randy Sterling (1974)	35
Kelly Stinnett (1994–95, 2006)	33, 36
George Stone (1973–75)	40
Pat Strange (2002–03)	38
Darryl Strawberry (1983–1990)	18
Scott Strickland (2002–03)	25, 28
John Strohmayer (1973–74)	39
Brent Strom (1972)	40
Dick Stuart (1966)	17
Tom Sturdivant (1964)	47
Bill Sudakis (1972)	9
John Sullivan (1967)	20
Darrell Sutherland (1964–66)	47, 43, 45
Craig Swan (1973–84)	27
Rick Sweet (1982)	8
Ron Swoboda (1965–1970)	14, 4

T

Pat Tabler (1990)	35
Shingo Takatsu (2005)	10
Jeff Tam (1998, 1999)	36, 38
Frank Tanana (1993)	29
Kevin Tapani (1989)	26
Tony Tarasco (2002)	40
Randy Tate (1975)	48
Jim Tatum (1998)	19
Frank Taveras (1979–1981)	11
Billy Taylor (1999)	26
Chuck Taylor (1972)	42
Hawk Taylor (1964–67)	19
Ron Taylor (1967–71)	42
Sammy Taylor (1962–63)	16
Dave Telgheder (1993–95)	38, 40
Garry Templeton (1991)	11
Walt Terrell (1982–84)	49
Ralph Terry (1966–67)	38
Tim Teufel (1986–1991)	11
George Theodore (1973–74)	18, 9
Frank Thomas (1962–64)	25
Ryan Thompson (1992–95)	44, 20
John Thomson (2002)	50
Lou Thornton (1989–1990)	4, 1
Marv Throneberry (1962–63)	2
Gary Thurman (1997)	10
Dick Tidrow (1984)	32
Rusty Tillman (1982)	34
Jorge Toca (1999–2001)	30
Jackson Todd (1977)	30

Andy Tomberlin (1996–97)	33
Joe Torre (1975–77)	9
Mike Torrez (1983–84)	30
Kelvin Torve (1990–91)	24, 39
Steve Trachsel (2001–06)	29
Bubba Trammell (2000)	33
Alex Treviño (1978–1981, 1990)	29, 6
Rick Trlicek (1996–97)	34, 50
Michael Tucker (2006)	22
Wayne Twitchell (1979)	36
Jason Tyner (2000)	11

U

Del Unser (1975–76)	25
Lino Urdaneta (2007)	19

V

Mike Vail (1975–77)	31, 6
Eric Valent (2004–05)	57
John Valentin (2002)	4
Jose Valentin (2006–07)	18, 2
Bobby Valentine (1977–78)	1
Ellis Valentine (1981–82)	17
Julio Valera (1990–91)	34
Jason Vargas (2007)	43
Mo Vaughn (2002–03)	42
Jorge Velandia (2000–01, 2003)	11, 13
Robin Ventura (1999–2001)	4
Tom Veryzer (1982)	11

Fernando Viña (1994)	1
Frank Viola (1989–1991)	29, 26
Joe Vitko (1992)	49
Jose Vizcaino (1994–96)	15

W

Billy Wagner (2006–07)	13
Bill Wakefield (1964)	43
Chico Walker (1992–93)	34
Pete Walker (1995, 2001–02)	49, 43
Tyler Walker (2002)	46
Donne Wall (2001)	33
Derek Wallace (1996)	47
Gene Walter (1987–88)	31
Claudell Washington (1980)	15
Allen Watson (1999)	30
Matt Watson (2003)	50
Dave Weathers (2002–04)	35
Hank Webb (1972–76)	42, 29, 30
Al Weis (1968–71)	6
Turk Wendell (1997–2001)	99
David West (1988–89)	46
Mickey Weston (1993)	43
Dan Wheeler (2003–04)	39
Rick White (2000, 2001)	51
Wally Whitehurst (1989–1992)	47
Ty Wigginton (2002–04)	9
Rick Wilkins (1998)	39
Carl Willey (1963–65)	28
Nick Willhite (1967)	29

Charlie Williams (1971)	35
Dave Williams (2006–07)	32
Gerald Williams (2004, 2005)	6, 21
Mookie Wilson (1980–89)	1
Paul Wilson (1996)	32
Preston Wilson (1998)	11
Tom Wilson (2004)	6
Vance Wilson (1999–2004)	3
Herm Winningham (1984)	21
Gene Woodling (1962)	11
Chris Woodward (2005–06)	4
David Wright (2004–07)	5
Billy Wynne (1967)	35

Y

Tyler Yates (2004)	32,* 33
Masato Yoshii (1998–99)	29, 21
Anthony Young (1991–93)	33, 19
Joel Youngblood (1977–1982)	18

Z

Pat Zachry (1977–1982)	40
Victor Zambrano (2004–06)	38
Todd Zeile (2000–01, 2004)	9, 27
Don Zimmer (1962)	17

ACKNOWLEDGMENTS

This book has been a long time coming. Since 1962, yes, but the Mets by the Numbers Web site (mbtn.net) has been up and running since 1999.

Neither the book nor the Web site would be possible without those who could run, hit, throw, and instruct well enough to be worthy of major league status. We may sometimes be flip in our assessments, but anyone good enough to wear a Mets uniform and number without having to pay $200 for the privilege automatically has our respect.

Our deepest gratitude is reserved for Mark Weinstein at Skyhorse Publishing, who erased three years of angst in three minutes by starting negotiations for this book the day after the Mets clinched the 2006 division title. Now that was a good day.

We sincerely thank Howie Rose for writing the foreword to this book. Also thanks to Lou Schwartz, president of the American Sportscasters Association, for putting us in touch with Eric Spitz at WFAN, who generously made entreaties on our behalf. Thanks to Andrew Fegyveresi at SNY and Victoria Estevez, Andrew Lombardi, and Matt Vigil from Tupelo Honey Productions/*Mets Weekly*. Special thanks also to the players who have addressed unsolicited questions over the years about their uniform numbers, especially the all-good-guy team of George Theodore, Lenny Randle, Joe McEwing, Ed Hearn, and Kelvin Torve.

And we couldn't have done it alone. Sources that were especially helpful beyond all the scorecards and media guides include the following reference works: *The Cultural Encyclopedia of Baseball*, 1st edition, Jonathon Fraser Light (Jefferson, NC: McFarland & Co., 1997); *The Baseball Encyclopedia*, 4th edition, Gary Gillette and Pete Palmer (New York: Sterling Publishing, 2007); *Total Baseball*, 7th edition, John Thorn, Pete Palmer, and Mike Gershman (Kingston, NY: Total Sports Publishing, 2001); and *The New Bill James Historical Baseball Abstract* (New York: The Free Press, 2001). And while our research was independent of the two definitive books on uniform numbers, the fact that these had been published didn't hurt: *Baseball by the Numbers*, Mark Stang and Linda Harkness (Lanham, MD: The Scarecrow Press, 1997), and *Now Batting, Number . . .* , by Jack Looney (New York: Black Dog and Leventhal Publishers, 2006).

Books on the Mets are many in number, but the ones that we referred to faithfully for this project were the following: *This Date in N.Y. Mets History*,

Dennis D'Agostino, (Briarcliff Manor, NY: Scarborough, 1981); *The Complete Year-by-Year N.Y. Mets Fan's Almanac*, Duncan Bock and John Jordan (New York: Crown, 1992); *The New York Mets: Twenty-Five Years of Baseball Magic*, Jack Lang and Pete Simon (New York: Henry Holt, 1986); and *The New York Mets*, Leonard Koppett (New York: Macmillan, 1974).

We bounced in and out of countless Web sites to track down information or just jog the memory. The most important of these hold the cryptic details of every game played, plus the stats of every player, and in some cases, uniform number info: baseball-almanac.com, baseball-reference.com, retrosheet.org, and ultimatemets.com. Let's not neglect the newspapers that do the dirty work daily and are available on the Web: newsday.com, northjersey.com, nydailynews.com, nypost.com, and nytimes.com. Marty Noble, whose great work at *Newsday* for many years showed a particular interest in the uniform number, continues his great work at mlb.com. Thanks also to Jeff Pearlman for graciously having a look at the book. Historical info and insight on the team we're here for was offered by cranepoolforum.net, faithandfear.blogharbor.com, loge13.com, mets-blog.com, and everyone else, and there are many of you. We love you all.

Matt:
Help with yearbooks and other materials came from Robert Pizzella, Brad Smith, and Syd Silverman, who bought and brought home plenty of materials in the Dark Ages of Mets baseball. It all would have been tossed away if not for my mother, Jan McNally Silverman, who went against the old stereotype and carefully stashed this Mets gold away against fire and time. And she didn't even like baseball. Also thanks to friends Bruce Markusen, Todd Radom, Linc Wonham, and Alec Dawson, plus colleagues Gary Gillette, Pete Palmer, Greg Spira, and Jim Walsh for their patience in handling my share of the workload while I labored through the night to find Red Kress's uniform number. Appreciation to Alan Silverman (no relation) as emergency starter for the computer and aid with the birth of metsilverman.com. An endeavor requiring much time scouring the archives for arcane—yet vital—information couldn't be possible without the moral assistance of family: Debbie, Jan, and Tyler Silverman. I'll pick the yearbooks, scorecards, and books off the floor now. Or tomorrow.

Jon:

When I say I don't know how to thank the people who made this possible, I mean that quite literally: I don't know who they are. But there have been, since 1999, hundreds of fans, most with long memories and good attention to detail, who have been in touch via email with suggestions, memories, questions, information, and evidence—every bit of which made it better and more accurate. Some are considerably more obsessive on this topic than I could ever be, and most are better organized. Of these, I owe special thanks to Ed Armstrong, who kept his own records dating from the 1960s and always shared them when asked. Jason from New Jersey has always been way ahead of me on research but kind enough to continually reach back and pull me forward again. His data on Mets personnel history is staggering and, I am certain, the best there is. Thanks also to Matt for twisting my arm.

A small and grossly incomplete list of others includes Matt Buscemi, Gordon Handler, Pete Mahoney, Doug Hoffman, Dennis D'Agostino, Michael Grimaldi, Michael Weil, Kasey Ignarski, Gene Fry, Andy Shinka, Joe Ruszkowski, Scott Pirrung, Steve Bulota, Joe Hickey, Bob Finkel, Mark Simon, Glenn Larsen, Kenny Bumbaco, Ken Mattucci, Aaron Weiss, Rich Kroebel, Ernie Alston, Mitchell Pak, Shari Forst, Jonathan S. "52" Weissman, Edward Hoyt, Kevin Carter, Richard DiStefano, Dave Murray, Jim Haines, David Whitham, "Paul C.," "Lazylou," "Irv," "Keith," "Ellis," "Glen," "Mike J.," "Mark in Japan," and "Jack." Thanks for everything. Paul Lukas (Uniwatch) and Greg W. Prince (Faith & Fear in Flushing) were early discoverers and supporters of the project and happen to be my favorite writers—whether they're tackling baseball or food and beverages. They completely get it.

I also owe thanks to my dad, Frank, and older brother Bill for having assembled an impressive amount of Mets material for me and my younger brother Chris to discover and for establishing a home where Mets fandom was a natural part of who we were. It was no accident that this research project began while I was home for the holidays. Since then I have a whole new family to thank, my wife, Heidi Shea, who indulges my fandom and noisy typing; Ivan, our awesome No. 1 son; and Skipper, who ate some notes and threw up on many others.